Machine Embroidery
with confidence
A beginner's guide

Nancy Zieman

©2005 Nancy Zieman

Published by

kp books
An Imprint of F+W Publications

700 East State Street • Iola, WI 54990-0001
715-445-2214 • 888-457-2873

Our toll-free number to place an order or obtain
a free catalog is (800) 258-0929.

Library of Congress Catalog Number: 2004097734

ISBN: 0-87349-857-7

Printed in China

Introduction

So you want to learn to embroider! The world of machine embroidery is stimulating, satisfying and exciting. There's an amazing wealth of options and designs just waiting for you and your embroidery machine.

I've come into many of your homes via my *Sewing With Nancy* television program, and some of you may have ordered supplies from my Nancy's Notions catalog and Web site. I recall that when I first started machine embroidering several years ago, the process seemed a little overwhelming. But, I've had so much fun embroidering that I have to admit that I started by purchasing "blank" (ready-made) garments and projects so I could immediately start embellishing with embroidery. Believe me, that is OK you don't have to sew every item you are embellishing. Time is precious ... do whatever inspires you in the most timely fashion!

As I've experimented with embroidery, I've learned a lot, and in this book I share that information so you can benefit from my successes—and my challenges. This book will teach you the basics of machine embroidery and give you confidence to explore more complex techniques and projects on your own. And look for my personal Motivating Memos and creative Nuggets of Inspiration.

As you page through this book I hope that you are motivated by all the lovely projects and that you will learn basic embroidery skills which will foster personal growth and self-assurance in this creative hobby.

Whether you are looking for information on choosing a stabilizer, combining designs, making your own templates, or quick and easy projects to embroider, you will find the information at your fingertips.

Ready, Set, Embroider!

Regards,

Nancy Zieman

Table of Contents

1 Machines.................... 6

Types of Machines...................................7
Machine Capabilities..............................8
  1 Media the Machine Uses 8
  2 Fonts 10
  3 Embroidery Fields.............................11
  4 Editing 12
  5 Thread Color Options 13
  6 "Bells & Whistles" 14
Instructional Tools 16
Checklist 17

2 Designs 18

Built-in Designs...................................19
Memory Cards....................................20
Single Format Floppy Disks...................20
Multiformat Floppy Disks.....................20
Multiformat CD..................................21
Downloading from the Internet..............22
Hardware & Software.........................25
Direct Transfer Systems.......................25
Reader/Writer Transfer Systems 26
Single Format Reader/Writer.................26
Multiformat Reader/Writer 26

3 Stabilizers & Tools........ 27

Stabilizers..28
Cut-Aways.......................................28
Tear-Aways.......................................30
Wash-Aways.....................................32
Heat-Aways......................................34
Adhesives and Fusible Sprays.............35
Marking Tools 36
Marking Pens and Pencils....................36
Embroidery Needles..........................37
Thread...38
Rayon Threads..................................39
Polyester Threads...............................40
Cotton Threads.................................40
Specialty Threads...............................41
Bobbin Thread..................................42
Tools for Testing 43
Sample Cloth....................................43
Embroidery Reference Cards.................43

4 Getting Started............ 44

Organizing and Choosing Threads..............45
Organizing Your Thread Collection 45
Organizing Thread for Stitching a Design.....45
Converting Thread Colors.....................45
Selecting Fabrics and "Blanks"...............46
Fabrics...46
Positioning Aids 48
Using Templates 48
Do-it-Yourself Templates 49
Embroidery T-square...........................50
Embroiderer's Positioning Board 51
Hooping Aids...................................52
Springs..52
Snappy..53
Proper Stabilizing 54
Hooping Both Fabric and Stabilizer 54
Hooping Stabilizer; Then Applying Fabric.....56
Using an Adhesive Spray......................58
Basting Fabric to Hooped Stabilizer 59
Window Technique.............................60
Attaching the Hoop to the Machine 62
Making a Test Swatch..........................63

5 Basics & Beyond 65

Using a Template for Proper Placement 66
Using Templates with The Perfect
   Placement Kit 66
Embroidering the Design 67
Finishing Steps 68
Pressing Designs 69
Caring for Embroidered Projects 69
Additional Embellishment 69

Editing Possibilities 70
Changing Colors 70
Skipping Colors 71
Mirror Imaging 72
Rotating for Design 72
Rotating for Convenience 73
Combining Designs 73
Creating a Scene 73
Connecting Linear Designs 74

Specialty Hoops 75
Hoops for Caps 75
Hoops for Socks 75
Multiposition Hoops 76
Hoop-It-All™ Products 76

6 Expanding Your Vision .. 77

Holiday Kitchen Collection 78
Embroidering Cotton Dish Towels 79
Embroidering Terry Towels or Bibs 82
Embroidering on Quilted Potholders 84
Embroidery on Cotton Aprons—
   Multiple Designs 86

Keen Jeans 88
Embroidered Jean Legs and Pockets 88

By the Seashore 91
Seaside Tote 92
Sea Shells Beach Towel 93
Six Panel Sun Hat 95
Swim Suit Cover-up 96

Dressing up Denim 97
Embroidering on Collar Points 98
Creating a Continuous Design
   on a Collar 100
Embroidering above Pocket Top 101
Embroidering on Cuffs 102
Embroidering on a Pocket 103

Quilting and Home Décor Medley 104
Charming Chickens Wall Hanging 104
Crayon Alphabet Quilt 106
Christmas Splendor Wall Hanging 108
Paper Leaf Appliqué 109

Baby Belongings 112
Bunny Blanket 113
Baby's Name Wall Hanging 115
Organizer Hang-up for the Nursery 117
Daisy Tufted Baby Quilt 119

Fish Stories 121
Big Fish Denim Shirt 122
Anchors Away Sweatshirt 123
My Fishin' Gear Polo 124
"A Luring" Fleece Pillowcase 125
Fleece Fishing Blanket 128
Fishin' Hat 129

Showcase 130

Troubleshooting 138

Glossary 141

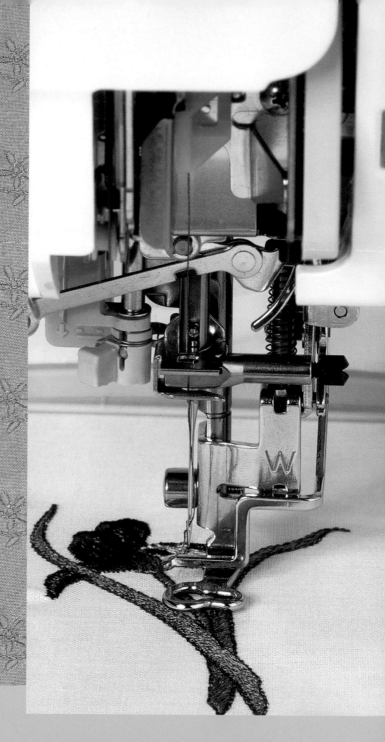

1 *Machines*

An embroidery machine equals power. Power to control the destiny of your embellishments and designs. Power to create in any color or pattern you desire. Power to go against the grain and express your individuality. And in order to harness this power, you must choose to conquer your fears and tame this wild beast.

Background: Amazing Designs ADC 1358

TYPES OF MACHINES

There are many different home embroidery machines on the market, each having its own special features. Before purchasing a machine, take some time to evaluate your needs and how you plan to use the machine.

Embroidery Only Machines—The most affordable embroidery machines on the market, these machines are for computerized machine embroidery only. They do not sew standard stitches. Embroidery only machines are appropriate if you're the type of person who is just starting to embroider, or if you only plan to do simple projects—such as embroidering sweatshirts or towels—that do not require sewing.

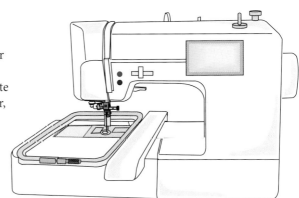

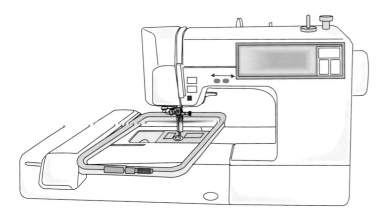

Sewing and Embroidery Machines with limited editing/combining capabilities—These machines have the capability of computerized machine embroidery, plus they also can be used for constructing garments, quilts or other projects. These machines are considered mid-range because they do have some editing capabilities, but not nearly as many as high-end machines. These mid-range machines typically have simple green and black LCD screens. Some have separate embroidery units that attach to the machine, while others have built-in embroidery functions that are out of the way when not in use.

Sewing and Embroidery Machines with editing/combining capabilities—The top of the line embroidery machines on the market, these machines have the capability of computerized machine embroidery, plus they also can be used for constructing garments, quilts or other projects. These high-end machines have the most editing/combining capabilities available, giving you more control over designs. Some have separate embroidery units that attach to the machine, while others have built-in embroidery functions that are out of the way when not in use. Typically, these machines have full-color screens.

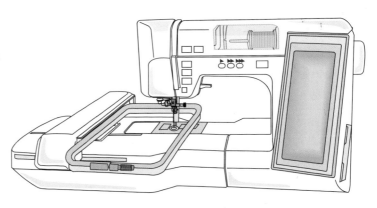

Machines

MACHINE CAPABILITIES

To familiarize you with the different types of machines, we've categorized them based on their capabilities. But what does that mean? Not all embroidery machines are created equal. Some machines perform more functions than others. You may not need and/or want all of these functions—some will be more important to you than others. The following pages detail different types of capabilities, such as media each machine uses, fonts and editing functions.

1 MEDIA THE MACHINE USES

Embroidery designs are available on several types of media. There are differences in how you use each and whether you need additional equipment.

> ### Motivating Memo
>
> *All of the machines we're talking about are home format machines, which are intended for home use, not for use in a business. For professional and commercial use, there are high-speed commercial embroidery machines. Designed to run for hours at a time, these machines stitch much faster than home machines.*

• Built-in Designs—Most embroidery machines have this capability. Some machines have more designs than others, and some also have exclusive designs that are only available for that particular machine. Built-in designs may include character designs, frames and alphabets.

• Memory Cards—The next step up from built-in designs is memory cards. Most embroidery machines have a slot for inserting the memory card. The memory card uses the sewing machine's built-in computer. Each memory card is designed to work with a specific machine format.

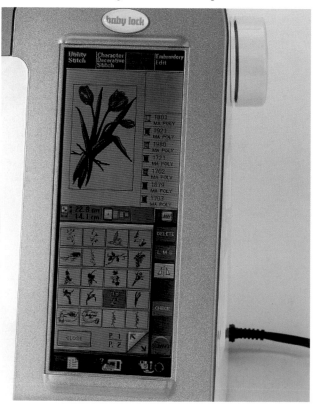

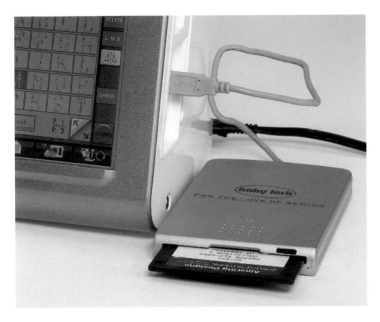

• Floppy Disk—Some machines have a floppy drive, which functions the same as a memory card drive. If the machine doesn't have a floppy drive, and you want to use designs from floppy disks, a separate computer with a floppy drive and a transfer system such as a reader/writer box specifically for the machine are required. That allows you to save the designs from the floppy onto a memory card.

• CD—Only a few machines have CD drives. For almost all embroidery machines, you need a separate computer to transfer the designs to a floppy disk, or a computer and specific software, or a transfer system such as a reader/writer box to save the designs to a memory card.

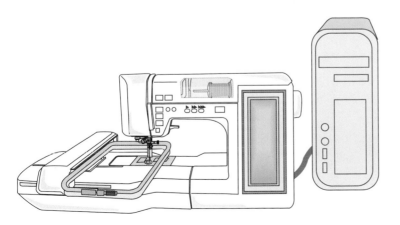

•Direct hookup to computer—Some brands of machines have a cable that connects the machine to a computer. In that case, you can access designs from floppy disks, CDs and your computer's hard drive without using a separate reader/writer system. Technology is changing rapidly. Some machines accept storage devices that allow you to transfer information between your computer and your embroidery machine. Their storage capacity is much greater than that of CDs, memory cards or floppy disks.

Machines

2 FONTS

Fonts vary by size and by style. You may already be familiar with fonts from word processing programs. Basically, font refers to the style of letters, for example, block or script.

• Size—Built-in fonts are generally available in three sizes: small, medium and large. Depending on the machine, these sizes are either fixed or adjustable. For example, on some machines you have just three choices: small, medium or large. However, on high-end machines, you can choose small, medium or large, and then fine-tune the size even more.

• Adjustable spacing—This refers to the spacing between individual letters. Again, it depends on your machine, as not all machines have this capability. Some fonts have specific spacing that you cannot change. For example, very basic machines have fixed spacing—you type in a word and that's that. High-end machines, however, have adjustable spacing—allowing you to move each letter independently to fine-tune the spacing.

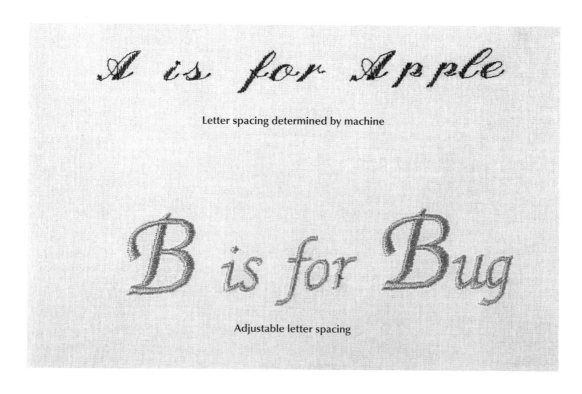

Font samples

Letter spacing determined by machine

Adjustable letter spacing

3 EMBROIDERY FIELDS
(size of stitch field)

The embroidery field is the area in which the machine stitches. Most designs are created to fit within a 4" embroidery field. Larger designs go outside of that field, some filling a space as big as 5" x 7" or larger. The important thing to remember is that your machine determines what size designs you can stitch. Some machines can only stitch designs that fit within a 4" stitch field, while others are capable of stitching larger designs. Using a larger hoop will not allow you to embroider outside of your machine's capability. For example, a machine with a 4" maximum stitch field cannot stitch designs larger than 4".

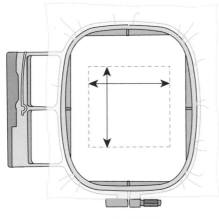

Stitch field

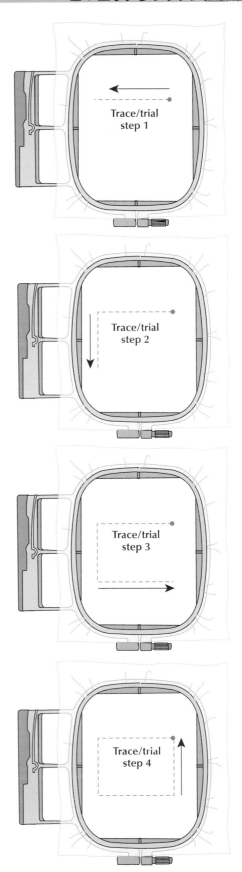

Trace/trial step 1

Trace/trial step 2

Trace/trial step 3

Trace/trial step 4

• Trace/trial function—This function checks the position of the design. The embroidery frame moves, "tracing" around the stitch field to help you position the design in the correct place and to make sure that there is enough space to stitch the design.

NUGGET OF INSPIRATION

Like any new language, the language of machine embroidery can often be a tricky one to learn. There are several different ways of saying just about everything. For example, say the term "embroidery field" to other embroiderers and they may look puzzled or even correct you. Embroidery field is just one way of saying it; other choices include stitch field, embroidery area, boundaries of the embroidery and trace/trial.

4 EDITING

Sometimes a design does not look exactly as you would like. Maybe it's facing in the wrong direction, the angle it's tilted at doesn't fit your project, or you want to combine several designs. That's where editing comes in. Rotating, mirror imaging and moving designs are basic editing functions found on most embroidery machines.

Rotating—Moves the design from a stationary axis, usually 90° at a time.

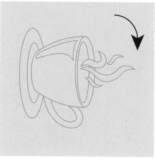

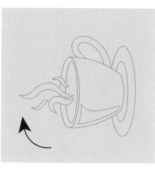

| Original position | Rotate 90° | Rotate 90° | Rotate 90° |

Mirror imaging—is the reverse image of a design obtained by flipping over a design. You can mirror a design horizontally or vertically.

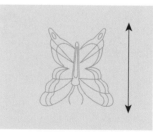

| Original position | Mirror horizontally | Original position | Mirror vertically |

Moving designs—Relocate the design in the stitch field, both horizontally and vertically.

| Original position | Move design left | Move design right | Move design up | Move design down |

5 THREAD COLOR OPTIONS

When selecting designs, always remember that you do not have to use the colors that the designers used. Changing the thread colors can dramatically change the look of a design. It's an exciting element to experiment with when first learning to embroider. Your machine can help you here. Whether you do your experimenting on-screen or on sample cloth, the following features will help you explore the possibilities of thread color.

Design with default colors

Design with custom colors

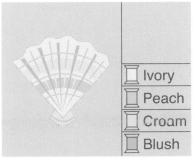

Design with default colors

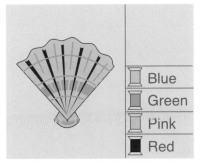

Design with alternate screen colors for better visibility

• Color selection; on-screen colors—Available only on high-end machines, this feature lets you change the colors on-screen so that you can see how designs will look with different colors before doing any stitching. Another benefit of this function is that if the original on-screen colors are difficult to see, you can save your eyes by changing the colors to more visible colorations.

• Ability to skip colors—You don't have to stitch every color of a design. For example, on a design with four colors, you can choose and stitch one, two, three or all four thread colors. To get an idea of what the various combinations will look like, stitch out the various thread color options on fabric samples. Your owner's manual will instruct you how to advance to the next thread color.

Colors 1–4

Colors 2 & 4

Colors 2–4

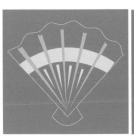

Colors 3 & 4

Color 4

Machines

6 "BELLS & WHISTLES"

This category of machine capabilities includes functions that are usually primarily found on high-end embroidery machines. You don't need these things to embroider successfully, but once you try them, you may wonder how you ever survived without them. Some of these functions give you more control over your designs, while others make your life easier. Either way, consider them the icing on the cake!

• **Advancing or backing up stitches**—allows you to move the needle forward or backward in the design. It's useful if the thread breaks while sewing or if you want to start again from the beginning. For example, if your thread breaks you can back up the number of stitches needed to move your needle at a position in the design before the thread broke and start stitching again.

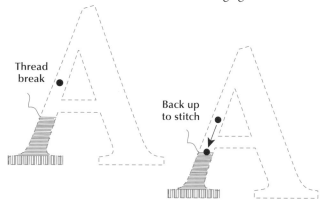

Thread break

Back up to stitch

• **Automatic needle threader**—helps you easily thread the needle. Because embroidery requires many thread color changes, this feature is extremely useful. It allows you to change the thread quickly and easily.

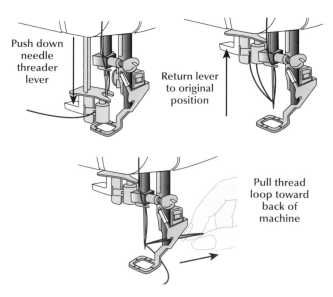

Push down needle threader lever

Return lever to original position

Pull thread loop toward back of machine

• **Automatic thread cutter**—clips both the upper and lower threads at the end of each color in the design.

• **Thread notification**—stops the machine within a few stitches if the upper thread breaks or the spool or bobbin runs out. Some machines will also give you a message directing you to check for a thread break or letting you know the thread has run out.

! Check and !
• rethread •
upper thread

CLOSE

• **Bobbin sensor**—monitors the amount of thread on the bobbin. Depending on your machine, a light will go on or a warning message will let you know that your bobbin thread is running low. This is useful because it prevents the possibility of stitching an entire color only to discover that part of it didn't stitch because you ran out of bobbin thread.

! There is not !
! much bobbin !
thread
remaining

CLOSE

• Rotating designs by degree increments—allows you to rotate designs in 90° increments, or on some machines, in 1° increments, giving you much more control and flexibility in positioning a design.

Original position

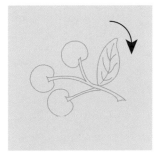
Rotate in 90° increments

Rotate in 1° increments

• Moving designs diagonally—lets you move designs diagonally, in addition to horizontally and vertically, features available on most machines. This gives you more control over the placement of the design.

Original position

Move design diagonally

In comparison, using a machine that doesn't have this feature, it would take two steps to move this design to the same position.

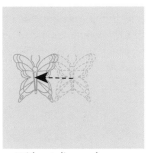
Without diagonal move feature; step 1

Without diagonal move feature; step 2

• Indication of total stitching time—calculates the approximate amount of time the machine spends actually stitching the design. NOTE: This calculation does not include time needed to change thread colors, etc. Some machines also give number of stitches in the design.

• Changing machine speed—allows you to change the stitching speed of the machine. It is very useful when stitching with specialty threads such as metallic, which require you to stitch at a slower pace for best results.

• **Color separation display**—shows you exactly how each color looks separated from the entire design as a design is stitching.

• **Combining designs**—allows you to position designs together on-screen before you start stitching.

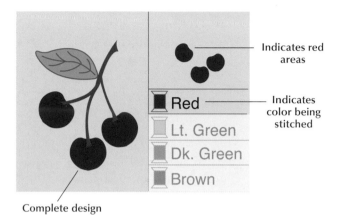

Indicates red areas

Red — Indicates color being stitched

Lt. Green

Dk. Green

Brown

Complete design

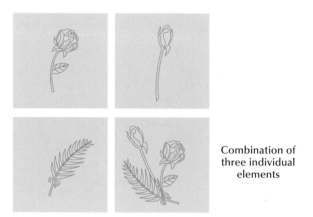

Combination of three individual elements

INSTRUCTIONAL TOOLS

After buying an embroidery machine, the next step is learning how to use it. There are several different types of instructional tools available to you.

Manual

Your owner's manual is a great resource for learning how to use and take care of your machine. Each manufacturer has its own techniques/instructions. Your manual also offers troubleshooting tips to help if you have problems with stitches or the machine's operation. Most manuals contain a list of accessories available from the manufacturer, such as special presser feet, bobbins, cleaning equipment and replacement parts.

Video/CD

Some machines also have an instructional video or CD that demonstrates how the machine works. If you are interested in a particular machine, your dealer may show you the video or CD at the store.

Dealer

Buying an embroidery machine from a dealer, as opposed to buying from the Internet, is a choice that will benefit you in the long run. A dealer will demonstrate the machine before you buy it, and most dealers offer classes/lessons to teach you how to use your machine. In addition to offering a warranty on the machine, the dealer is also your resource for machine maintenance.

◼ NUGGET OF INSPIRATION

Personalize your owner's manual by putting sticky notes on pages you refer to often. It's amazing how many times you'll go back to certain pages; the markers really speed up this process.

CHECKLIST FOR PURCHASE/REVIEWING YOUR MACHINE

As with any major purchase, you want to do it right the first time and get the best value for your money. Shopping for an embroidery machine may seem overwhelming at times. Research your options and compare different brands. Ask yourself the following questions to determine your sewing needs before entering a store.

? *What types of embroidery projects do you plan to make?*
Are you only interested in embroidering designs, or do you also want the ability to sew? Will you make gifts for holidays and special occasions? Will you only use the machine a couple times a year? Knowing how you plan to use the machine and what types of projects you plan to make will help you identify which features are important.

? *What features do you want?*
Are you interested in doing a lot of design editing? Do you plan to add words and letters to many of your projects? Consider which features best meet your embroidery needs. Talk to your dealer and try out several different machines.

? *Do you own a computer?*
Do you plan on looking for designs on the Internet or using designs from floppy disks and CDs?

? *What kind of support do the dealer and manufacturer offer?*
Does the machine come with a workbook and/or a video/CD that explains how to use it? Does the dealer offer classes? Is there someone you can call with questions? Is service available? What sort of warranty does the manufacturer offer on the machine?

? *What price range are you considering?*

After carefully considering these questions, it's time to take a test drive. Ask your friends, family members and co-workers to recommend a dependable embroidery machine dealer. It's important to purchase a machine from a reliable dealer, as the dealer will offer support, classes and continued assistance with the machine.

■ NUGGET OF INSPIRATION
Buying an embroidery machine is much like buying a car. Think about what you want, do your research and then take some machines for a test drive.

2

Designs

Designs allow you to add your creative touch to a project. Designs give you the power to transform plain fabric or blank items into projects with personality. Designs allow you to express yourself, to play out your fantasies and to capture your dreams.

Background: Amazing Designer Series™ Jessica McClintock Collection I
Inset: Amazing Designer Series™ Accents for Style by Nancy Zieman

You can find embroidery designs in many different places and forms. The majority of machines have a library of built-in designs. Embroidery designs are also available on several types of media: memory cards, floppy disks and CDs.

Designs are also available in different formats, or languages. (The terms format and language are interchangeable.) Each machine speaks a different language and will only read designs "written" in that language. Therefore, when you purchase designs, it is crucial that you get the correct format designs for your embroidery machine. ALWAYS check the packaging to ensure that you have the correct format. Generally, once you open the design package, it is not returnable. It is in your best interest to double check that you bought the correct format. The chart at right lists a sampling of home embroidery machines and their formats.

Machine Format	Machine
PES	Baby Lock®, Bernina® Deco, Brother®, Simplicity®, White
PCS	Pfaff 7560, 7562, 7570
EMD	Elna Xquisit™, Singer® XL-5000
HUS	Viking 1+, Iris, Rose, 605
SHV	Viking Designer I
ART	Bernina® Artista
JEF	Janome 10000
PSW	Singer® XL-100, XL-1000

Built-in Designs

By far the most basic type of design, the built-in design is also the easiest to use. As soon as you take your machine out of the box and turn it on, you have access to built-in designs. Since these designs are built into the machine, you don't have to worry about formats. Different brands of machines often have several similar designs.

Some machines, usually high-end ones, also feature designs exclusive to that machine model or to that brand of machine. Designs can include character designs such as animals, flowers and seasonal motifs.

Your machine may also include alphabets, as well as frames with different shapes and types of lines (straight, wavy, scallop, etc.)

▇ NUGGET OF INSPIRATION

Built-in designs are great to use—they give you pretty much instant gratification as soon as you unpack the machine from the box. Built-in designs are especially useful when you're just getting to know your machine. Before you start investing in design collections, practice stitching out the designs included on your machine. You'll learn how to work with your machine, choose stabilizers and change thread colors. By the time you're ready to purchase design collections, you'll be embroidering with confidence.

Designs

Memory Cards

After you've explored your machine's built-in designs and are ready for something new, the next step is memory cards. Also called embroidery cards, they fit directly into the slot in the sewing machine and use the sewing machine's built-in computer. Each memory card is designed to work with a specific brand of sewing machine. Memory cards differ in size depending on the format. Be careful not to assume that two memory cards of the same size will work in different machines. For example, memory cards for Viking 1+, 605, Iris, Rose and Baby Lock® are the exact same size. But, the language on the Viking card is different than that on the Baby Lock® format. A Viking machine will not be able to read the designs on the Baby Lock® card and vice versa.

Single Format Floppy Disks

If your machine has a floppy disk drive, then a single format floppy disk functions the same as a memory card. You simply insert it into the correct slot on your machine. If your machine does not have a floppy disk drive, then you need an IBM compatible computer with a floppy disk drive and a software program with hardware component designed specifically for your sewing machine, or a reader/writer box. In order to use the designs, insert the floppy disk into your computer, and then save them to a memory card using the software component.

Multiformat Floppy Disks

Even if your machine has a floppy disk drive, you cannot insert a multiformat disk into the machine and expect it to work automatically. Because the disk has multiple formats on it, you need an IBM compatible computer with a floppy disk drive to "unzip" or install the designs in the single format for your machine.

• For embroidery machines with a floppy disk drive, save the unzipped designs in your computer to a blank floppy disk. Insert this disk into your machine.

• If your machine has a memory card slot, you will need an IBM compatible computer with a floppy disk drive, as well as a software program with hardware component designed specifically for your sewing machine, or a reader/writer box. Save the unzipped files to a memory card. Insert the card into your machine.

Multiformat CD

Because a CD has multiple formats on it, you need an IBM compatible computer with a floppy disk drive to unzip or install the designs in the single format for your machine. A multiformat CD works similar to a multiformat floppy disk, but a CD holds more information.

• For embroidery machines with a floppy disk drive, save the unzipped designs in your computer to a blank floppy disk. Insert this disk into your machine.

• If your machine has a memory card slot, you will need an IBM compatible computer with a floppy disk drive, as well as a software program with hardware component designed specifically for your sewing machine, or a reader/writer box. Save the unzipped files to a memory card. Insert the card into your machine.

• Note: There are a few machines that have a CD drive. Check with your dealer for the specifics of using a multiformat CD with your machine.

NUGGET OF INSPIRATION

After all of this discussion of different formats, you now know the extreme importance of checking and double checking the package before opening it. Are you tired of all the reminders yet? Just like your mother always used to say, "This is for your own good." Remember to make sure that you've purchased the correct format for you machine, because once you start tearing open that delicate cellophane wrapping, there's no turning back.

Designs

Downloading from the Internet

The Internet offers you a wealth of embroidery design options. You'll find free designs and ones for purchase, designs from professional digitizing companies and others from private designers. A word of caution: If you're using a free design from an unknown or private designer, the quality of the design is not guaranteed. Make sure to test free designs from the Internet before using them on your projects.

To teach you how to download designs, we'll use a free design from the Sewing With Nancy® Web site as an example. Once you learn how to download here, you'll be able to do it anywhere.

To download a snowflake design using an IBM computer:

1 Open your Internet connection and go to

> http://sewingwithnancy.com

2 Click on "Television Show."

NANCY'S NOTIONS
800.833.0690
sewing with nancy

SHOP   LOGIN
VIEW BASKET   SPECIALS
CHECKOUT   QUICK ORDER
ORDER HISTORY CATALOG REQUEST

SEARCH [ ] GO HOME | TELEVISION SHOW | RETAIL STORE | ONLINE EXTRAS | EVENTS

3 Click on "Free Embroidery Designs."

Then select and click on "Free Embroidery Design—Snowflakes."

4 Scroll down to the bottom of the page. Click on your embroidery machine format from the list below the design. (Example: PES is the Baby Lock® format.)

5 A dialog box will appear similar to the one below.

File Download
Some files can harm your computer. If the file information below looks suspicious, or you do not fully trust the source, do not open or save this file.

File name: SGLsnowflakespes.zip
File type: ZIP file
From: www.nancysnotions.com

Would you like to open the file or save it to your computer?

[Open] [Save] [Cancel] [More Info]

☐ Always ask before opening this type of file

NUGGET OF INSPIRATION

If you're being a good embroiderer and testing each design before stitching it on a project, then you no doubt have piles and piles of stitch-outs laying idly about your sewing room. What should you do with them? Think of creative ways to incorporate those stitch-outs into projects. For example, you could create an entire quilt top by piecing together different stitch-outs, adding sashing strips to connect them. Or, stitch test designs on pillowcases or tea towels to give as gifts.

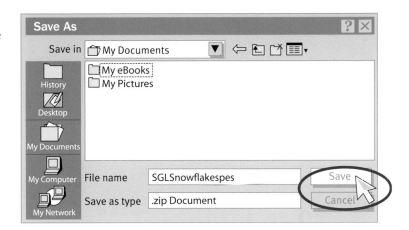

6 Click "Save." The following dialog box appears. You can now choose where to save the zipped design file on your computer. We suggest you save it to your "My Documents" folder.

7 After you pick a download location, click "Save."

8 The file will then be downloaded from the Internet to the location you chose. Click "Close" to close the download window.

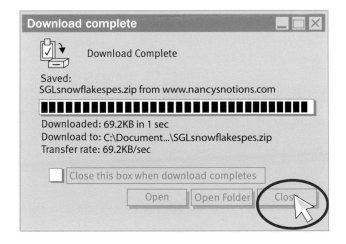

NUGGET OF INSPIRATION

The downloaded file is a zipped embroidery design file. Basically, a zipped embroidery design file is the design compressed to save space and time when downloading. To use the design you need to unzip the file using an unzipping program, such as WinZip®. If you do not own an unzipping program, go to www.winzip.com to download a free evaluation version. The following instructions use WinZip®.

9 Go to your "My Documents" folder and double click the saved version of your design. Your WinZip® program should open automatically. Click "Use Evaluation Version," "I agree," "Next," or whatever prompt is fitting for your version.

10 Select the design files and click "Extract."

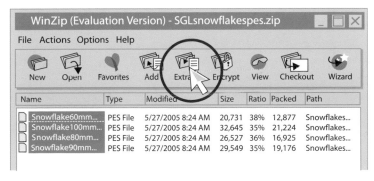

Downloading from the Internet   23

Designs

11 Choose (Click) where you want to save the designs. Options could be "My Documents" or a floppy disk or other location of your choice. Click Extract. The designs will automatically be saved to that location. For example, if you have chosen your "My Documents" folder, it will create a file folder in that location that contains your unzipped designs. Close any open windows.

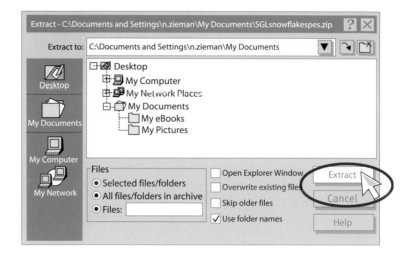

12 Go to "My Documents" to verify that a file folder was created with the unzipped files in it. The zipped version (SGLsnowflake) which also appears on the screen can be deleted if you wish.

13 You can save the designs to a floppy disk, memory stick, transfer directly to your embroidery machine, or use software such as Amazing Design® The Amazing Box™ or The Mini Amazing Box™.

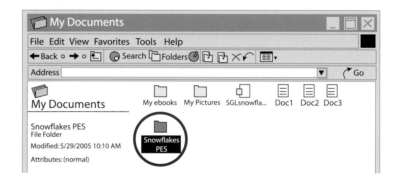

14 If you are saving the designs to a memory card, open your sewing machine software. Select and open the designs from the saved location. Note: Check with your machine instruction manual or dealer to determine what type of reader/writer box or software is needed to transfer the design to a memory card for that machine. (For example, you may be able to use Amazing Designs® Box™ or The Mini Amazing Box™.)

15 Follow the instructions to transfer the design to the memory card.

16 Insert the memory card in the machine. You're ready to embroider!

HARDWARE & SOFTWARE

As we mentioned, sometimes you need a separate IBM compatible home computer and a software program with hardware component to transfer designs from their original form to a memory card so that you can use them in your embroidery machine. That's where hardware and software come in. Hardware is an external component that connects to your computer through a port and reads designs from and writes to memory cards.

Each hardware component comes with its own companion software program that must be installed on the computer. A transfer system opens the door to the world of embroidery, one where you are no longer limited to memory cards. A transfer system gives you access to designs on many different types of media. Note: If you wish to do any editing to designs, such as resizing or combining, you'll need additional computer software.

When purchasing hardware, you first need to identify the type of port your computer has. A port is a plug-in that allows the hardware to communicate with the computer. There are two types of ports: serial or USB. After identifying the type your computer has, purchase hardware with the same type of port.

When purchasing software, check machine formats and computer requirements. It's very important to know these things before purchasing hardware and/or software, because as we've mentioned several times before, once opened, they're often not returnable.

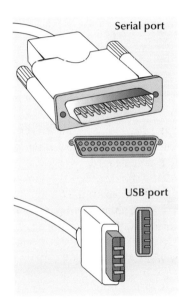

Serial port

USB port

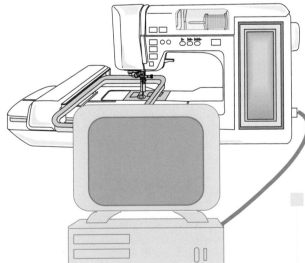

Direct Transfer Systems

Some machine models have a cable that connects the machine directly to a computer. The cable is a "hardware" device that works together with its own software program, similar to a reader/writer box. In that case, you can load designs from floppy disks and CDs onto your computer, then transfer them directly into the memory of your embroidery machine or a memory card inserted in the machine.

◼ NUGGET OF INSPIRATION
You'll notice that when speaking about computers, we only mention IBM compatible computers, not Macintosh. That's because most embroidery machine company's software/hardware programs are only compatible with IBM. Currently, software compatible with Macintosh computers is very limited.

Designs

Reader/Writer Transfer Systems

Reader/writers are the most common types of embroidery hardware. As the name implies, they allow you to read designs from a computer hard drive, floppy disk, CD and memory card, and write designs to a blank memory card. For most reader/writer transfer systems, a computer is required.

Single Format Reader/Writer

Generally sold by machine dealers for a specific machine brand, a single format reader/writer box has only one slot and works with only one format. This type of box performs two main functions. First, it allows you to save designs from your computer to a blank memory card, which you can insert into your machine for stitching. Second, it allows you to read designs from a memory card into the computer so that you can edit designs in the computer software program. Then, resave the newly edited designs to a blank memory card for stitching.

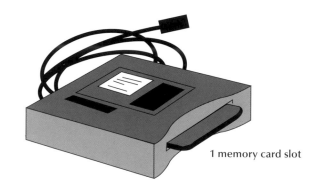

1 memory card slot

Single format reader/writer box

Multiformat Reader/Writer

The multiformat reader/writer box works with several different formats and has more slots, generally two or four. This box performs the same functions as the single format reader/writer box; it allows you to save designs to a blank memory card. However, since it reads multiple formats, you can also convert designs on a memory card from one format to another. For example, say that you own a Baby Lock® machine. You want to use a design collection but it's only available in the Pfaff format. What to do? Do you give up and find another collection? NO. You insert the Pfaff format memory card into the Pfaff slot in your reader/writer box. Insert a blank memory card into the Baby Lock® slot on the reader/writer box. Read the designs from the Pfaff card and write to the Baby Lock® card. Then, you're ready to stitch.

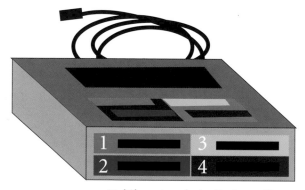

Multiformat reader/writer box with 4 card slots

With a multiformat reader/writer box, you can save designs from your computer hard drive, CD and floppy disk drives; read other format cards and convert them to your machine's language; and save designs from your own format memory card (if you've edited designs).

3

Stabilizers & Tools

Tools help you to stitch flawless-looking designs.
They provide a firm foundation of support, assist you
in accurately marking design placements, and enable
you to cleanly trim jump threads. Every stabilizer
you use, every thread color you choose, every cut
that you make brings you one step closer to the
realization of your creative vision.

Background: Amazing Designs ADC 1345
Inset: Amazing Designs ADC 1345

Stabilizers and Tools

STABILIZERS

By definition, a stabilizer is designed to support or even replace fabric under the stress of stitching. Sounds easy enough, right?

Wrong. Many different stabilizers are currently on the market, and making the correct choice can make or break your project. Eliminators of fabric distortion and puckers, stabilizers are important staple products for every well-equipped sewing room.

We've organized stabilizers into four categories, based on how you remove them—cut-aways, tear-aways, wash-aways and heat-aways. If you're just starting out, familiarize yourself with the different types of stabilizers by doing some serious exploring. It's important that you take the time to test, test, test! Stitching test samples will give you an accurate idea of how stabilizers will perform, and will save you from tearing your hair out after making a potentially disastrous mistake on your actual project.

Cut-Aways

Cut-away stabilizers are like your best friend. They are always there for you to get you through all of life's ups and downs. Cut-aways are permanent and remain on fabric through multiple washings. As you might guess from the name, to remove cut-away stabilizers, simply trim them from the edge of your embroidery after the design is stitched and the fabric is unhooped.

Cut-aways are appropriate for knits, unstable fabrics and designs that might be distorted by tearing away the stabilizer. Since the stabilizer is trimmed away after stitching, the remaining stabilizer is there just to support the design.

Motivating Memo

Cutting stabilizer can dull your good fabric shears. It's best to use a paper scissors to cut away the excess stabilizer.

Type	Product name	Characteristics	Ideal For . . .
Translucent textured nonwoven	• Sheer Stay • Simply Stable Poly-mesh Cut-away • Sulky® Cut-Away Soft 'n Sheer™	• Lightweight • Resists stretching • Eliminates show-through; semi-transparent • Comfortable next to skin	• Lightweight knits or wovens; sheer fabrics • Dense embroidery designs, open-weave fabrics or complex designs on lightweight fabrics
Iron-on nonwoven	Fusible No Show Mesh	• Lightweight • Fuses to fabric with a low temperature iron • Resists stretching; eliminates pulling or sagging of designs • Eliminates show-through; semi-transparent • Comfortable next to skin	• Lightweight knits • Dense embroidery designs, open-weave fabrics or complex designs on lightweight fabrics
Nonwoven	• Mega Stay • Pellon® Sof-Stitch® • Simply Stable Cut-away • Sulky® Cut-Away Plus™	• Midweight • Resists stretching; soft hand and excellent stability • Eliminates pulling or sagging of designs • Provides optimum support	• Outerwear: knits, sweaters, sweatshirts and jackets • Open-weave fabrics with a large or complex design, high detail embroidery designs, or dense designs
Water-activated adhesive	• Hydro-stick™ Cut-away	• Heavyweight • Eliminates hooping fabric. Hoop stabilizer, moisten with moist sponge; fabric sticks to stabilizer • Replaces spray adhesives; eco-friendly • Leaves no gummy residue on needle or machine parts	• Avoiding hoop marks on fine fabrics, napped fabrics, synthetic suedes, leathers and fleece • Small or irregularly shaped items difficult to hoop • Unstable fabrics

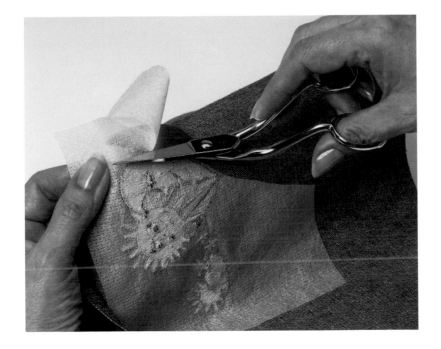

NUGGET OF INSPIRATION

When removing cut-away stabilizer, it's really easy to slip and cut through your base fabric. Oops! Unfortunately, that mistake is very difficult to correct. To prevent cutting through your fabric, hold the stabilizer as shown, cupping the fabric around your hand. Trim using an appliqué scissors. Its wide bill lifts the stabilizer as you trim. No more unexpected cuts!

Stabilizers and Tools

Tear-Aways

Tear-away stabilizers are like the crazy new hair color you tried or a wild shade of lipstick. They are only temporary but lots of fun! After the stitching process, they are torn away from the design. Tear-aways are temporary, and it's generally easy to remove the excess because the needle perforates the stabilizer during embroidery. They are ideal for dense stitching where tearing won't distort embroidery stitches or the fabric.

> ### Motivating Memo
> *If a tear-away stabilizer stretches and tears in one direction, layer two pieces at a right angle to achieve proper tension.*

When you think of stabilizers as the foundation of your project, it's only natural to assume that they go on the bottom. But, did you know that some tear-away stabilizers can also be used as toppings? Toppings are used on top of the fabric being embroidered. They prevent stitches from sinking into high loft or looped fabrics. For example, Dry Cover-Up™, a permanent vinyl stabilizer, keeps the base fabric from showing through embroidery.

■ NUGGET OF INSPIRATION
When removing tear-away stabilizers, it's tempting to just rip the stabilizer away. That can place unnecessary and damaging stress on the stitches and fabric. Instead, place your thumb on the edge of the stitching as you tear away the stabilizer. You'll protect your stitching and fabric, and get closer removal of the stabilizer.

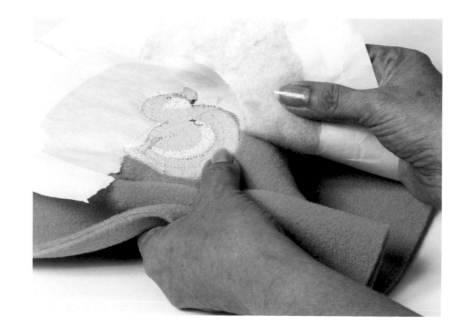

Stabilizers and Tools

Type	Product name	Characteristics	Ideal For . . .
Iron-on translucent film	Kleer-Fuse™	• Very lightweight • Fuses to fabric with a low temperature iron; opaque until fused, then turns clear • Eliminates fabric shifting, sliding, puckering • Stabilizer under stitches is permanent; helps support embroidery design	• Fabrics requiring low temperature iron • Lightweight knits; stretchy or delicate fabrics
Nonwoven	Pellon® Lightweight Stitch-N-Tear®	• Lightweight • Prevents show-through; available in two colors • Multiple layers provide added support	• Lightweight wovens and knits • Small motifs on blouses, jackets or windbreakers, denim shirts or knit turtlenecks
Iron-on nonwoven	• Firm Hold Lite™ • Sulky® Totally Stable™	• Lightweight • Fuses to fabric with a medium temperature iron • Eliminates shifting, sliding and puckering; holds fabric straight and taut in hoop • Leaves no residue on fabric	• Lighter weight fabrics that can be ironed • Knits and wovens; stretchy or delicate fabrics • Delicate embroidery stitches
100% cotton	Cotton Soft by Madeira	• Midweight • All-purpose stabilizer • Soft and gentle to the touch, yet strong and firm for hooping and stitching • Won't stretch or distort stitches when removed	• Virtually any fabric • Baby and children's garments • Where stabilizer touches skin
Nonwoven	• Ultra Tear • Pellon® Stitch-N-Tear® • Simply Stable Tear-away	• Midweight • Eliminates puckering and stitch distortion • Multiple layers provide added support	• Virtually any fabric • Small motifs on blouses, jackets, denim shirts, windbreakers or knit turtlenecks
Iron-on nonwoven	Firm Hold™	• Midweight • Fuses to fabric with a medium temperature iron • Provides firm hold • Eliminates shifting, sliding and puckering of fabric; holds fabric straight and taut in hoop	• All weights and types of fabrics that can be ironed • Knits and wovens • Stretchy or heavyweight fabrics
Colored vinyl	Dry Cover-Up™	• Midweight • Keeps base fabric color from showing through embroidery • Prevents embroidery from sinking into high loft fabrics; gives three-dimensional lift • Permanent; does not wash out	• Using on top of fabric to match thread color, enhancing embroidery • Most fabrics, prints, patterns and fabric colors that will show through embroidery • Areas where the back of embroidery shows
Water-activated adhesive	Hydro-stick™ Tear-away	• Heavyweight • Eliminates hooping fabric. Hoop stabilizer, moisten with sponge; fabric sticks to stabilizer. • Replaces spray adhesives; eco-friendly • Leaves no gummy residue on needle or machine parts	• Avoiding hoop marks on fine fabrics, napped fabrics, synthetic suedes, leathers and fleece • Items too small or irregularly shaped to hoop such as cuffs, collars, pockets and children's garments • Stable fabrics
Adhesive stabilizer with release paper	• Filmoplast Stic • SIA™	• Heavyweight • Eliminates hooping fabric. Hoop stabilizer; score and remove release paper to expose adhesive; fabric sticks to stabilizer • Replaces spray adhesives; eco-friendly • Leaves no gummy residue on needle or machine parts	• Avoiding hoop marks on fine fabrics, napped fabrics, synthetic suedes, leathers and fleece • Items too small or irregularly shaped to hoop • Preventing stretching while embroidering on knits

Stabilizers and Tools

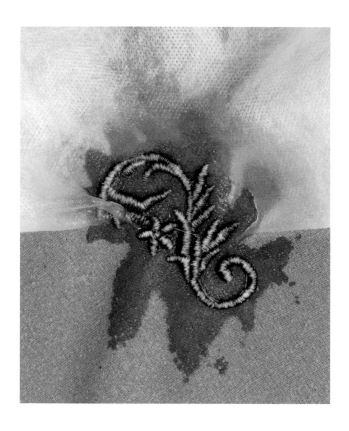

Wash-Aways

Wash-away stabilizers are like soap operas, romance novels, chocolate and ice cream. They are there when you need a quick fix, then just disappear with the click of a switch, or a spoon when you don't need them!

Wash-aways are designed for use on washable fabrics, are easily removed by water and leave no visible residue. Most wash-away stabilizers are packaged as transparent film. When exposed to air, some wash-away stabilizers can dry out and become brittle. Conversely, in very humid conditions, wash-away stabilizers may actually begin to dissolve. To prevent this, store your wash-away stabilizers in airtight containers.

Many wash-away—or water-soluble—stabilizers can also be used as toppings to prevent stitches from sinking into high loft or looped fabrics. For example, if you were embroidering a set of terry cloth towels, that would be a great opportunity to use a wash-away stabilizer on top. Your stitches will stand tall and proud!

◼ NUGGET OF INSPIRATION
There are two main methods for removing wash-away stabilizers.

1) Soak the fabric in water. Soaking works best for heavyweight stabilizers.

2) Mist the stabilizer using a spray bottle. Misting is best used with lightweight stabilizers.

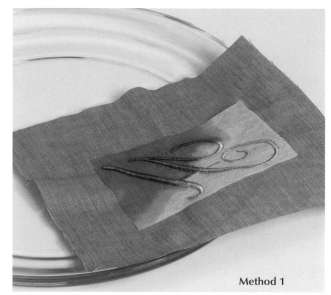

Method 1

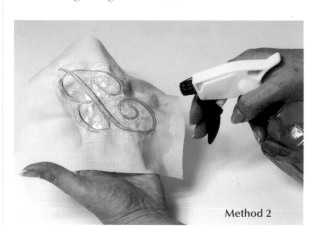

Method 2

Type	Product name	Characteristics	Ideal For . . .
Transparent film	Clear Away *Lite*	• Very lightweight • Leaves no residue; eco-friendly • Prevents loops from pulling on knitted or looped fabrics	• Virtually any lightweight, delicate washable fabric • Using on top of fabric to prevent stitches from sinking into fabrics
Transparent film	Avalon® by Madeira	• Lightweight • Prevents loops from pulling on knitted or looped fabrics • Can draw design and stitch directly onto multiple layers of film for free-style machine embroidery	• Appliqués, terry toweling, knits and buttonholes • Dense embroidery; free-style machine embroidery • Using on top of fabric to prevent stitches from sinking into fabrics
Liquid Spray	Perfect Sew™ Spray	• Allows you to customize amount of stiffness • Eliminates puckering on embroidery and appliqué	• Sheer and delicate fabrics • Most washable fabrics that need stability
Water-soluble nonwoven	• Wash-Away • Aqua-Melt™	• Midweight • Provides extreme stability; does not stretch • Flexible and soft; easy to handle for cutting and hooping; can be easily hooped with fabric	• Blankets, napkins, handkerchiefs or any single layer of fabric where a traditional backing would show • Baby clothes; lace work and monogramming • Using on top of fabric to prevent stitches from sinking into fabrics
Adhesive nonwoven	• Aquabond • Wash-Away Extra	• Midweight • Soft and stable, with the added bonus of a paper-backed adhesive • Eliminates hooping fabric. Hoop stabilizer; score and remove release paper to expose adhesive. Fabric sticks to adhesive.	• Avoiding hoop marks on any washable fabric • Items too small or irregularly shaped to hoop, such as cuffs, collars, pockets and children's garments
Transparent film	• Clear Away • Sulky® Ultra Solvy™	• Mid- to heavyweight • Provides extreme stability; does not stretch • Can draw design and stitch directly onto multiple layers of film for free-style machine embroidery • Dissolve to use as a brush-on or spray-on stabilizer	• Sheer and/or high loft fabrics; lace work and monogramming • Hoopless embroidery; free-style machine embroidery • Using on top of fabric to prevent stitches from sinking into fabrics
Adhesive, transparent film	S-dSV™	• Heavyweight • Provides extreme stability; bonds to fabric without heat • Replaces spray adhesives; eco-friendly; leaves no residue • Removing release liner exposes adhesive • Used together with hooped adhesive stabilizer or reinforced plastic with cut-out window. Back window with S-dSV™; fabric sticks to adhesive	• Sheer and lightweight fabrics; bridal tulle, lace work, etc. or whenever the back of the fabric may be visible • Temporary stabilizer when embroidering delicate fabrics, fleece and other stretch fabrics • Placing on top and bottom of high nap fabrics to prevent nap from showing through embroidery and stabilizer from remaining on back

Stabilizers and Tools

Heat-Aways

Heat-aways are very similar to wash-away stabilizers. Like wash-away stabilizers, heat-aways are there when you need them; then disappear when you don't. Heat-aways are temporary; they disintegrate with heat and are removed without washing or spraying with water. In fact, you shouldn't get them wet. Doing so can transfer chemicals from the stabilizer to the base fabric. Then when you use an iron, the base fabric disintegrates. That's something you definitely don't want to happen.

Heat-aways are great for use with fabrics that aren't washable (such as velvet), with special techniques like making lace, and with delicate fabrics.

As you can see from the following chart, there are not many heat-away stabilizers currently on the market. We've only listed one. You probably won't need to use heat-away stabilizers very often.

Type	Product name	Characteristics	Ideal For . . .
Heat sensitive woven	Sulky® Heat-Away™	• Midweight • Disintegrates with a hot, dry iron, then brushes away easily • Easy to see through and trace designs onto for stitching • Firm	• Spun lace, cutwork, faux woven fabric, 3-D appliqué • Any project where wetting or tearing would distort stitches or damage base fabric

■ NUGGET OF INSPIRATION

When removing a heat-away stabilizer, don't be alarmed when you see the stabilizer turning brown. I promise you; that's supposed to happen! When the stabilizer heats up, it literally burns up. Then, you just simply brush it away and move on.

ADHESIVES AND FUSIBLE SPRAYS

These sprays do just what their names imply. Use them to turn nonadhesive cut-away and tear-away stabilizers into adhesive ones.

Use adhesive sprays to adhere the stabilizer to your fabric for greater stability, but do not use them with wash-away or heat-away stabilizers. The dampness of the spray could damage or dissolve the stabilizer. NOTE: Be careful not to spray adhesive near your machine. If any overspray gets into your computerized machine, it could adhere to machine parts and cause lots of problems.

Fusible sprays function slightly differently than adhesive ones. Apply fusible spray onto stabilizer. Let it dry; position the stabilizer over the fabric; and press to temporarily fuse the stabilizer to fabric. After embroidering, you can cut or tear the excess away.

Type	Product name	Characteristics	Ideal For . . .
Temporary spray adhesive	Sulky® KK2000™ • Dritz® Spray Adhesive • Sullivans Adhesive Spray • Madeira MSA 1100	• Temporary; allows you to reposition the fabric before stitching it in place • Bonding disappears in 2–5 days • Odorless, ozone friendly, will not stain • Doesn't gum up needles or scissors	• Temporarily bond stabilizer to fabric
Fusible spray	606® Spray and Fix	• Spray on stabilizer, let dry for three minutes, iron to fuse to fabric. • Cut or tear excess away. • Colorless, stainless • Spray both fabric and stabilizer for a permanent bond. • Leaves no residue; won't gum up needles or scissors	• Temporarily or permanently bond stabilizer to fabric

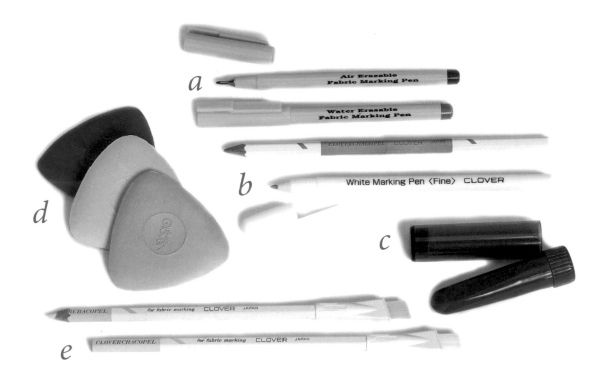

MARKING TOOLS

Marking Pens and Pencils

a Fabric marking pens are available in air- and water-soluble forms. Air-soluble pens (generally purple ink) contain disappearing ink that vanishes within 12–24 hours. Water-soluble pens (generally blue ink) contain ink that can be removed with cold water.

b Fabric marking pencils have super-thin lead specifically designed for fabric. Since they contain less graphite than standard pencil leads, they resist smearing and wash out. Marks erase with a drop of cold water. Pencils are also available with white lead for marking dark fabrics.

> ### Motivating Memo
>
> *Air- and water-soluble pens are very convenient, but pressing can permanently set these marks into fabric. To avoid this, completely remove marks before pressing, even if that means using water on air-soluble marks. After all, you don't want today's helper coming back to haunt you tomorrow!*

DO NOT use regular ballpoint pens or regular lead pencils, as marks are difficult to remove.

Chalk is available in several colors to contrast with every fabric; it comes in several forms.

c Chaco-Liner—looks similar to a tube of lipstick. Dispenses accurate, thin powder lines on any fabric. It's available in white, pink, yellow or blue for light and dark fabrics.

d Triangle Tailor's Chalk—has a chalk base in a firm triangular form. It comes in a variety of colors, and it never leaves a stain.

e Chacopel Pencils—tailor's chalk in a fine line pencil.

Chalk marks brush or wash out easily. They come in white, yellow and pink/blue. Pencil caps with brushes and sharpener are also available.

EMBROIDERY NEEDLES

Using the correct needle for embroidery will ensure smooth stitching and clean finished embroidery. Using a new needle for each project is an inexpensive way to avoid stitching problems.

Change your needle after every three hours of stitching. Changing the needle regularly contributes to clean, accurate stitching and saves you from broken threads and other embroidery problems.

- Use size 75/11 needles for lightweight to medium weight fabrics and size 90/14 needles for medium to heavyweights.

- In general, select a needle that is designed to work with the specific fabric you're using in your project. For example, use a ballpoint needle with knit fabrics and a sharp needle with wovens. However, if you're using a specialty thread, select a needle to work with that thread. For example, use a metallic or metafil needle with metallic thread, and a topstitching needle with heavier threads such as glow in the dark thread.

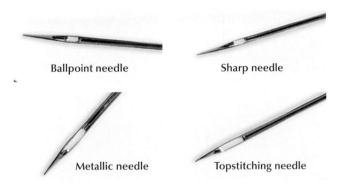

Ballpoint needle   **Sharp needle**

Metallic needle   **Topstitching needle**

- Machine Embroidery Needles feature a specially designed needle scarf and eye to virtually eliminate thread breakage when stitching dense embroidery designs. Metallic machine embroidery needles feature a fine shaft and sharp point to eliminate thread breakage, a specialized scarf to prevent skipped stitches and an elongated eye to prevent thread-stripping.

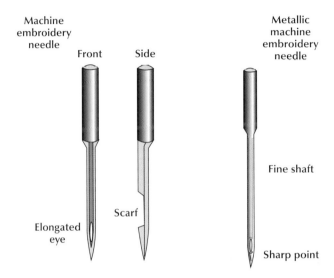

Machine embroidery needle — Front — Side — Metallic machine embroidery needle

Elongated eye — Scarf — Fine shaft — Sharp point

- Titanium Coated Embroidery Needles are strong, durable needles that work well with all projects. They work especially well with adhesive stabilizers because they resist the adhesive. Titanium needles have a lifespan five times longer than conventional machine embroidery needles.

Stabilizers and Tools

THREAD

Thread comes in a plethora of different colors and runs through every design that you stitch, but how much do you really know about this sewing room staple? Just like fabric, thread is available in different weights and fibers. The lower the weight, the thicker the thread. For example, 30 wt. thread is thicker than 40 wt.

Ply refers to the number of strands that are twisted together to create the thread. Unlike weight, a higher ply number means thicker thread. So for example, 3 ply thread is thicker than 2 ply thread. Most professionally produced embroidery designs are digitized for standard 40 wt./2 ply embroidery thread.

Embroidery threads are usually made of rayon, polyester or cotton fibers. Each has unique characteristics. Experiment with different threads to get the perfect look for your project.

Rayon Threads

- Rayon threads have a unique tight twist which creates a lustrous sheen. Durable, rayon threads have superior tensile strength and exceptional colorfastness. They're great for almost any project you can dream up!

- *Care: Machine wash and dry, hot water safe to 203° F (95 °C). Use a warm iron when needed. Use any bleach except chlorine bleach. Or, dry clean with any solvent except trichloroethylene.*

- Rayon threads are available in both solid colors and multicolored. Multicolored rayon threads range from the subtle to the dramatic. Use them to add depth, texture and dimension to your embroidery designs. They're very effective when used in combination with solid colored threads to highlight parts of a design. For example, use a multicolored thread to stitch flowers, and use a solid rayon to stitch the stems and leaves to make the flowers pop. Each type has different characteristics and works well in different types of designs.

TWEED LOOK THREAD

Tweed look thread is created by twisting two different colored strands of solid colored thread together. This subtle, multitone thread gives natural color and contour to any design. The texture of this thread is consistent. Because two different colored strands of thread are twisted together, the color of the thread is the same throughout the spool. It is ideal for highlighting realistic features on designs such as animals, fur, birds, feathers, grass, trees, flowers, rocks, water, etc.

SPECKLED THREAD

Speckled thread consists of a solid base color mixed with multicolor speckles that add depth, texture and pizzazz. The texture of this thread is sporadic because the colored speckles are randomly spaced on the base color. This thread is ideal for designs with a country feel, apples, water, flowers, butterfly wings, seashells, etc.

VARIEGATED THREAD

Variegated thread features gradations of tone-on-tone or multicolor hues. The look of variegated thread can be either subtle or very obvious, depending on how you use it. The thread consists of evenly spaced bands of color. For example, a regular line of satin stitching will appear striped. A flower bouquet design, with very small blooms, will look as if each flower is a slightly different color. Because of the consistent color changes, variegated thread is best for smaller designs. It's less desirable as a fill stitch on a large area, as the design will appear striped and the color changes will be anything but subtle.

RANDOMLY VARIEGATED THREAD

Randomly variegated thread features randomly changing lengths of color, making it different from variegated, which has consistently changing lengths of color. Unlike standard 40 wt. thread, randomly variegated thread is 30 wt. Because it is thicker, this thread helps stitches appear fuller, but it should not be used in very dense designs. It is ideal for sketchy backgrounds in landscape designs. It also livens up simple outline designs. (For example, use it to outline a design stitched with regular thread. Randomly variegated thread is much more exciting than a plain black outline and will really change the overall look of a design.)

Stabilizers and Tools

Polyester Threads

• Vibrant polyester threads resist abrasion and breakage. They remain brilliant even after repeated exposure to sunlight, chlorine and washing. They're great for baby items or often used on laundered projects. Polyester threads are available in almost as many solid colors as rayon and they look and feel similar. Multicolored options are also available.

• *Care: Machine wash and dry. Hot water safe to 203°F (95°C); safe to use chlorine bleach. Use a cool iron when needed. Or, dry clean with any solvent except trichloroethylene.*

Cotton Threads

• Cotton threads have a soft matte finish ideal for heirloom projects when you do not want the sheen or bright colors of rayon or polyester threads.

• Cotton threads are available in a variety of weights: The 80 wt. is a fine, soft, lightweight thread, ideal for delicate, dense stitching such as enhancing pillowcases or handkerchiefs. The 30 wt. is much thicker and is ideal for less dense embroidery designs and lace making.

• *Care: Machine wash and dry cool (85°F/30°C). Use any bleach except chlorine bleach. Use a hot iron when needed. Or, dry clean with any solvent except trichloroethylene.*

Specialty Threads

Life (and embroidery) is so much more enjoyable with a little bit of sparkle and pizzazz. Using specialty threads is like dressing your designs in their finest eveningwear and getting them ready for a night on the town! Create a variety of effects, ranging from silly to dramatic. Use metallic thread to add a touch of elegance to a design, or use threads that glow in the dark to create a spooky Halloween project. As with multicolor threads, these specialty threads are quite effective when used in combination with other types of thread. They'll bring attention to specific areas of designs, making them pop out and get noticed! The following threads are just the tip of the iceberg of all the fun and unique threads available.

TEXTURED METALLIC THREAD

- Gets its sparkle from a slightly textured twist, adding richness to your designs. Use a vertical spool holder: the thread unwinds better and feeds into the machine more smoothly. For best results, use a metallic embroidery needle. Stitch slowly and loosen the tension.

- *Care: Machine wash and dry (hot water safe to 140° F/60° C). Do not bleach. Use a cool iron when needed. Or, dry clean.*

SMOOTH METALLIC THREAD

- Catches light in a lustrous glow with its smooth finish. Use a vertical spool holder; the thread unwinds better and feeds into the machine more smoothly. For best results, use a metallic embroidery needle. Stitch slowly and loosen the tension.

- *Care: Machine wash and dry (hot water safe to 140° F/60° C). Do not bleach. Use a cool iron when needed. Or, dry clean.*

GLOW IN THE DARK THREAD

- Recharges with available light and glows to brighten up any project. Feeds as smoothly as regular thread. Some brands are thicker and not very manageable, so do your homework. For best results, use a regular machine embroidery needle.

- *Care: Machine wash cool/machine dry low. Do not bleach, dry clean or iron directly on embroidery.*

RIBBON-LIKE THREAD

- Is a thin, flat, polyester film that is metalized with an aluminum holographic layer to give it a shimmering, brilliant shine. Use only on a vertical spool pin. For best results, use a 14/90 metallic, topstitching or embroidery needle, and stitch slower than usual.

- *Care: Machine wash cool or warm/machine dry low. Use a warm iron when needed; do not iron directly on embroidery. Or, dry clean.*

Stabilizers and Tools

Bobbin Thread

Bobbin thread is one of the most important parts of creating high quality embroidery. Bobbin thread is thinner than conventional embroidery thread—it's specifically weighted to work with embroidery thread. It may be thin, but it's strong enough to keep densely embroidered designs flexible. Using a thinner thread in the bobbin reduces bulk and helps embroidery lie smooth.

Bobbin thread is available both on spools and on prewound bobbins. Bobbin thread on a spool must be wound onto your machine's bobbins. Prewound bobbins save time, are convenient and generally hold more thread (up to three times more) than self-wound bobbins. However, make sure to check whether prewound bobbins fit your machine. And before starting your actual project, always stitch a test sample to determine which type of thread works best.

Here are some general guidelines and tips for working with bobbin thread:

• If bobbin thread shows on the top of the design, check for incorrect threading, then reduce the top thread tension.

• If you're concerned about matching your bobbin thread to the top thread, use cotton prewound bobbins, available in multiple colors. This is ideal for projects on which the back of the design will show.

• Prewound bobbins are sometimes filled too full to fit in some machines. If this is the case, spool off several yards of thread so the bobbin fits in the machine.

• If your machine has a low bobbin indicator, it is best to change bobbins before reaching the very end of the bobbin. Thread is often very tight at the end of the bobbin and this could cause serious stitching problems. When the bobbin indicator first indicates that the bobbin thread is running low, change it at the next opportunity.

• The sides on cardboard prewound bobbins are removable. If you have a low bobbin indicator that reads through the bobbin side, remove one side, (the side which faces the sensor light), and the automatic bobbin sensor will work. Leaving the second side on will prevent the bobbin from jumping around as it reaches the end of the bobbin.

• Wind spooled bobbin thread onto bobbins at half speed to get an even, consistent wind and to avoid stretching the fibers.

• Using prewound bobbins with cardboard sides in machines with drop-in bobbins is not recommended.

▌ NUGGET OF INSPIRATION

Talk about unsung heroes! Bobbin thread rarely takes center stage, but it definitely plays a strong supporting role in determining the quality of your finished embroidery. Using a quality bobbin thread reduces bulk, helps top stitches lie smoothly and helps prevent breaking, knotting and shredding. Experiment, and test several bobbin threads. Use the thread that gives you best results, and it will keep you "bobbin' along" Broadway!

TOOLS FOR TESTING

Test your design before stitching on your project. You'll save time in the long run, and you'll dramatically increase the chances that your finished embroidery will be just what you anticipated. Check stitch density, colors and placement. Remember the old adage: a stitch in time saves nine.

Sample Cloth

Embroidery sample cloth is a white prestiffened muslin designed specifically for testing designs. Stitch each design exactly as you want it on the finished project, backing the sample cloth with the same stabilizer you plan to use with your project. Write details such as thread colors and design number directly on the cloth. Note additional details on an embroidery reference card.

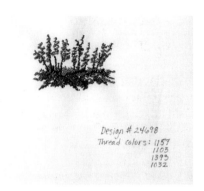

Design # 24698
Thread colors: 1157
1103
1399
1032

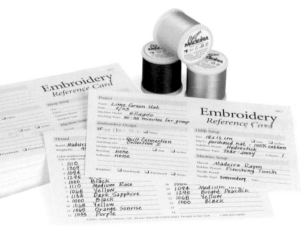

▮ Nugget of Inspiration

What measure 4" x 6", have lots of lines and make your life much easier? Embroidery reference cards! Get in the habit of using them to list the important details of every embroidery project. Once you do, you'll agree that using them is one habit you'll never want to kick.

Embroidery Reference Cards

Can you remember the color order, stabilizer type and stitching time of that design you embroidered two months ago? Yesterday? Neither can we, and that's why we use embroidery reference cards. The two-sided cards have spaces to document all the details such as stitching time, the design's original size, its new size, software used, thread colors and more.

Use reference cards with embroidery sample cloth to test designs and make templates. To store the cards, samples and photos of finished projects together for future reference, simply slip them into a plastic page protector. They'll be dust-free and organized whenever you need them. The next time you use the design you may change it again, or use it exactly as before, but by having the card, sample and photos, you don't have to repeat your work (or your mistakes)! Samples store flat for reference.

▮ Nugget of Inspiration

As an alternative to using these cards, write notes on sticky notes and leave them all over your sewing room. But, when you need them, you might find that they've disappeared! To get information about a design, you'll have to pull it up on the computer and desperately try to remember the changes you'd made. You'll basically have to repeat all of your work—a complete waste of time. Once you start using embroidery reference cards in your sewing room, you won't even consider using sticky notes!

Getting started is a matter of looking deep within and finding the desire to move forward. It means preparing for the journey ahead, choosing your path and taking the first step toward your dreams. Then, you breathe, and begin—with the realization that only you can accomplish your goals.

4 Getting Started

ORGANIZING AND CHOOSING THREADS

So you're ready to start embroidering! Make your life (and embroidery) easier by organizing your threads before you begin.

Organizing Your Thread Collection

If you're following the thread colors recommended on a design collection when you embroider, in most cases you'll be looking for thread color numbers. To simplify and speed thread selection, organize your threads by color number instead of color family. For example, arrange all of your threads in rows, with one row being the 1100s, the next 1200s and so on.

Getting your threads in order may not seem like a necessary step, especially if your design doesn't use a lot of different colors. But, the one time you don't do it may just be the time you get distracted and lose track of your thread order. Just think, one careless mistake could result in a green pig or an orange-faced baby or some other strange looking design that you never intended. Trust me—it's a good idea to have your threads in order before you start stitching the design!

Organizing Thread for Stitching a Design

Before stitching an embroidery design, get all of the threads you'll need for that design ready and in order. Whether you're following the colors recommended on the design collection or choosing your own colors, putting them in order before stitching will save you time and prevent mistakes.

• An easy way to organize threads is to use a mini thread rack. Number each peg on the rack. Then place the threads on the rack in the order listed on the thread sequence chart.

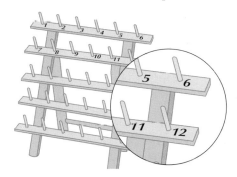

• If a color is used more than once, place an empty bobbin on the peg as a placeholder.

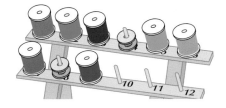

Converting Thread Colors

Each design collection recommends thread colors for stitching that design. Some collections recommend thread made by a specific manufacturer. For example, a collection may recommend Madeira threads or Sulky® threads. In both instances, the collections list the threads according to color number, for example, Red 1147, True Blue 1042, etc.

Now, that can pose a problem if the design card you're using recommends Sulky® numbers and you own Madeira thread: The numbers and colors will NOT match. Therefore, you'll need to convert the numbers. You can easily do this using a thread conversion chart.

Getting Started

You'll find thread conversion information in many books, as well as on some computer software. For example, the *Threads, Threads & More Threads! Volume I* book by Sue Green-Baker and Patty Seevers includes information on converting colors from 10 major rayon machine embroidery thread companies. The *Threads, Threads & More Threads! Volume II* CD gives similar information for converting colors between 14 polyester and cotton thread manufacturers. Look for similar information in books or computer software at your favorite sewing center or from Internet embroidery sources such as nancysnotions.com.

Other design collections indicate only generic color names, such as red, blue, orange, etc. In these cases, select colors that you like or that coordinate with your project. Test the colors you choose by stitching a sample to make sure they work well together and you like the finished design. If not, you can modify the colorations before stitching your actual project.

SELECTING FABRICS AND "BLANKS"

Now that your thread is organized, decide where you'll embroider your design. Start with fabric yardage and make a project with tender loving care. Or, for an even easier option, select a "blank." Blanks are ready-made garments and items on which you can embroider. Since the construction is already finished, you can devote your time to personalizing that item and making it one of a kind.

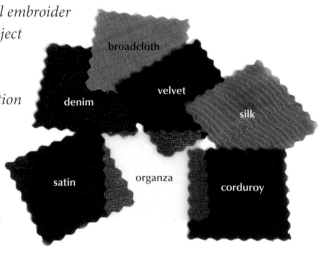

Fabrics

You can embroider on almost any type of fabric. The trick is choosing the correct stabilizer and design to suit that fabric. So, here are a few things you need to know about fabric in order to make wise stabilizer and design choices.

Fabrics are made in three ways: woven, knit and nonwoven. Blanks, those ready-made garments and items, also fit into these categories, since they're constructed from fabric.

• Woven fabrics—Yarns go over and under one another.

Examples of woven fabrics:
- denim
- corduroy
- broadcloth
- batiste
- organza
- challis
- wool coating
- silk
- satin

Examples of woven blanks:
- denim or chambray garments
- towels
- canvas totes

Choosing designs for woven fabrics:
Some woven fabrics (such as denim and broad-cloth) are so sturdy, you can use designs that are quite dense. Other woven fabrics (for example, organza) are very thin and sheer, so it's better to use less dense designs.

A dense design is suitable for a sturdy fabric

Choose a less dense design on sheer fabric

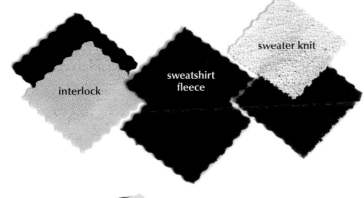

sweater knit

sweatshirt fleece

interlock

• Knit fabrics—One loop of yarn is pulled through another loop. Most knits stretch.

Examples of knit fabrics:
  • interlock
  • sweatshirt fleece
  • sweater knits

Examples of knit blanks:
  • T-shirts
  • sweatshirts
  • socks

Choosing designs for knit fabrics:
Knits have a tendency to stretch, so choose designs that are less dense for best results.

If the knit has a lot of loft, (for example, with sweatshirt fleece or high loft fleece), try using a stabilizer on top of the fabric as well as on the bottom to prevent the design from sinking into the fabric.

Select a less dense design on knit

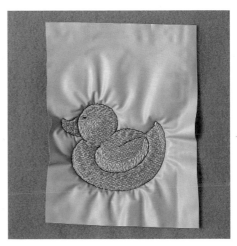

Use stabilizer on top and bottom with lofty fabrics

Getting Started

• Nonwoven fabrics—Heat, moisture and pressure are applied to fibers, forcing them close together. Sometimes chemicals are added to hold the fibers together.

Examples of nonwoven fabrics:
  • many interfacings
  • synthetic suede
  • felt

Examples of nonwoven blanks:
  • synthetic suede garments or accessories
  • felt hats

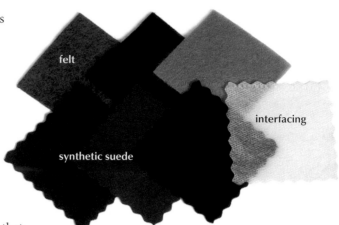

Choosing designs for nonwoven fabrics:
You can use most designs on nonwovens. Avoid designs that are extremely dense. Combined with the thickness of the fabric, the stitching may bunch up and create a thread nest on the underside of the fabric

POSITIONING AIDS

After you select a design for your embroidery project, the next crucial step is positioning it on your project. Doing that accurately will help avoid worrisome surprises—a design slightly off center, or worse yet, a design somewhere other than you expected.

You can position a design randomly or in an exact location. For many commonly embroidered items, such as T-shirts, sweatshirts, hats, table linens, towels, bed linens, blankets and boxer shorts, there are industry guidelines for embroidery placement. For example, on a T-shirt, the embroidery design is usually placed on the left chest or at the center front.

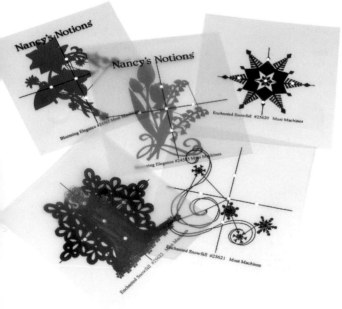

Using Templates

If you decide to position designs in specific locations, you'll find templates extremely helpful. Templates help you precisely place designs on your projects. There are several types of templates. Some design collections offer ready-made templates, but you can also make your own.

Using templates definitely takes some of the worry out of positioning embroidery designs, especially on flat fabrics. But as you gain experience, you'll undoubtedly want to embroider more challenging projects that include multiple layers of fabric—T-shirts, sweatshirts, linens, shirts, etc. You'll find a variety of products available to help you efficiently, consistently and accurately position embroidery. Spend less time preparing for embroidery and more time getting compliments once the embroidery is complete!

Purchased Templates are extremely convenient. Often made of durable plastic, each template has a printed silhouette of a design, a center hole and cross marks. They're ready to use as soon as you open the package.

The Perfect Placement Kit—designed by Eileen Roche and Deborah Jones of *Designs in Machine Embroidery* magazine—includes purchased templates specifically designed to simplify positioning on ready-made items such as embroidery blanks.

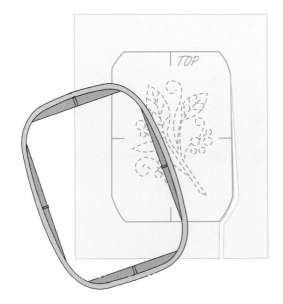

Do-it-Yourself Templates

If purchased templates aren't available, you can make your own. Try one of the following techniques:

1 Stitch the design or the outline of the design on a heavy or densely woven test fabric such as embroidery sample cloth. Before removing the stitched design from the hoop, mark the horizontal and vertical centers of the hoop and trace around the inside of the hoop. Also indicate the top of the hoop. After removing the fabric from the hoop, cut around the traced line and use the cutout as a template.

2 Stitch the design and mark the horizontal and vertical centers while it's still in the hoop.

3 Print out templates using your computer. To do this, you must have a software program that enables you to get the design into the computer. For example, for designs on a CD, you'll need a CD ROM Drive; for Memory cards you'll need The Amazing Box™. Most software programs, such as Amazing Designs® Smart•Sizer Platinum™, also can provide print to-scale templates. Check your settings.

Getting Started

Embroidery T-square

An embroidery T-square such as Embroiderer's Buddy helps position designs on items like T-shirts and sweatshirts. It's designed according to industry standards, and you'll get consistent results every time.

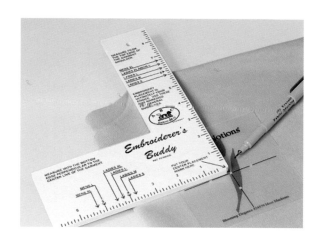

1 With the Buddy facing right side up, locate the size of the T-shirt on both the vertical and horizontal sides.

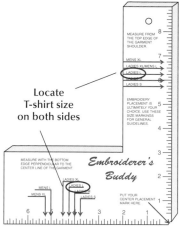

Locate T-shirt size on both sides

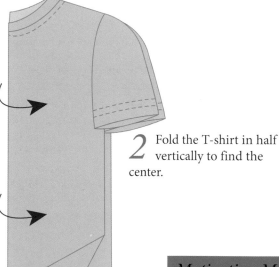

2 Fold the T-shirt in half vertically to find the center.

3 Place the vertical side of the Buddy along the shoulder, aligning the size mark with the shoulder seam.

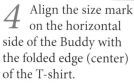

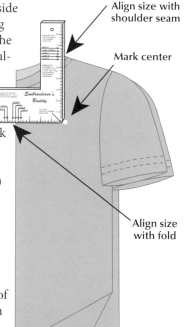

Align size with shoulder seam

Mark center

Align size with fold

4 Align the size mark on the horizontal side of the Buddy with the folded edge (center) of the T-shirt.

5 Using the Buddy as a guide, mark the center placement. This mark indicates where the exact center of your embroidery design should go.

Motivating Memo

When you remove the Buddy from the T-shirt, you're left with only a center mark, not any cross marks. Align the vertical edge of a quilting ruler with the folded edge of the shirt. Move the ruler over to the center mark and mark the vertical line. Use these marks to line up the T-shirt in the hoop.

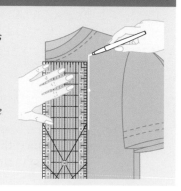

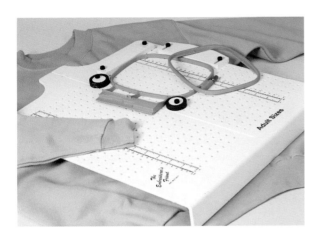

Embroiderer's Positioning Board

A board such as the Embroiderer's Friend is ideal for positioning designs on a variety of garments. It both helps you hold onto the garment as you align the design and prevents you from hooping the back of the garment. After marking the position of the design, use this board to easily hoop garments like T-shirts and sweatshirts.

1 Determine design placement on the shirt, and mark with a cross mark. Place a dot at the center point of the cross mark.

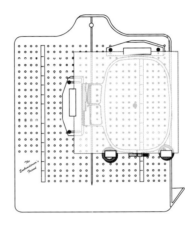

5 Tape your stabilizer onto the brackets so that it completely covers the outer ring of the hoop. This keeps the stabilizer in place while the garment is mounted onto the Embroiderer's Friend.

2 Lay the T-shirt in position over the Embroiderer's Friend, making sure to align the shoulder and front. Transfer the mark from the T-shirt to the Embroiderer's Friend.

6 Slide the garment over the board, aligning the neckline with the marked line on the board. The lip on the bottom edge of the Embroiderer's Friend fits against the edge of a table, preventing the board from sliding around.

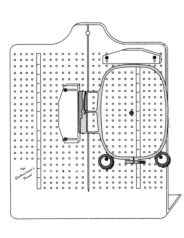

3 Place the outer hoop so that the center marking on the Embroiderer's Friend is in the center of the hoop. Arrange the brackets on the pegboard to fit your hoop.

4 Position and attach brackets according to instructions that come with the Embroiderer's Friend.

7 Place the inner hoop into the outer hoop, aligning the cross marks.

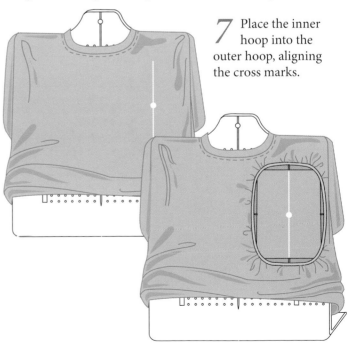

HOOPING AIDS

Springs

These little metal springs help keep your outer hoop open so it's easier to get the inner hoop in place. Putting them onto your hoop takes only seconds, but the benefits will pay off for years.

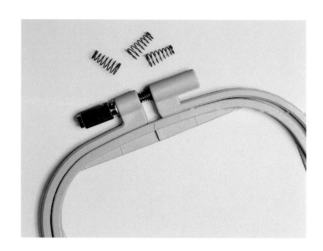

1 Remove the tension screw from the hoop.

4 Put the screw through the second part of the hoop and tighten.

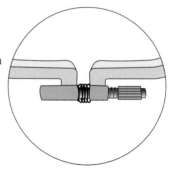

2 Put the screw through the first part of the hoop.

Place screw through first side of hoop

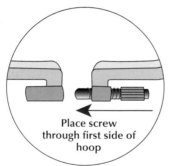

■ NUGGET OF INSPIRATION
You've heard of looking for a needle in a haystack? Well, looking for a misplaced screw or a nut isn't fun, either. When you're inserting springs, do so over a cleared work area. That way you'll be able to more easily find anything that escapes, and your hooping will be a lot more trouble-free.

3 Slide one spring onto the screw.

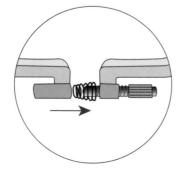

Snappy

If you're doing lots of embroidery, hooping can put a lot of strain on your hands. This hooping aid puts even pressure on all four sides of the hoop; it really saves your hands. Snappy works with most home sewing/embroidery machine hoops. Informative instructions come with Snappy, detailing precisely how to get best results. Here's a brief outline of how to use Snappy in conjunction with the Embroiderer's Friend to hoop a T-shirt.

1 Set up Snappy to accommodate your hoop.

2 Place the inner hoop in the brackets. The brackets should be snug enough that they hold the hoop in place even when you turn the Snappy over.

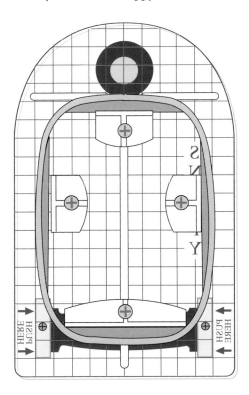

3 Position your outer hoop, fabric and stabilizer for hooping.

4 Place the Snappy over the outer hoop, with the inner hoop side facing down. Guide the hoop using both hands on the Snappy.

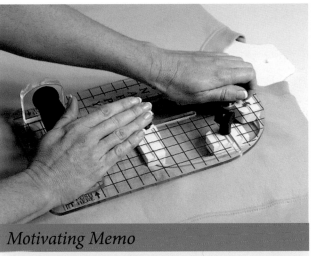

Motivating Memo

Be sure to use the bottom handle at the corners, rather than pressing down in the middle. Gripping the middle will fatigue your hands just as much as hooping without the Snappy would.

5 Tilt the Snappy and apply pressure just at the top of the inner hoop.

6 Using the handle at the bottom of the Snappy, apply pressure to one corner and then the other, snapping each corner into place.

Getting Started

PROPER STABILIZING

Although some may beg to differ, I believe that no seamstress is an island. Everyone needs support at some point in life. Nowhere is that statement truer than in the world of machine embroidery. Proper stabilization is the very foundation of good embroidery. Without proper support, designs can pucker, pull or sag. Sometimes the outline doesn't line up with the other areas of the design. That's called "poor registration." Unstable and unsupported fabric can also result in stitches sinking into the fabric or fabric stretched beyond recognition.

Using the appropriate stabilizer will result in smoother running projects, increased productivity and professional-looking projects.

Of course, after you choose the correct stabilizer, you have to get it into the hoop properly. You'll generally hoop the fabric and the stabilizer together for best results. However, there will be times when hooping the fabric and stabilizer together is not the best option (for example, when working with delicate fabrics). In those cases, choose one of the other hooping alternatives detailed.

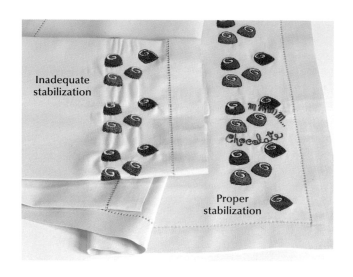

Inadequate stabilization

Proper stabilization

■ NUGGET OF INSPIRATION

Be sure to use quality stabilizers designed for embroidery. You may hear rumors of people using substitutes such as coffee filters or dryer sheets. As tempting as that may sound (especially if it's 4 a.m. and you don't have the correct stabilizer on hand), it's a bad idea. Inadequate stabilizers can cause many problems; they prematurely dull needles and generate excessive lint. So, keep the coffee filters in the kitchen, where they belong.

Hooping Both Fabric and Stabilizer

Whenever possible, always use this hooping method. Hooping the fabric and stabilizer together is the most stable choice, and it's also the easiest to master.

■ NUGGET OF INSPIRATION

A word of advice: Hooping and long sleeves don't mix. If you were ever to accidentally hoop, say, the sleeve of your sweater along with your fabric, rest assured that you're not the first embroiderer to do so. But to avoid that little mishap, just make sure that your sleeves are out of the way before sinking the inner hoop into place.

1 It's often helpful to add a layer of fusible interfacing to the wrong side of the fabric before adding stabilizer(s) and stitching an embroidery design.

• Interfacing adds body to a fabric, and it prevents the stabilizer from showing through after stitching is completed. For example, use interfacing when embroidering on delicate fabric such as silk douppioni.

• Select a weight of interfacing similar to or lighter than the base fabric. Follow the manufacturer's instructions for fusing.

2 Select a stabilizer. (See pages 28–35.)

3 Hoop the fabric.

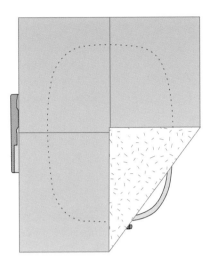

- Mark the vertical and horizontal centers of the embroidery design.

- Place the outer hoop on a flat surface. Loosen the tension screw.

- Position the fabric and stabilizer over the hoop, aligning the fabric's vertical and horizontal centers with the vertical and horizontal center cross marks on the hoop.

■ NUGGET OF INSPIRATION

When hooping fabric, it is mighty tempting to tug and pull on the fabric to get it taut in the hoop. Be careful not to pull too much, or you'll stretch and distort the fabric. Then you'll end up with a horribly puckered design, and you'll just have to do the whole thing over again.

- Press the inner hoop into place using one of the following methods:

- Position the inner hoop on the fabric. Gather some fabric on each side of the hoop in your hands while you grasp the hoop, and pick up the hoop, fabric and stabilizer all at once. Tilt the top of the inner hoop into the top of the outer hoop, pressing it into place. Work your way down to the bottom.

- Position the fabric and stabilizer on the outer hoop. Tilt the bottom of the inner hoop into the outer hoop. Using your thumbs, apply pressure on the lower sides of the hoop, fanning your hands out to hold the fabric taut. With your index fingers at the top of the hoop, slowly apply pressure and push the top of the inner hoop into the outer hoop.

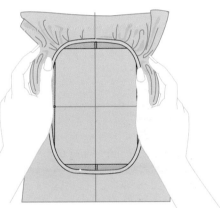

Gather fabric on each side of hoop as you grasp it

Motivating Memo

Check the outer hoop tension as you hoop the fabric. If the hoop is too tight, loosen the screw; if it's too loose, tighten the screw. Adjusting the screw concentrates all the tension in the screw area, so for best results, you need to evenly distribute the tension. Remove the fabric from the hoop and repeat the hooping process. The tension should now be spread evenly through the hoop. This reduces hand fatigue and prevents fabric stretching.

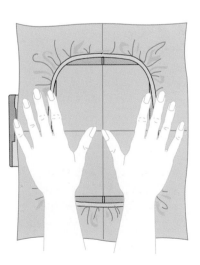

Press inner hoop firmly in place

• Countersink the inner hoop, pushing it down about ⅛"
for added stability.

•Turn the hoop over. Verify that the stabilizer is completely hooped and that no extra fabric is caught in the hoop. If
necessary, rehoop the fabric and stabilizer.

Motivating Memo

*If you're using a round hoop, use a gridded surface such
as a rotary cutting mat to help keep fabric grainline
straight when hooping. Place the hoop on the cutting
mat, aligning a straight edge of the hoop with a line on
the mat. Position the
fabric, again align-
ing the straight edge
of the fabric with a
line on the mat. Then
insert the inner hoop
and proceed.*

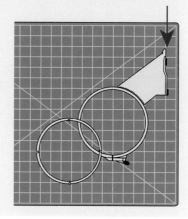

Hooping Stabilizer; Then Applying Fabric

This hooping method is ideal when you want to avoid hoop marks on delicate fabrics, napped fabrics, synthetic suedes,
leathers, and fleece. It's also great for embroidering items too small or irregularly shaped to hoop (for example, cuffs, collars, pockets, and children's garments).

USING A PAPER-BACKED ADHESIVE STABILIZER

• Hoop stabilizer (SIA™, Wash-Away Extra or Aquabond), with the paper side up.

• Use a pin point to score the paper covering on the
stabilizer. Remove sufficient paper to provide a sticky
surface for positioning the fabric.

Paper side
of stabilizer

Remove
paper to
expose
adhesive

Adhesive

Motivating Memo

*When scoring the paper on the stabilizer, be careful that
you only score the paper, not the stabilizer. Any holes in
the stabilizer will reduce its effectiveness, decreasing its
stability.*

• Position the fabric over the sticky surface; finger press it in place to secure it.

• Stitch the design. Then remove the fabric from the adhesive-backed stabilizer, tearing or cutting away the design from the underside of the stabilizer, but leaving the remaining stabilizer in the hoop.

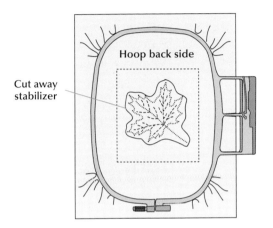

Cut away stabilizer

• Patch the hole in the stabilizer in the hoop by cutting a piece of the adhesive-backed stabilizer large enough to cover the hole, allowing at least ½" overlap on each side.

- Score a corner and remove the paper backing.

- Apply the adhesive-backed stabilizer patch to the underside of the hooped stabilizer.

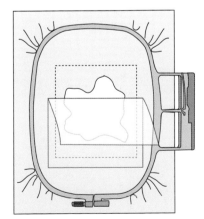

Patch hole with more stabilizer

USING A STABILIZER WITH WATER-ACTIVATED BACKING

• Hoop Hydro-stick™ stabilizer, adhesive (shiny) side up.

• Attach the fabric to the stabilizer.

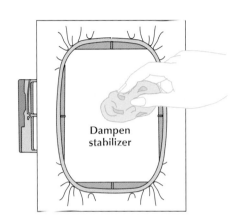

Dampen stabilizer

- Dampen the stabilizer with a wet (but not dripping) sponge. NOTE: Be careful not to use too much water. The wetter the stabilizer, the tighter bond it will form with the fabric. Using too much water makes removing the fabric very difficult.

- Position the fabric over the now-sticky stabilizer. Smooth with your hands.

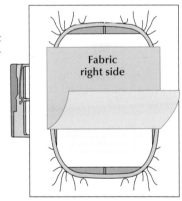

Fabric right side

Motivating Memo

If you need to reposition your project, gently peel away the fabric, rewet the stabilizer and reposition.

• Stitch the design. Then remove the hoop from the embroidery unit.

• Gently remove excess stabilizer by tearing or cutting it away.

• Patch the hole in the hooped stabilizer as detailed at left, cutting another piece of the stabilizer with the water-activated backing and covering the hole.

Getting Started

Using an Adhesive Spray

Use this hooping method when you want to convert a nonadhesive cut-away or tear-away stabilizer into an adhesive one. Adhesive sprays temporarily "baste" the stabilizer to your fabric for greater stability. Always spray the adhesive onto the stabilizer, rather than onto the fabric. And remember, a little goes a long way. More isn't necessarily better. Examples of adhesive sprays include Dritz® Spray Adhesive and Sulky® KK2000™.

USING A WET ADHESIVE SPRAY

- Hoop the stabilizer.

- Spray the adhesive spray lightly onto the stabilizer, following manufacturer's instructions.

- Position and smooth the fabric onto the stabilizer.

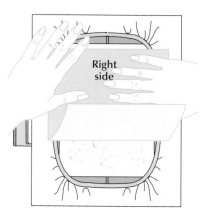

USING A FUSIBLE SPRAY ADHESIVE

- Hoop the stabilizer.

- Spray a fusible spray lightly onto the stabilizer; let it dry.

- Position the fabric over the stabilizer and press it in place with an iron.

Spray fusible spray onto stabilizer

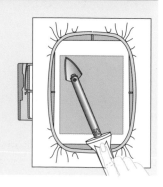

Basting Fabric to Hooped Stabilizer

Use this hooping method when you want to further stabilize your project. Basting allows you to stabilize your fabric without using any sprays, and the large stitches are easy to remove.

BASTING BY HAND

- Hoop the fabric and stabilizer together.

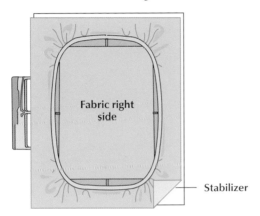

- Stitch evenly spaced, large stitches outside of the embroidery design area.

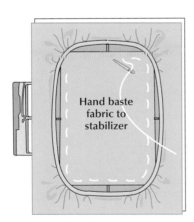

- Embroider design.

- Remove the basting stitches.

BASTING BY MACHINE

- Hoop the fabric and stabilizer together.

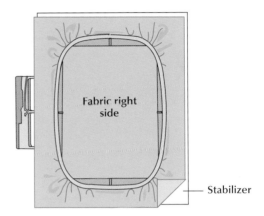

- Set your sewing machine for a long basting stitch.

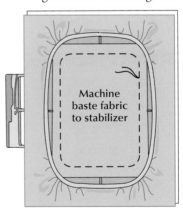

- Stitch around the outside of the embroidery design area.

- Embroider design.

- Remove the basting stitches.

Some embroidery machines have the capability to baste the fabric and stabilizer together with the touch of a button. Check your owner's manual to see if your machine has that feature.

If your machine has built-in frames, as well as the option to embroider them with a straight stitch, that's another option for basting the fabric to the stabilizer.

Getting Started

Window Technique

This method is ideal for unhoopable projects or fabrics such as fleece or other high loft fabrics where hooping could leave an unsightly impression. It also works well when embroidering synthetic suede, sheer or lacy fabrics, fabrics that stretch, items or areas that are too small to hoop (collars, cuffs, pockets), and areas where hooping would be awkward (totes, hats, purses).

1 Cut a piece of reinforced plastic approximately 1" larger on all sides than the hoop.

2 Hoop the reinforced plastic to provide a stable base for the fabric that will be embroidered.

3 Prepare a window in the plastic.

• Cut an opening large enough for the embroidery design, centering the window in the reinforced plastic and leaving ¾"–1" of plastic on each side of the window.

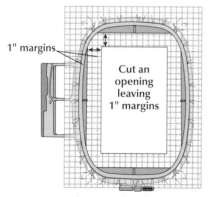

• Using a window sized to fit the design will give better design resolution. For example, for a 4" (100 mm) design, use a 4½"–5" window.

• Label the reinforced plastic window with the size of the cutout. This makes it easier to select and reuse a window of an appropriate size for future embroidery projects.

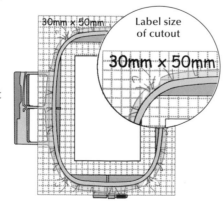

• Optional: Seal the inside cut edges of the window with masking tape to reinforce and stabilize the edges and give the opening more visibility.

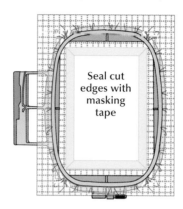

4 Cut a piece of sticky-backed stabilizer (for example, SIA™, S-dSV™ or Wash-Away Extra) at least ¾" larger on all sides than the window.

5 Place the stabilizer behind the window.

• Remove the backing from the sticky-backed stabilizer. Mark the side that was next to the sticky side of the stabilizer. This is the "release side" of the backing.

• Turn over the hoop so the underside faces up. Center the stabilizer, adhesive side down, over the reinforced plastic window, covering the cut-out window evenly on all four sides. Make sure the stabilizer is taut and has no ripples. Use your fingertips to gently secure corners of the stabilizer.

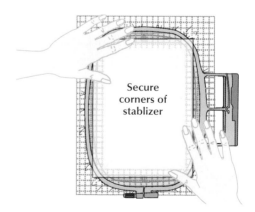

• Turn the hoop over so it is right side up.

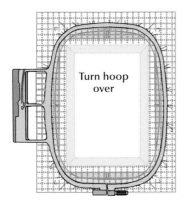

Turn hoop
over

• Position the release side of the backing from the stabilizer over the sticky surface; securely finger press all outer edges of the stabilizer to the reinforced plastic.

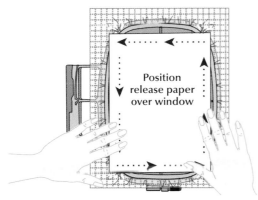

Position
release paper
over window

This helps ensure that the stabilizer is very secure and stable in the window. Then carefully remove the backing.

6 Stitch the design.

• Position the fabric over the sticky area, right side up; smooth fabric in place. The fabric adheres to the adhesive and is stabilized within the hoop.

• Stitch the design.

• Carefully remove the fabric from the stabilizer, keeping the reinforced plastic hooped.

7 Economize by reusing the reinforced plastic and stabilizer in the hoop, either immediately or in the future.

• After removing the majority of the stabilizer from the stitched design, fill the hole that remains by cutting another piece of stabilizer slightly larger than the hole.

• Turn over the hoop. Center the stabilizer patch over the hole in the original stabilizer, meeting the adhesive side of the stabilizer to the underside of the hole. Make sure the stabilizer is taut and wrinkle-free. Then you're ready to embroider another design.

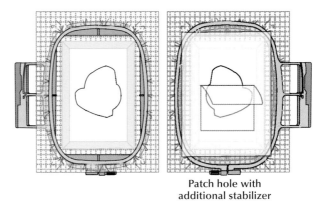

Patch hole with
additional stabilizer

8 You can refill the stabilizer window several times before completely replacing it.

• Replace the stabilizer when:
  - The stabilizer is no longer sticky.

  - Buildup of stabilizer layers could interfere with stitch quality.

  - The stabilizer loses its stability.

• Replace the reinforced plastic when:
  - The plastic loses its stability and no longer is tight in the hoop. Note: Before discarding the plastic, try rehooping it. Sometimes this will make it possible to reuse the plastic.

  - The plastic is "wavy," rather than taut and drum-like.

  - The plastic is damaged by needle holes, cuts or tears.

9 Save reinforced plastic windows and reuse them at a later date when embroidering designs of similar sizes.

• Store windows flat when they're not being used.

• When you need a window of a particular size, measure the design; then check your window inventory to see if you have an appropriate size. If so, merely rehoop the plastic, making sure the design fits within the window.

Getting Started

ATTACHING THE HOOP TO THE MACHINE

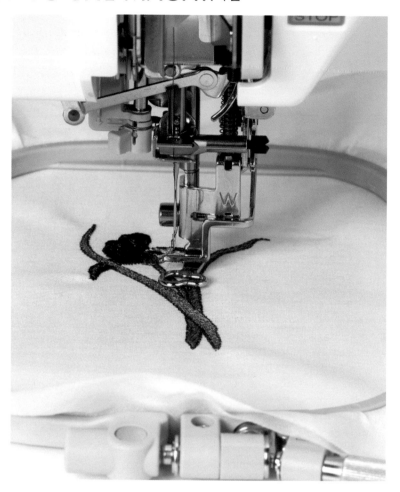

Now that you know how to hoop your fabric, you need to think about attaching the hoop to the machine. Learning a few key pointers about attaching the hoop can make the difference between a smooth embroidery experience and one riddled with problems.

First, make sure the hoop is facing in the correct direction. It should be facing right side up, with the side that connects to the machine facing in the correct direction. Some machines have hoops that attach on the right side, and others, on the left or top.

Before hooping, look at the item you'll be embroidering. Is it flat like a piece of fabric or a blanket? Or does it have an opening, such as a pillowcase or a sweatshirt?

• If the piece is flat, position the hoop so that the bulk of the fabric is on the left side of the machine. This keeps the extra fabric out of the way of the embroidery unit.

• If the piece has an opening, position the hoop so that the side that connects to the machine faces an opening.

• To attach the hoop to the machine, position it horizontally as you slide it into the machine.

• If it's necessary to tilt the hoop to get it under the foot, make sure the hoop is horizontal after it passes under the foot.

• Make sure the hoop snaps in all the way so it doesn't vibrate and come out during the embroidery process.

• The hoop should snap into place easily. If you have to use force, check to ensure that no fabric or stabilizer is in the way, preventing the hoop from snapping into place.

Before you begin to stitch, double check that there isn't anything underneath the hoop that shouldn't be there. Clear away any extra fabric that might have moved under the hoop while you were attaching it to the machine.

MAKING A TEST SWATCH

Before stitching a design on your actual project, always do a test swatch. Use the same or comparable fabric, stabilizer, hoop and thread that you'll use for the finished design. After stitching the swatch, you can make changes before stitching your actual project. For example, based on the looks and quality of the test swatch, you can do things such as choose a different stabilizer, change thread colorations, adjust tensions or try a different type of bobbin thread to make the design look just like you want it to look.

1 Using the design chosen, select and organize your threads. (See page 45.)

2 Choose a stabilizer.(See pages 28–35.)

3 Hoop the fabric and stabilizer. (See pages 54–61.)

4 Set up the machine to embroider. Follow these general guidelines; refer to your owner's manual for specific instructions for your machine.

- Attach the embroidery unit.

- Replace the conventional presser foot with an embroidery foot.

- Use a new machine embroidery needle.

- Thread the top of the machine with machine embroidery thread. Use a prewound bobbin or a lightweight thread such as Madeira Bobbinfil Thread in the bobbin.

- Slightly loosen the top tension by two numbers or notches. This keeps the bobbin thread on the wrong side of the fabric and prevents it from showing on the right side. Some machines may do this automatically; on others you may need to make the adjustment.

- Attach the hoop to the embroidery unit.

5 Embroider design.

- Lower the presser foot. Bring up the bobbin thread. Hang onto both the top and bobbin thread tails when you start to stitch to avoid tangled threads. Refer to your owner's manual for the specific procedures for your machine.

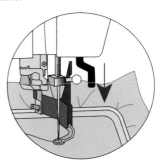

Motivating Memo

Before you begin to stitch, and occasionally during the stitching process, check to make sure that both the needle and foot screws are tight. Both sometimes loosen during long periods of stitching. Remember the old adage: An ounce of prevention is worth a pound of cure.

- Sew a few stitches; then stop to secure the thread.

Clip the thread tails.

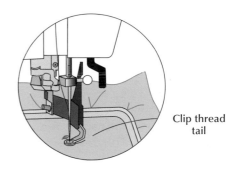

Clip thread tail

Getting Started

- Stitch the remainder of the first color.

- Follow the prompts on the machine. These instructions will tell you when to change thread colors.

  - To change threads, raise the presser foot. Then clip the needle thread at the thread spool. This prevents the thread from springing up into the machine.

  - Next, clip the thread at the needle, and remove the thread by pulling it out through the needle. This flosses the machine tension disks and prevents lint from being drawn into the machine mechanism. It's not necessary to clip the bobbin thread.

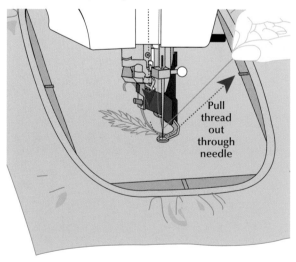

Pull thread out through needle

  - Thread the top of the machine with the next thread color; continue stitching.

- Repeat until all colors have been stitched and your machine indicates the design is complete.

6 Check the swatch.

- Look at the embroidered design carefully.

  - Are there any puckers?

  - Do the stitches look even and well formed?

  - Does the bobbin thread show on top?

  - Did the stabilizer provide sufficient support?

  - Are the colors pleasing?

- Make any necessary changes. If you make significant changes, make a second test swatch to ensure the finished design is exactly what you want.

Basic techniques are the building blocks of self-reliance, enabling you to achieve things you might never have thought possible. Knowledge of the basics empowers you to accomplish embroidery tasks with boldness and conviction. Basic techniques give you the ability to embellish your own world with whatever colors and designs you choose.

5

Basics & Beyond

Basics & Beyond

USING A TEMPLATE FOR PROPER PLACEMENT

In the previous chapter, you learned about templates, including how to make your own templates. Now let's use those templates to help precisely position a design.

Motivating Memo

Here's a gentle reminder: Naturally, you'll always want to stitch a test sample of any design before positioning and stitching that design on your project. Doing so takes a lot less time than trying to remove a stitched design that isn't quite right!

1 Position the template for the design on the fabric. Move the template around until you are pleased with the placement. Tape the corners of the template to the fabric using Sewer's Fix-it Tape.

2 Hoop the fabric and stabilizer, carefully aligning the cross marks on the hoop with those on the template. Attach the hoop to the machine.

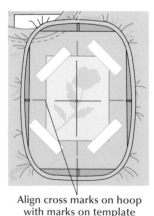

Align cross marks on hoop
with marks on template

3 Position the needle at the center mark of the design. Remove the template and stitch the design.

Using Templates with The Perfect Placement Kit

The Perfect Placement Kit (see page 49) makes it easy to position designs on 15 different types of ready-made items such as embroidery blanks. Although you can use The Perfect Placement Kit to place designs on many different items, we'll illustrate how it works on one of those items: a napkin. We'll embroider a monogram onto a corner of a napkin (sometimes referred to as "on point" placement). Note: The template recommends using a 2¼" letter for the monogram, and the guidelines printed on the template are for 2¼" letters. But, as you'll see, you can use almost any letter size.

1 Place the napkin on a flat surface. Position the Perfect Placement Napkin on Point Template on the napkin, aligning the template's "Napkin Edge" line with the outer edge of the napkin.

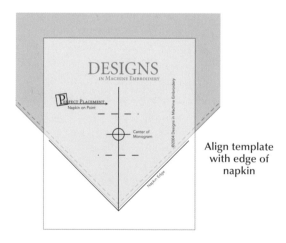

Align template with edge of napkin

2 Position the target sticker (included in the kit).

• If embroidering a 2¼" letter, slide the target sticker under the template crosshair. This marks the center of the design. Then remove the template.

• If you're using a letter size other than 2¼", create a template of the actual monogram. (Use one of the methods detailed on pages 48–49.) Place the template on top of the Perfect Placement template, aligning the lower edge of the monogram with the lower edge of the Perfect Placement line.

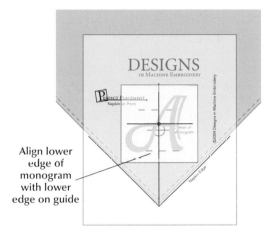

Align lower edge of monogram with lower edge on guide

• Slide a target sticker under the monogram template crosshair. Then remove the template.

3 Hoop the napkin, making sure it is square in the hoop. (We recommend using the Window Technique, pages 60–61, since it will most effectively stabilize the small napkin corner.) Use the mini ruler (included in the kit) to check your alignment. Move the hoop to center the needle over the target sticker, remove the sticker and embroider the design.

You could use this same process using almost any embroidery design. And even though The Perfect Placement template tells you exactly where to place the center of the design, there is some room for creativity. For example, compare the two napkins pictured below. On the first napkin, we placed the design exactly as indicated on the template. On the second, we placed the design exactly as we did on the first napkin; then tilted the design slightly for a different effect.

Embroidering the Design

Follow the instructions for stitching the test design as detailed on page 63. The process is exactly the same. The only difference is that you now will be embroidering on your actual project.

Since you are embroidering on the actual project, take time to check that everything's in order before you start to stitch. Ask yourself the following questions:

• *Are my thread colors in order?*
  —Whether you use a mini thread rack or a muffin tin to organize your threads, make sure that you have the correct thread colors and that they're arranged in order.

• *Do I have a new needle in my machine?*
  —For best results, change your needle after every three hours of stitching. Doing so contributes to clean, accurate stitching and prevents broken threads and other embroidery miscues.

• *Did I hoop anything besides the fabric and stabilizer?*
  —Turn over the hoop and check the underside. It's very easy for an extra layer of fabric to get caught in the hoop.

• *Are my stabilizer and fabric hooped properly?*
  —Tap your fingers on the bottom of the hooped fabric/stabilizer. It should sound hollow like a drum and feel taut.

■ NUGGET OF INSPIRATION
The Golden Rule of embroidery is this: Check twice; stitch once. If you accidentally hooped an extra layer of fabric—or your shirt—once you start stitching it's very difficult and time consuming to get back to the starting point. The same rule applies to organizing your thread colors. It's much easier to make changes and correct mistakes before you begin stitching.

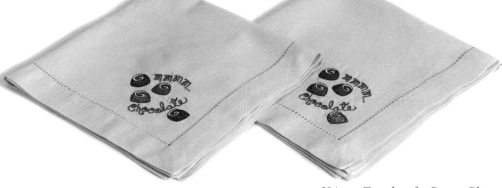

Basics & Beyond

- *Is there enough thread on the top spool to complete the design?*

  —If not, you may want to check whether you have a second spool of that color, or you may prefer to select a different colored thread spool that has sufficient thread. If you run out of thread halfway through the embroidery design, your only options are to stop embroidering and purchase more thread or to try to finish the design with a similar color.

- *Do I have enough bobbin thread to stitch my entire design?*

  —This is especially important if you're stitching a large or very dense design and your machine has a drop-in bobbin. To rethread the bobbin, you'll have to remove the hoop from the machine, interrupting the stitching process and opening the door for possible problems. If in doubt, change to a new bobbin before starting to stitch the design. You can always use up partial bobbins on smaller designs.

- *Do I have the correct thread in the needle?*

  —Even if your threads are arranged in the correct order, you may have forgotten to thread the first one. You don't want to start stitching your design using the last color from the previous design that you stitched.

Finishing Steps

So you've just stitched the last color. Where do you go from here? Although you'll be very excited about completing your first embroidery design, remember that the design is not yet finished. There are just a few final details.

1 Remove the hoop from the machine—but don't remove the fabric from the hoop. If by chance you notice that the design is not finished, don't panic. Simply reattach the hoop to the machine. As long as the fabric hasn't shifted, the design should stitch out perfectly aligned.

2 Trim off jump stitches. Jump stitches are long stitches that skip over the fabric between color changes, or between different areas when using the same thread color. Using a sharp pointed embroidery scissors, carefully trim away those stitches. Take your time. You don't want to cut through the actual design or the base fabric.

Jump stitches

Motivating Memo

For best results, trim jump stitches before unhooping the fabric. When the fabric is still in the hoop it remains tight, making it easy to find and cleanly trim the jump stitches. Use a sharp pointed scissors to trim the threads to avoid getting any frayed ends.

3 Double check that the design has been completed before you remove it from the hoop. Do NOT unhoop the fabric until you're absolutely sure the stitching is finished. It's nearly impossible—as well as time consuming—to rehoop the fabric and get it aligned enough to complete the stitching.

NUGGET OF INSPIRATION

This is another case where you're probably thinking, "Of course I wouldn't remove the design from the hoop before it's complete." Well, many seasoned embroiderers have thought the same thing, only to do just that: remove the design from the hoop and discover—oops! They forgot to stitch out the last color change.

4 Remove the fabric from the hoop. If you need to apply pressure to separate the two parts of the hoop, push on the hoop, not the fabric. It would be a shame to stretch out the fabric after you've done the embroidery.

5 Remove the stabilizer.

6 Remove pen/pencil/chalk marks.

7 Remove hoop marks using one of the following methods. NOTE: Let the base fabric guide your choice of removal method. For example, if a fabric is not washable, do not use water to remove marks.

- Press or steam the hoop marks.
- Use a spray bottle to lightly spritz the hoop marks with water. Use your hands to smooth out the marks and/or wrinkles, then allow the fabric to dry.

Basics & Beyond

Pressing Designs

Sewing and pressing just naturally go together. After you sew, you press.

Embroidery is no different. Pressing the embroidery design after stitching it is important. It helps to set the design into the fabric and gives your project a polished, professional look.

Motivating Memo

Before pressing your embroidered piece, make absolutely sure to remove all air- and water-erasable pen marks. Pressing can permanently set these marks into fabric.

- Always press the design from the wrong side. If you press from the right side, you could flatten the threads.

- Place the embroidered fabric face down on a padded pressing surface or towel.

- Cover the fabric with a press cloth.

- Use a steam iron at the lowest setting; gently press.

Motivating Memo

Instead of using a regular steam iron, consider using a garment steamer to press your embroidered pieces. It's a quick and easy alternative to traditional pressing. And remember—always set the temperature at the lowest setting.

Caring for Embroidered Projects

Consider two main factors when caring for an embroidered piece: fabric and thread. Check the care instructions for both. If they conflict, follow the one that is the most restrictive. You obviously don't want to use a cleaning method that will shrink your garment or damage your embroidery design.

NUGGET OF INSPIRATION

If you're planning to give your embroidered project away as a gift, write the care instructions on an index card and tuck it in with the gift. Doing so helps the recipient care for the item properly, and helps keep the gift in good condition. You could also create a "Made by" label to sew into the project to serve as a reminder that you made the gift. Sign your name to the label, along with any other information, such as dates, a personal message or a small embroidery design.

Additional Embellishment

When creating embroidered projects, you don't have to stop after the stitching is completed. You can enhance your embroidery with objects such as crystals, beads, pearls and more. Sometimes, adding the tiniest crystal or bead can completely change the look of a design, making it glimmer and shine! For example, put crystals on an angel's wings to make them sparkle, add elegant accents to a holiday tree, or create the effect of glistening snow. By adding a few simple touches, you can make your projects come alive and shine.

Basics & Beyond

EDITING POSSIBILITIES

Now that you know how to add a basic embroidered design, don't stop there. Your embroidery machine has a wealth of potential, just waiting for you. Here are some ideas to get you started.

Changing Colors

Embroidery design collections usually include a listing of the colors used to stitch the pictured designs. But don't think for a moment that those colors are the only ones you can use. If you don't like the colors featured on the card—or even if you do—experiment with choosing your own color schemes. You'll be amazed at how dramatically a design can change simply by substituting a few different colors.

For example, we used three designs from the Amazing Designer Series™ Nature's Bouquet Collection by Nancy Zieman. We stitched each design three different times, each time using a different color for the flower. As you can see, depending on the thread colors you choose, the blooms could represent any number of flowers. For example, stitched in purples they could be tulips, in red they could be roses, or stitched in golds, they're black-eyed Susans ready to spring open.

The colors originally suggested on this card were a lovely color palette of velvety violets, soft greens and earthy browns inspired by the gentle advance of fall. However, by changing just four of the eight colors, you can create a completely different look. For example, you can use shades of red for a warm and cheery Christmas feel. Or, use shades of gold for an earthy, harvest look that perfectly catches the feeling of a sun-kissed, late autumn day.

Designs #24721, #24724, #24742
Madeira Rayon colors:
Purples: 1112, 1143, 1311, 1330
Reds: 1385,1186, 1119, 1070
Golds: 1257, 1025, 1068, 1145

Colors 1—4

Colors 2 and 4

Colors 2—4

Colors 3 and 4

Color 4

Skipping Colors

Just because a design includes, for example, four colors, that doesn't mean you have to stitch four colors. You can choose and stitch one, two, three or all four thread colors. We call this technique "Pick 'n Choose." If your machine has this feature, your owner's manual will instruct you how to advance to the next thread color. To get an idea of how this effect looks, experiment with various color combinations, stitching them out on fabric samples.

So why would you want to Pick 'n Choose? There are several instances when this technique comes in very handy:

1 To *add interest*

You may want to stitch only certain colors of a design to add interest. For example, if you're stitching the same design several times on one project, varying the colors you use will add interest and will make the design appear to be different, rather than an exact duplicate.

2 To *quilt*

Did you know that you can use your embroidery machine for quilting through all three layers of a quilt? You can, and it's quick and easy to do. The trick is to choose the correct embroidery design. You want a design that's only an outline. Some designs are created specifically for quilting, but you can also use the Pick 'n Choose technique to stitch only the outline of any design, making it suitable for quilting.

3 To *make templates*

Using the Pick 'n Choose Technique can also save you time when making your own templates. If you stitch the design to use as a template, stitching only the outline will save you a lot of time and thread.

Basics & Beyond

Mirror Imaging

Mirror imaging means just what it says—it's like looking at a reflection or something in a mirror. Everything is the opposite of the original: what's on the right is now on the left and vice versa. Mirror imaging a design means, in essence, flipping it over.

Mirror imaging comes in handy in many different situations. It can provide balance to a project, as well as break up the monotony of many repeated designs. For example, we created the pages at the beginning of each chapter in this book by stitching tone-on-tone embroidery on fabric. If you embroider only one design, mirror imaging some of the designs is an easy way to create subtle differences in the designs, adding interest, as well as making the entire project visually more interesting.

As another example, compare the two collars pictured here. On the first collar, both designs are facing the same direction. Notice how much more natural the second collar looks, with the second design mirror imaged so both designs face toward the center.

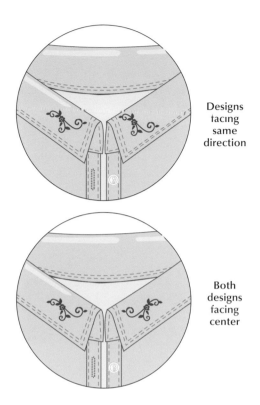

Designs facing same direction

Both designs facing center

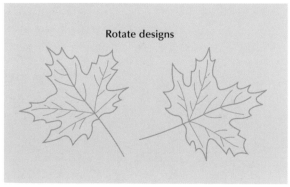

Rotate designs

Rotating for Design

Rotating involves pivoting a design from a central axis or starting point. The most obvious reason for rotating a design is to position it in a specific way on your project. Like mirror imaging, rotating can break up the monotony of repeated designs. Rotating, especially in small increments, can also make a design more interesting. For example, compare the two designs pictured here. On the first project, each leaf is in its original position. On the second project, we rotated each leaf. Notice how those small changes give the project a more fun and relaxed feeling.

Rotating for Convenience

Rotating also serves a more practical purpose. It can help you solve hooping problems associated with projects that are bulky or awkward to hoop, such as totes and hats. To add embroidery to these types of projects, you must hoop them a specific way. However, when you do that, you may find that the design faces the wrong way. Rotating lets you solve this problem with the touch of a button.

For example, to embroider this tote:

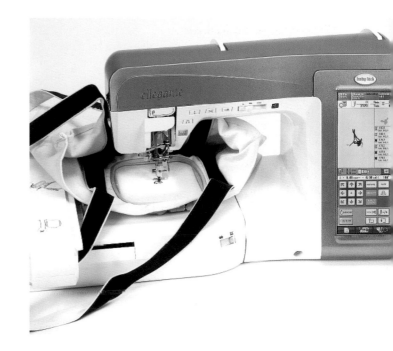

1 Hoop the tote so the bulk of the fabric is to the back of the machine.

2 Choose the design on the machine. Notice that if you were to stitch the design at this point, it would be positioned vertically (upside down).

3 Rotate the design 180°. Check that you've rotated it in the correct direction. Stitch.

Combining Designs

As you become more experienced, you may want to combine designs on your project. You can combine designs to create a scene or to embroider connected linear designs.

Creating a Scene

This technique is useful for creating landscape-type scenes. Combining designs such as flowers, fences and shrubbery can create lovely garden and landscape effects.

1 Use templates to create the scene. Here is where you really become the designer. You can use the designs as they are, and if your machine has the capability, you can mirror image, or even rotate the designs to make the scene look more realistic.

2 Position each template and mark its position.

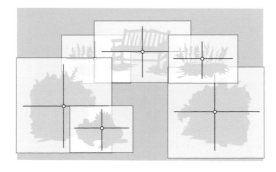

3 Before hooping, determine the order in which you'll stitch the designs, working from the background to the foreground. Then, hoop the fabric. Use the template markings to align the fabric in your hoop so that the design is in the center. Or, if your machine has the capability of moving designs in the hoop, try to hoop so that more than one design fits in the hoop. Rehoop for each group of designs until they're all stitched.

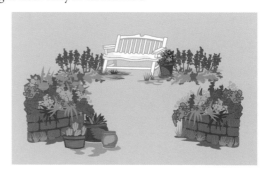

Basics & Beyond

Connecting Linear Designs

Use this technique to add borders to home décor items like sheets, pillowcases and table linens. Or, use it to add borders to garment sections such as skirt or tunic hems, yokes, cuffs or center fronts.

1 Draw a center positioning line on your project. For example, to stitch the border design on a pillowcase, draw a line parallel to the hem all the way around the pillowcase.

2 Make several templates of the design for easier and more accurate positioning. (See pages 48–49.)

3 Position the first template on the line. Mark.

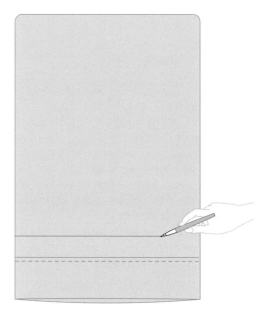

Draw positioning line

Position first template on mark

4 Position the remaining templates, using the center line and the other templates to line up the designs.

5 Hoop the fabric. Try to fit as many designs in one hooping as possible. Rehoop for each design until they're all stitched. When rehooping, make sure to line up the marks on the hoop with the center positioning line for greater accuracy.

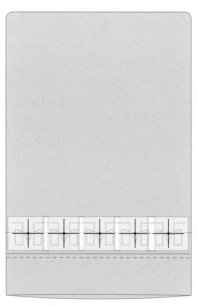

Position remaining templates

Basics & Beyond

SPECIALTY HOOPS

As their names imply, specialty hoops are designed for specific purposes. Whether you want to embroider a cap, sock, or just want to stitch lots of designs without rehooping every time, specialty hoops can really make your life easier.

Hoops for Caps

Primarily designed for stitching caps, cap hoops also work with oddly shaped items that are difficult to hoop such as fanny packs, purse flaps, collars and quilt squares. Hoop an adhesive stabilizer such as SIA™, secure your embroidery item, and stitch. The trick to working with cap hoops is getting the item you want to embroider correctly positioned. You'll probably need to spend some time working with the item, and this may include folding, squishing and other manipulations to get the item securely in the hoop, with its other parts (such as a cap's brim) out of the way.

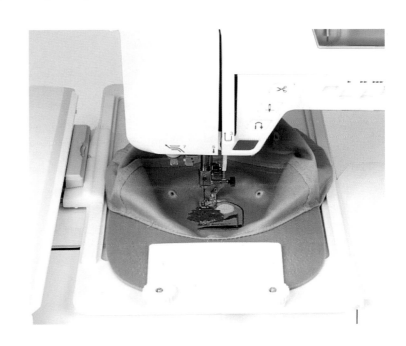

Hoops for Socks

Sock hoops are useful for embroidering socks, as well as other narrow items such as cuffs, gloves and sleeves. Like cap hoops, the trick with the sock hoop is getting the item onto the hoop. Once you've done that, you're home free. Adjustable pins on the hoop let you adapt it for both child and adult sizes. After hooping the item, attach the sock hoop to your standard embroidery hoop.

NUGGET OF INSPIRATION

When positioning a sock onto a sock hoop, especially a challenging one like a child's sock with lace trim, it is possible that you'll get slightly frustrated. One or two seasoned embroiderers have even been known to consider throwing the device across the room in frustration. But rest assured; once you successfully hoop that sock, your frustrations will fade and you'll already be moving on to hooping the next one.

Basics & Beyond

Multiposition Hoops

Multiposition hoops come with some machines. Larger than the standard 4" embroidery hoop, they enable you to stitch multiple designs within the same hooping. You must physically move these hoops to the next position to stitch the next design. Some hoops slide to the next position, while others must be moved and clicked into place. The process differs by manufacturer, so check your owner's manual.

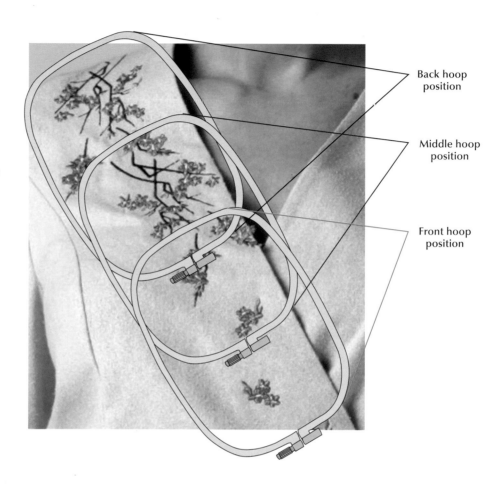

Back hoop position

Middle hoop position

Front hoop position

Hoop-It-All™ Products

The Hoop-it-All™ company manufactures several styles of multiposition hoops, including the Giant Hoop-It-All™ Set, the Super Giant-L Hoop-It-All™ Set and the Giant Double Wide Hoop-It-All™ Set. The main difference between models is machine compatibility. Each hoop works only with specific machines. The Giant and Giant Double Wide work with machines on which the embroidery unit attaches on the right side, while the Super Giant-L works with machines on which the embroidery unit attaches on the left side.

These hoops have much larger stitch fields that allow you to embroider multiple designs without having to stop and rehoop as often. Depending on the model, the stitching field can be as large as 8" x 23". That's a real timesaver! Since the Hoop-It-All™ products are frame hoops—they don't have an inner ring—you never have to worry about hoop marks. An adhesive stabilizer applied to the back of the hoop securely holds fabric during stitching.

Use the hoops to embroider napkins, towels, table linens—the hoops work great for any project, especially scenes and linear designs. The possibilities are endless, but the number of times you'll have to rehoop isn't!

Expanding your vision is part of the natural progression of this journey. You may take baby steps at first, but soon you will be moving by leaps and bounds, stretching your imagination. Many of the following projects have been embroidered on ready-made blanks; you need only add a little creativity. Enjoy!

6 Expanding Your Vision

Background: Amazing Designer Series™ Kayla Kennington Collection I
Inset: Amazing Designer Series™ Accents for Style by Nancy Zieman

Expanding Your Vision

Holiday
Kitchen Collection

Embroider Blanks…It's a timesaving way to create an embroidered item with a touch of personality—Yours! Blanks are those ready-made items that are just calling out for a touch of fun. The following projects have all been embroidered on ready-made blanks so you only need to add a little creativity. Have fun!

Holiday Kitchen Collection

Warm up your holiday gifts with embroidered kitchen accessories! The snowmen will melt your heart, and the gingerbread cookies will bring a nostalgic air to your holiday. All hearts will come home to amazing embroidered gifts!

Embroidering Cotton Dish Towels

- To position the design on the towel:

Fold to mark center

- Fold towel vertically to find center; mark.
- Measure 3"–5" from bottom edge of towel to position your horizontal marking (depending on your design). The + marking will be your cross mark.

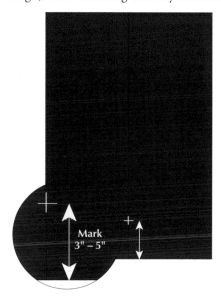

Mark 3" – 5"

Position

- Make sure that the design you choose is proportionate to the size of the towel or area being embroidered. On some embroidery machines you can adjust the size of a design with a simple touch of a button. Check your owner's manual.

- Embroider a sample of the design you plan to use, or an outline of the design. Or, make and use templates. (See pages 48–49.) Place the sample/template on the towel to see how it looks before you actually embroider on the towel. This will aid in placement as well as provide a check on size and coloration.

- Embroidery on kitchen towels is traditionally placed in the middle of the towel, centered approximately 3"–5" from the bottom. This may vary depending on how the towel is folded for display.

- For additional template options see pages 48–49.

Expanding Your Vision

Stabilize

- Choose a paper-backed adhesive stabilizer such as SIA™ that is easy to remove and won't "gum up" your needle.

- Use Dry Cover-Up™ on dark towels as a topping when embroidering with light thread colors. Choose a color that will coordinate with the main area of the design. For example, use white Dry Cover-Up™ on a dark towel on which you are embroidering a snowman. This eliminates "show through."

"Show through"

Dry Cover-Up™ eliminates "show through"

Hoop

Motivating Memo

Hooping only the stabilizer prevents hoop marks and allows you to move your design closer to the bottom of the towel without catching the hem.

- Hoop stabilizer only; then apply towel.
  - Hoop stabilizer with paper side up.

  - Use a pin point to score the paper covering on the stabilizer. Be careful that you score only the paper and not the stabilizer! Remove sufficient paper to provide a sticky surface for positioning the towel.

  - Center towel on top of sticky stabilizer, right side up. Align the cross mark with the horizontal and vertical markings on the hoop. Hint: Keep the towel folded in half vertically; position according to center hoop marking. This will ensure the design is straight.

NUGGET OF INSPIRATION

"Toppings" are much like frosting on a cake...they cover up the background (cake) and make the stitching (decorator icing) look "yummy"!

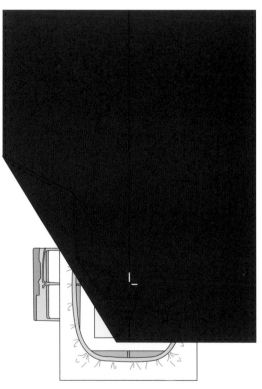

Center towel; align cross marks

Hoop stabilizer

Score; peel back stabilizer

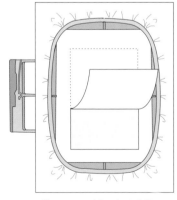

• Add a topping!
- Spray a piece of Dry Cover-Up™ with a temporary adhesive spray such as Sulky® KK2000™.

- Position topping over the embroidery area.

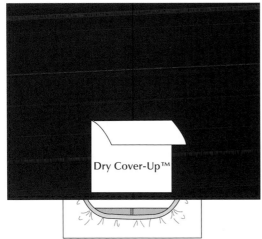

Dry Cover-Up™

NUGGET OF INSPIRATION

It's best to spray the stabilizer instead of the fabric whenever possible. This eliminates having a sticky hoop, and prevents you from getting an overabundance of adhesive on your fabric. Make a "glue box" for embroidery by finding a box a little bit bigger than your largest hoop. When you spray a piece of stabilizer, put it into the box before you spray. Then you won't have to worry about getting glue all over your hands, countertop, floor, clothes...you get the picture!

Embroider—Ready, Set, Stitch…Finish!

Motivating Memo

If you are embroidering on a dark towel, you might want to use black or a coordinating color bobbin thread so that your design blends on the reverse side of the towel.

• Set up your machine for embroidery.

• Attach the hoop with layered towel and stabilizer to your machine.

• Embroider the design. Remove the excess Dry Cover-Up™ after embroidering the coordinating color. If necessary, add pieces of Dry Cover-Up™ of different colors when stitching areas of those colors.

• Trim jump stitches and gently tear away excess stabilizer.

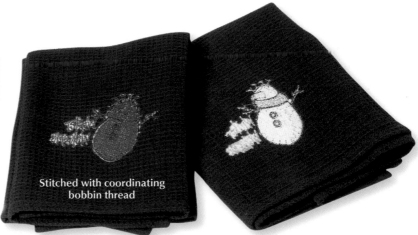

Stitched with coordinating bobbin thread

Design Collection used for towels:
Amazing Designs® Christmas Collection III
Designs #25389, #25390 and #25398

Expanding Your Vision

Embroidering Terry Towels or Bibs

Position

- For terry towels: Refer to positioning directions for cotton towels, page 79.

- For bib:

  - Fold bib in half lengthwise to find vertical center cross mark.

  - Place horizontal cross mark in desired position, depending on size of design.

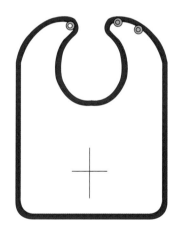

Stabilize

- Use a tear-away stabilizer such as Simply Stable and a spray adhesive similar to Sulky® KK2000™ to secure the terry bib or towel to prevent the nap from being distorted.

- Add a topping to prevent stitches from sinking into the high nap terry fabric. A good choice would be a clear wash-away stabilizer such as Finishing Touch™ Clear Away Lite.

Hoop

- Hoop stabilizer only.

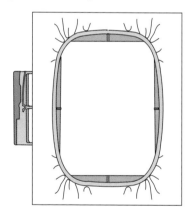

- Spray lightly with spray adhesive .

Expanding Your Vision

• Position and smooth the terry bib or towel onto the stabilizer.

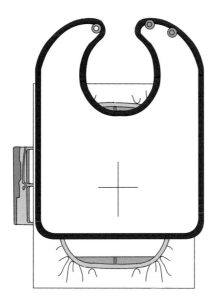

• Lightly spray a piece of clear wash-away stabilizer with a spray adhesive and position it over the embroidery area on the bib or towel.

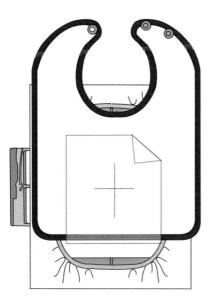

Embroider—Ready, Set, Stitch…Finish!

• Set up your machine for embroidery.

• Embroider your design, trim jump stitches and gently remove excess stabilizer.

• Spritz remaining wash-away stabilizer topping with water, or rinse to remove.

NUGGET OF INSPIRATION

Make a "hoop bib" by cutting a piece of lightweight cardboard a little larger than the hoop. Place the hoop on the cardboard; outline the inner ring. Cut out the inside of the cardboard approximately ½" from the marked outline. Place this bib over the hoop when you spray, and any overspray will not get on the hoop.

Design Collection used for terry towels and bibs:
Amazing Designs® Christmas Collection VIII (ADC1341)
Designs #53258 and #53260

Expanding Your Vision

Embroidering on Quilted Potholders

Position

- Center the design by folding the potholder on point (through the center, point to point); mark.

- Make the cross mark toward the bottom of or in the middle of the potholder, depending on size of the design.

- We enlarged the gingerbread cookie on the potholder using the machine's sizing feature. Check your owner's manual to see if your machine has this ability.

Motivating Memo

When sizing a design on your machine, make sure that you stitch it out on sample fabric before stitching on your project, as sometimes the density is affected.

Stabilize

- Use Hydro-stick™ Tear-away stabilizer. This eliminates using an adhesive spray.

- Use Dry Cover-Up™ as a topper to eliminate "show through" on a dark colored potholder.

Hoop

- Hoop stabilizer only, with shiny side up.

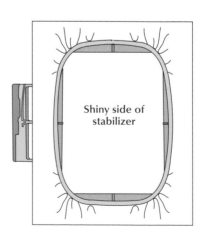

Shiny side of stabilizer

• Use a dampened sponge to wet the shiny side of the stabilizer, making it sticky. (Remember: a little water goes a long way.)

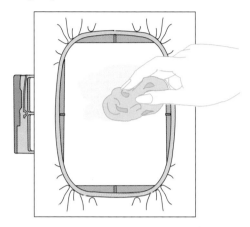

• Center potholder on top of sticky stabilizer, right side up, aligning cross marks.

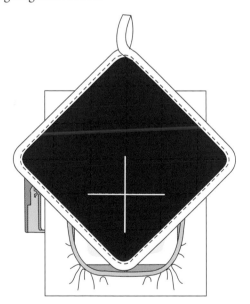

• Lightly spray a piece of Dry Cover-Up™ with a temporary adhesive spray such as Sulky® KK2000™. Position stabilizer over the embroidery area on the potholder.

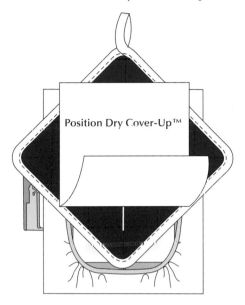

Embroider—Ready, Set, Stitch…Finish!

• Match the bobbin thread to the potholder so that the design back will be less visible.

• Set up your machine for embroidery.

• Attach the hoop with layered potholder and stabilizers to your machine.

• Embroider your design. Trim jump stitches; gently remove excess stabilizer.

Design Collection used for potholders and aprons:
Amazing Designs® Christmas Collection III
Design #25388.

Motivating Memo

If you used too much moisture on the stabilizer, making it hard to remove now that it has dried, wet a corner of the stabilizer. The moisture will wick through the stabilizer, making it easier to remove.

Expanding Your Vision

Embroidery on Cotton Aprons—Multiple Designs

Position

- Make a template. (See pages 48–49.) This will help position houses and cookies so that they don't overlap. Mark center of each design on the apron.

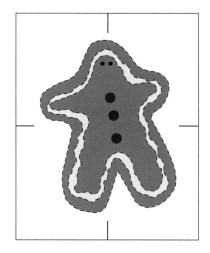

- Combine designs on your machine. Add middle design, then left, and finally right design (mirror imaged). If your machine doesn't have the capability to combine designs, use your largest hoop so you don't have to rehoop as often.

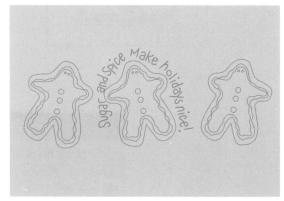

Combine designs on screen

Expanding Your Vision

Stabilize

Use Hydro-stick™ Tear-away stabilizer and Dry Cover-Up™, as for the potholder, pages 84–85.

Hoop

Center apron over sticky stabilizer, matching cross marks of the middle design with hoop cross marks.

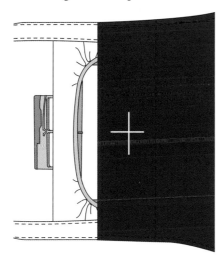

Embroider—Ready, Set, Stitch…Finish!

- Stitch complete center design, including the lettering.

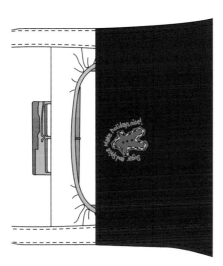

- Stitch left design, aligning cross marks. Skip the lettering.

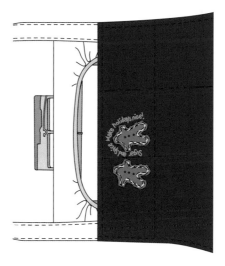

- Stitch right design (mirrored), aligning cross marks. Skip the lettering.

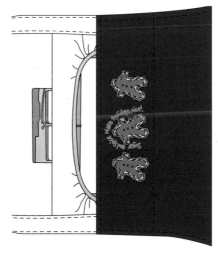

- Trim jump stitches and gently remove excess stabilizer.

Design Collection used for potholders and aprons:
Amazing Designs® Christmas Collection III
Designs #25388 and #25395

NUGGET OF INSPIRATION

On the apron with the houses, stitch each house with a different color so it looks like a holiday village. Which house is Santa's?

Expanding Your Vision

Nothing's better than your favorite pair of jeans—unless, of course, it's your favorite jeans accented with embroidery or trims. Combine and mirror image a few simple designs to create a garment that looks like it walked right out of the pages of the latest fashion magazine.

Embroidered Jean Legs and Pockets

Prepare the Jeans

- Open the leg seams to obtain a flat area for easy stitching.

  - Look for a simple seam that is not flat felled (usually the inner leg seam).

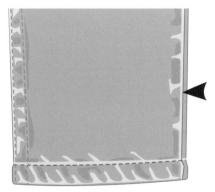

  - Open the seam; release the hem using a seam ripper.

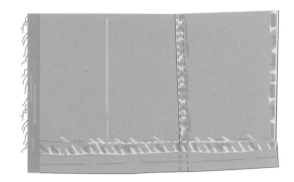

- Open the pocket area using one of the following methods:
  - With a simple seam, open the seam so the pocket can be flipped up and out of the way.

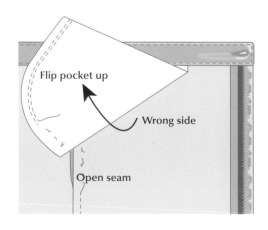

Flip pocket up

Wrong side

Open seam

- With a flat felled seam, cut along the pocket seam on the inside to release the pocket. Then fold it out of the way. Restitch that section after embroidery is completed.

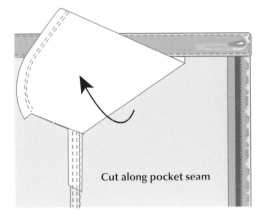

Cut along pocket seam

Position

• Combine several designs if desired for an elegant embroidery. Some machines are able to save combined designs as a new single design. Check whether your machine has this capability. We combined two designs into an "L" shape, but feel free to modify designs or arrangements to create your own unique designs.

• Stitch template(s) for the design components. See pages 48–49 for details. Be sure to make cross marks to aid in positioning the template(s).

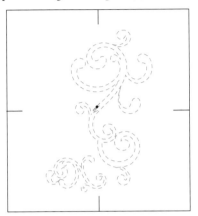

Stabilize

• Use a sticky-backed wash-away stabilizer such as S-dSV™, or an adhesive nonwoven with release paper such as Aquabond or Wash-Away Extra.

• Use the window technique. (See pages 60–61.)

Hoop

• Use the largest hoop available.

• Position one leg of the jeans over the sticky stabilizer; finger press in place.

Motivating Memo

It's important to prevent the weight of the jeans from pulling or distorting the embroidery. Support the jeans by resting the fabric on a table, or "nest" the fabric around the embroidery hoop. Just don't allow the jeans to hang off the table!

Expanding Your Vision

- Use a template to position the design.

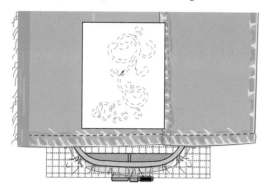

Embroider—Ready, Set, Stitch…Finish!

Use your arrow keys to position needle over cross marks for each design before stitching.

- Embroider the design on one pant leg.

- Trim jump stitches and gently peel and remove excess stabilizer, leaving the reinforced plastic and remaining stabilizer in the hoop.

- Patch the hole in the hoop with another piece of S-dSV™. Position the opposite side of the pant leg to embroider.

- Mirror image the designs. Position and embroider designs on the second side of the pant leg.

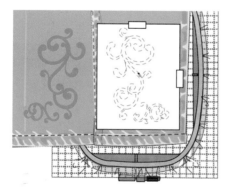

- Trim jump stitches and gently remove excess stabilizer.

- Repeat, embroidering the second pant leg. Trim jump stitches and gently remove excess stabilizer.

- Rinse jeans to remove remaining stabilizer.

Jeans Pocket Embroidery

- To hoop and embroider the pocket area:
  - Use window method for hooping and the same stabilizers as for embroidering legs, pages 60–61.

  - Manipulate the jeans so the pocket area adheres to the sticky-backed stabilizer. Sometimes it's necessary to turn the jeans wrong side out.

  - Embroider the pocket, checking to ensure inner pocket isn't caught in the stitching.

- Trim jump stitches, remove hoop and gently peel and remove excess stabilizer.

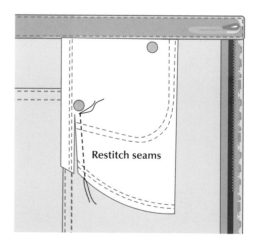

- Repeat, embroidering second pocket if desired. Trim jump stitches and gently remove excess stabilizer.

- Rinse jeans to remove remaining stabilizer.

- Restitch seams. (If the pocket seams were cut open, fold under cut edges and edgestitch to close the pocket opening, stitching only through the pocket.)

Restitch seams

Design Collection used for Keen Jean Designs:
Amazing Designer Series™ Accents for Style Collection I
Designs #28818 and #28824

By the Seashore

Your inner child comes out when you're walking along the seashore. Create those seaside memories with your embroidery, and you'll remember them all year round. These projects take a bit more time, but they won't burn your enthusiasm for embroidery!

Expanding Your Vision

Seaside Tote

Use an existing pattern for your favorite beach tote. Add embroidery before constructing the tote. You may want to press a fusible interfacing to the wrong side of the area you will embroider for extra stability.

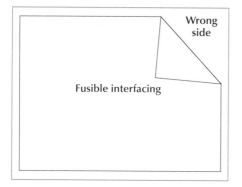

Position

• Select embroidery designs that fit well together and look realistic as far as proportion.

• Prepare templates for the designs to aid in positioning on the tote or pocket of the tote. Arrange the templates until you are pleased with the combination. (See pages 49 and 73.)

Make sure to mark cross marks of each design so that you know where to start each embroidery pattern.

• Transfer the template markings directly to your tote with a washable marker or stickers designed for centering such as Perfect Placement Target Stickers.

NUGGET OF INSPIRATION

Designs aren't always pictured in proportion on CD or memory card cases. That's another good reason to stitch out your designs first before positioning them on your project. You need to make sure your beach chair fits under the umbrella!

Expanding Your Vision

Stabilize

- Use a mid- to heavyweight tear-away stabilizer such as Ultra Tear or Pellon® Stitch-N-Tear®.

Hoop

- Hoop fabric and stabilizer together.

Embroider—Ready, Set, Stitch…Finish!

- Use your arrow keys to position needle over cross marks for each design before stitching.

- Embroider the various designs. Trim jump stitches and remove excess stabilizer.

- Finish stitching your tote together according to pattern directions.

- Go looking for some seashells to put in your new tote!

Sea Shells Beach Towel

Wrap yourself in treasures of the sea!

We combined four different shell designs from the same design collection to make the shell border.

Position

- Select an interesting combination of shells or other designs that go well together and fit in the border band of the towel.

- Prepare a template for each design to aid in positioning on the towel border. (See pages 48–49.) Arrange templates until you are pleased with the combination.

- Rotate and mirror shell designs to give you a more interesting arrangement and make the shells look dissimilar.

Rotate and mirror designs

Mark centers of each design so that you know where to start each embroidery pattern.

Expanding Your Vision

Stabilize

Use a tear-away stabilizer such as Firm Hold Lite™ or Sulky® Totally Stable™. The "waxy-backed" stabilizers are best on towels, as they don't pull or distort the fabrics pile.

Motivating Memo

If you are using a towel without a woven border, hoop a midweight nonwoven adhesive-backed stabilizer such as Wash-Away Extra or Aquabond. Score and peel away the protective liner to expose the adhesive inside the hoop and position the towel over the stabilizer. Add a topping such as Avalon® by Madeira or Clear Away. To hold the topping in place, spray it with a small amount of temporary adhesive spray such as Dritz® Spray Adhesive or Sulky® KK2000™.

Hoop

Hoop stabilizer and towel together. A topping is not necessary, as you will be embroidering in the woven band of the towel and not directly on the pile.

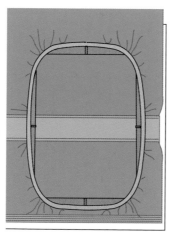

Motivating Memo

Subtle color changes make the shells look different. Changing the color order on duplicate shells is sometimes all that is needed for pleasing results.

Embroider—Ready, Set, Stitch...Finish!

• Use your arrow keys to position the needle over the cross marks for each design before stitching.

• Embroider the various designs, rotating and mirroring designs as necessary. Trim jump stitches, remove hoop and gently peel and remove the excess stabilizer.

Design Collection Memory Card used for the Towel designs: Amazing Designer Series™ Memories by the Shore Collection Designs #29009, #20912, #29013 and #29014

Expanding Your Vision

Six Panel Sun Hat

No special hoop needed for this hat!

Use an existing pattern for your favorite sun hat. Add embroidery before constructing the hat. For extra stability, you may want to press a fusible interfacing on the wrong side of the panels that you will embroider.

Position

• Select embroidery designs that coordinate and fit within the panels of the hat.

• Arrange design templates until you are pleased with the combination. Be sure to mark centers of each design with cross marks so that you know where to start each embroidery pattern.

• Transfer the template markings directly to your hat panels with a washable marker or stickers designed for centering such as Perfect Placement Target Stickers.

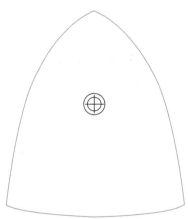

Stabilize

We used tear-away Hydro-stick™ stabilizer for this hat to securely hold and stabilize the small cap panels.

Hoop

• Hoop stabilizer only, with shiny side up.

• Use a dampened sponge to wet the shiny side of the stabilizer, making it sticky. Remember: a little water goes a long way!

• Center cap panel on top of sticky stabilizer, right side up.

Embroider—Ready, Set, Stitch…Finish!

• Position your needle using the cross marks on the panel for each design.

• Embroider the designs, hooping as necessary for each panel.

• Clip jump stitches, and gently remove excess stabilizer.

• Finish constructing the hat using your pattern for reference.

Design Collection used for the Sun Hat designs:
Amazing Designer Series™ Memories by the Shore Collection
Designs #20137, #20138, #20134, #29008 and #29010

Expanding Your Vision

Swim Suit Cover-up

Embroider an oversized T-shirt—it makes a perfect cover-up!

Position

- Make templates of the designs. (See pages 48–49 for details on making templates.) We used two different designs on our cover-up.

- Use a tool such as Embroider's Buddy or Perfect Placement Kit to simplify positioning. Center placement mark on the left chest of the cover-up using industry standards instead of guesswork.

- Arrange templates around the placement mark on left chest of cover-up. Mark centers of the designs.

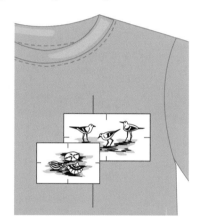

Stabilize

- Use a stabilizer that won't stretch and distort stitches on knits, for example, Kleer Fuse™ or cut-away Fusible No Show Mesh. Both are great on knits and comfortable next to the skin.

- If using a fusible cut-away stabilizer, press the stabilizer to the wrong side of cover-up, over the design area.

- If using a standard cut-away stabilizer, cut a piece large enough to hoop with the cover-up.

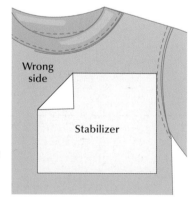

Motivating Memo

If you are stitching on a heavier knit you may need to use more than one layer of stabilizer.

Hoop

- Turn cover-up "inside out" so that the right side of the shirt is on the inside. This makes hooping much easier.

- Hoop shirt and stabilizer together, centering the placement position mark in the center of the hoop, aligning with marks on hoop.

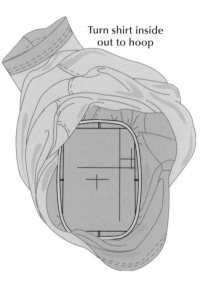

Turn shirt inside out to hoop

Embroider—Ready, Set, Stitch…Finish!

- Use your arrow keys to position needle over cross marks for each design before stitching.

- Embroider the designs. Trim jump stitches and gently remove excess stabilizer.

Design Collection Memory Card used for Swim Suit Cover-up designs:
Amazing Designer Series™ Memories by the Shore Collection Designs #20137 and #29010

Dressing up Denim

Adorn a collar with delicate floral designs, or a seasonal motif such as candy corn or snowflakes. Whatever design you choose…you'll stretch your style! Create some fun in your "ho hum" closet—embroider several of these detachable collars for your shirts.

Expanding Your Vision

Embroidering on Collar Points

Position

- Select an embroidery design that fits the collar area. Remember, you need only small bits of embroidery.

- Prepare a template for the design to aid in positioning. Commercial templates are available for some embroidery designs, or make your own template based on your test stitching.

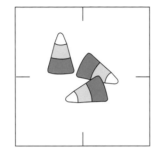

- Trace the outline of the stitched design onto a transparent template material. We used Templar®, a heat-resistant template material.

- Remember to transfer the hoop's vertical and horizontal cross marks to the template.

Stabilize/Hoop

- Use the window technique to stabilize the embroidery as detailed on pages 60–61. Since the collar doesn't fill the hoop, this alternate hooping method will stabilize the fabric, as well as eliminate hoop marks.

  - Hoop a piece of heavyweight vinyl or reinforced plastic.

  - Cut a window in the reinforced plastic leaving a ¾"–1" frame on each edge. Optional: Seal the edges of the frame with masking tape. This reinforces the edges and allows you to reuse the frame multiple times.

  - Cut a piece of sticky-backed stabilizer such as S-dSV™ at least ¾" larger on all sides than the window.

  - Remove the backing from the sticky-backed stabilizer. Mark the side which was next to the sticky side of the stabilizer. This is the "release side" of the backing.

  - Turn over the hoop so the underside faces up. Center the stabilizer, adhesive side down, over the reinforced plastic window, covering the cut-out window evenly on all four sides. Make sure the stabilizer is taut and

has no ripples. Use your fingertips to gently secure corners of the stabilizer.

  - Turn over the hoop so it is right side up. Position the release side of the stabilizer backing over the sticky surface; securely finger press all outer edges of the stabilizer to the reinforced plastic. This helps ensure that the stabilizer is very secure and stable in the window. Then carefully remove the backing.

- If possible, position both ends of the unembellished collar next to each other over the sticky stabilizer. Finger press, adhering the collar to the stabilizer.

- Place a layer of tear-away stabilizer under the hoop.

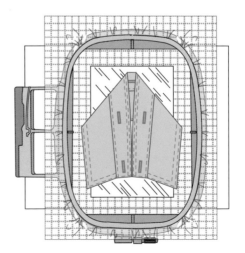

Embroider—Ready, Set, Stitch…Finish!

- Set up the machine for embroidery as detailed in your instruction manual.

- Position the template over one end of the collar. Move the needle to the starting point of the design.

- Remove the template and stitch the design.

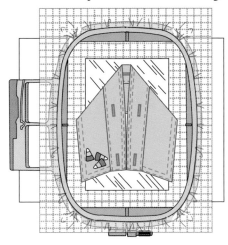

- Flip the template over to provide a mirror image of the design so both ends of the embroidered collar will look similar. Place the template on the second end of the collar.

- Mirror image the design on the embroidery machine, following instructions in the machine manual.

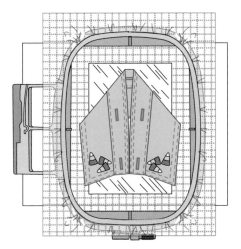

- Use the machine's arrow keys to position the needle at the design's starting point.

- Stitch the design on the second end of the collar.

- Trim jump stitches, remove hoop and gently remove excess stabilizer.

- Rinse collar to remove remaining S-dSV™ stabilizer.

Design Collections used for Collar Points:
Amazing Designer Series™ Hearts for All Seasons Memory Card
Design #28669
Amazing Designer Series™ Autumn in the Air
Design #22108

Motivating Memo

Always do a trial run before stitching on your actual project to ensure you like the design, thread colorations and positioning. Stitch on a scrap of an interesting fabric so you can use the test design later for another project such as a label, an appliqué, etc. Before removing the fabric from the hoop, also mark the hoop's vertical and horizontal cross marks.

Expanding Your Vision

Creating a Continuous Design on a Collar

Position

• Stitch out the design and measure to see how many times you are able to repeat it on the collar. Our design was repeated three times, and the whole design was mirror imaged for the second half of the collar. Notice how the hearts meet at the center.

Motivating Memo

If your machine does not have the capability to combine designs and/or mirror image you will need to make a template of your design. (See pages 49, 72 and 74.) Make sure to mark the center of each repeated design so that you know where to start each time you repeat the design. Making a template is a good positioning tool even if your machine is capable of combining and mirroring stitches.

Stabilize/Hoop

• Use a large hoop for this collar design. We use a 160 mm x 260 mm hoop.

• Use the window technique to stabilize the embroidery. (See pages 60–61.) This alternate hooping method will stabilize the fabric, as well as eliminate hoop marks.

• Position one half of collar in window, centering the design combination. Finger press, adhering the collar to the stabilizer.

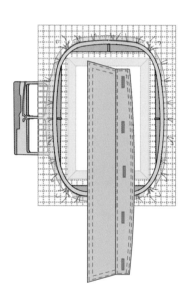

Embroider—Ready, Set, Stitch…Finish!

• Set up the machine for embroidery as detailed in your instruction manual.

• We used metallic thread to stitch the heart outlines. Use a vertical spool pin, reduce your top tension and stitch at a slower speed (350 stitches per minute or less) for best results.

• Position the template over one end of the collar. Move the needle to the starting point of the design.

• Remove the template and stitch the design. If necessary, reposition the template and stitch the remaining portions of the half design, ending at the center back.

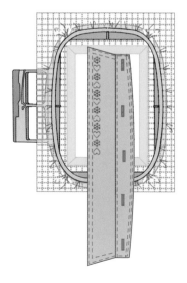

NUGGET OF INSPIRATION

Try helping the metallic thread to spool off the pin as you embroider, so that it doesn't twist or get caught—It takes a little extra effort, but the results are worth it! If you've ever experienced thread fraying and needle breakage you'll appreciate the difference this makes!

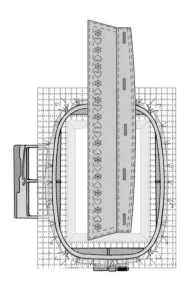

- Flip the template over to provide a mirror image of the design so both ends of the embroidered collar will look similar. Place the template on the opposite end of the collar.

- Mirror image the design.

- Remove stabilizer/collar from hoop leaving reinforced plastic hooped. Patch the hole as detailed on page 61.

- Position opposite end of collar in the window, centering the mirrored design combination. Finger press, adhering the collar to the stabilizer.

- Stitch the design on the second end of the collar. Trim jump stitches and remove stabilizer.

Design Collection used for Continuous Collar Design: Amazing Designer Series™ Hearts for All Seasons Collection Design #28661

Embroidering above Pocket Top

Position

- Some designs are especially designed to look like they are peeking out of the pocket top.

- Mark the position for the design with a cross mark above the top of the pocket.

- You may need to take a few stitches out of the sides of the pocket top and pin it down to keep it out of the way as you embroider.

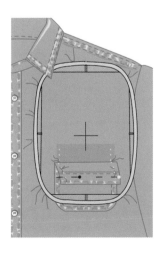

Remove several stitches; pin down pocket top

Stabilize

- Use a cut-away stabilizer like Pellon® Sof-Stitch™.

Hoop

- Hoop shirt and cut-away stabilizer together.

Embroider—Ready, Set, Stitch…Finish!

- Set up the machine for embroidery as detailed in your instruction manual.

- Embroider design, trim jump stitches and remove stabilizer.

- Restitch sides of pocket after embroidery is complete.

Design Collection used for pocket:
Amazing Designer Series™ Autumn in the Air
Design #22103

NUGGET OF INSPIRATION

Use a cut-away stabilizer on any designs that will be touching your body from the wrong side. Tear-away stabilizers tend to be scratchy. It's very uncomfortable to have an itch under your pocket!

Expanding Your Vision

Embroidering on Cuffs

Position

• Mark the center of the cuff for design placement.

Stabilize

• We used tear-away Hydro-stick™ stabilizer to securely hold and stabilize the cuffs, as they are too small to hoop.

Hoop

• Hoop the stabilizer only, with shiny side up.

• Use a dampened sponge to wet the shiny side of the stabilizer, making it sticky. Remember: a little water goes long way!

• Center cuff on top of sticky stabilizer, right side up.

Embroider— Ready, Set, Stitch…Finish!

• Set up the machine for embroidery as detailed in your instruction manual.

• Attach the embroidery hoop.

• Use the machine's arrow keys to position the needle at the design's starting point.

• Embroider the design on the cuff, making sure to line up design with center markings.

• Trim jump stitches, remove hoop and gently peel and remove excess stabilizer.

• Rehoop and embroider the second cuff following the same process.

  - Mirror image the design on your embroidery machine, if you have this function. Follow the instructions in your machine manual.

  - Stitch the mirrored design on the second cuff.

• Trim jump stitches, remove hoop and gently peel and remove excess stabilizer.

Design Collection used for cuffs:
Amazing Designer Series™ Autumn in the Air Collection
Design #22103

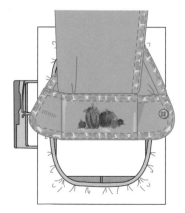

Expanding Your Vision

Embroidering on a Pocket

Position

- Remove the pocket from the garment so that it will still be functional after embroidering.

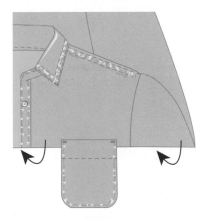

- Mark the center of the design where you would like it placed on the pocket.

Stabilize

- We used tear-away Hydro-stick™ stabilizer for this pocket to securely hold and stabilize the pocket.

Hoop

- Hoop the stabilizer only, with shiny side up.

- Use a dampened sponge to wet the shiny side of the stabilizer, making it sticky. (Remember: a little water goes a long way!)

- Center the pocket on top of the sticky stabilizer, right side up.

Embroider—Ready, Set, Stitch…Finish!

- Set up the machine for embroidery as detailed in your instruction manual.

- We used two different designs on our pocket (spiderweb and ghost). Position background design first. In this case we positioned the spiderweb first so it wouldn't cover up the poor ghost.

- Use the "trace around" feature on your machine to decide whether you want the design centered. This also helps you see how much space the design will take. Use arrow keys to position the design higher or lower.

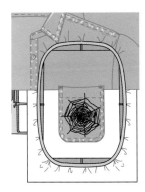

- Position the ghost in the same manner. We positioned ours toward the bottom and closer to the side of the pocket.

- Embroider. Trim jump stitches and remove stabilizer.

- Reposition pocket and stitch in place.

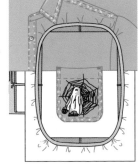

Design Collection used for pocket:
Amazing Designer Series™ Autumn in the Air Collection
Designs #22115 and #22089

Expanding Your Vision

Quilting and Home Décor Medley

If you embroider and quilt, why not combine your creative endeavors! You'll expand your horizons with an avocation that is fun and stimulating. These quilting projects will whet your appetite for greater challenges.

Charming Chickens Wall Hanging

Use your favorite wall hanging pattern to incorporate these Charming Chickens. The center square showcases an embroidered design. The remaining two squares include only the outline of the embroidery design; that stitching also quilts the layers of the wall hanging together.

Position

- Fold the center quilt square (for the completely embroidered design) in half vertically and horizontally to find the center. Press. Cross mark the center.

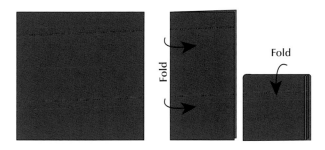

Fold

Fold

- Repeat, marking centers of remaining quilt squares that will include outlined embroidery designs.

Stabilize/Hoop

- Use the window hooping technique to stabilize the embroidery. (See pages 60–61.) This alternate hooping method stabilizes the fabric, and eliminates hoop marks when stitching the outline designs.

- Center the quilt square for the "funky chick" (complete embroidery design) on top of the sticky stabilizer. Center cross marks with hoop markings to ensure designs are properly centered.

- Slide a piece of tear-away stabilizer under the hoop for added support and to prevent puckering.

- After assembling and layering the wall hanging, hoop the area for the outlined chick designs using the window hooping technique and an adhesive-backed stabilizer.

Embroider—Ready, Set, Stitch…Finish!

- Set up the machine for embroidery as detailed in your instruction manual.

- Use the machine's arrow keys to position the needle at the first design's starting point.

- Embroider the funky chick. Trim jump stitches and gently remove excess stabilizer.

- Spritz to remove remaining S-dSV™ stabilizer.

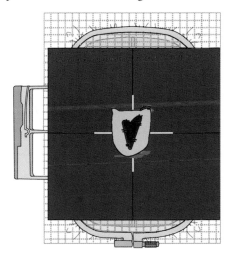

- Patch the hole in the hoop window with another piece of adhesive-backed stabilizer.

Quilt the Wall Hanging

Assemble and layer the wall hanging before embroidering the outline chicks, as they provide the quilting stitches that hold the layers together.

Embroider—Ready, Set, Stitch…Finish!

- Use the arrow keys to position the needle in the center of the first outline design. Forward through the design to the outline stitch.

• Stitch the outline designs through all layers of the wall hanging. This eliminates the need for a separate stabilizer.

• Clip jump stitches and gently remove excess stabilizer.

• Repeat, embroidering outline design added to the wall hanging.

• Spritz to remove remaining S-dSV™ stabilizer.

Design Collection used for Charming Chickens Wall Hanging:
Amazing Designs™ Whimsical Chicken Collection I (ADC1305)
Design #64380, #64382 and #64388

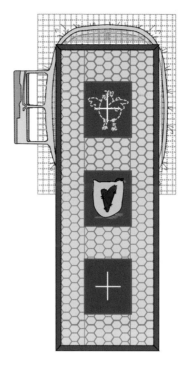

Crayon Alphabet Quilt

Make a simple log cabin quilt pattern and embellish it with colorful crayon alphabet letters. It's perfect for a child's first big bed! We alternated embroidered alphabet blocks with brightly colored bear prints and added embroidered violets. Choose the child's birth flower for added charm. It's a comfy "learn your letters" keepsake quilt!

Assemble the log cabin blocks before doing the embroidery.

• Fuse interfacing to the wrong side of center blocks following manufacturer's directions. This adds a little extra stability for the embroidery.

• Assemble log cabin blocks according to your favorite pattern.

Position

- Decide which blocks will have embroidered letters, print fabric or embroidered flowers.

- Cross mark the center of each embroidery square.

Stabilize

- Use a tear-away stabilizer such as Pellon® Stitch-N-Tear® or Cotton Soft by Madeira.

- Cut the stabilizer a little larger than the hoop.

Motivating Memo

Hold the stitches with your forefinger and thumb of one hand while gently tearing the stabilizer with your other hand. This helps eliminate pulled stitches.

Hoop

- Hoop log cabin squares and tear-away stabilizer together.

- Center cross marks with hoop markings.

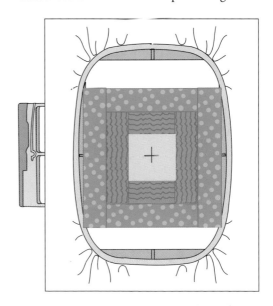

Embroider—Ready, Set, Stitch…Finish!

- Choose thread colors to complement the wall hanging fabric colors.

- Set up the machine for embroidery as detailed in your instruction manual.

- Use the machine's arrow keys to position the needle at the first design's starting point.

- Add sashing and finish the quilt following pattern instructions.

- Embroider designs, rehooping as necessary. Trim jump stitches and gently remove excess stabilizer.

Designs used for Crayon Alphabet Quilt:
- Amazing Design Collection™ Crayon Alphabet I (ADC1083)
- Pfaff Creative Fantasy Card 1
Design #15

Expanding Your Vision

Christmas Splendor Wall Hanging

Incorporate the splendor of the holiday season in your favorite wall hanging with this exquisite embroidery. Change the colors of the fabrics and designs to coordinate with your décor, and add a touch of gold metallic thread for an elegant shimmer.

Assemble the face of the wall hanging before doing the embroidery.

- Fuse interfacing to wrong sides of muslin embroidery squares following manufacturer's directions.

- Add sashing and borders according to pattern directions.

Position

- Make templates to help determine the placement of the embroidery designs. (See pages 48–49.)

- Cross mark the center of each embroidery square.

Stabilize

- Use a tear-away stabilizer such as Pellon® Stitch-N-Tear® or Cotton Soft by Madeira.

- Cut the stabilizer a little larger than the hoop.

Hoop

- Hoop wall hanging face and tear-away stabilizer together.

- Align cross marks with hoop markings.

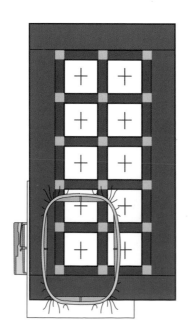

Design Collection used for Holiday Splendor Wall Hanging:
Amazing Designer Series™ Christmas Splendor Collection I by Nancy Zieman
Designs #25529, #25532, #25535 and #25549

Expanding Your Vision

Embroider—Ready, Set, Stitch…Finish!

• Choose thread colors to complement the wall hanging fabric colors. We used metallic thread to stitch the bells.

• Set up the machine for embroidery as detailed in your instruction manual.

• Use the machine's arrow keys to position the needle at the first design's starting point.

• Embroider designs, mirror imaging and rehooping as necessary. Trim jump stitches and gently remove excess tear-away stabilizer.

• Finish the wall hanging as suggested in your pattern.

Paper Leaf Appliqué

Fabric isn't the only medium for embroidery—try paper! Think "outside the embroidery box" as you create this lovely appliquéd paper picture! Use similar techniques to make scrapbook pages.

Expanding Your Vision

Position

- Make leaf templates to aid in positioning the embroidery.

  - Tape cardstock to the back of the hoop. Make sure it is taped securely.

  - Set up machine for embroidery referring to your machine manual.

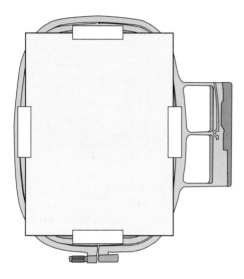

- Stitch only the leaf outlines, without thread in the machine.

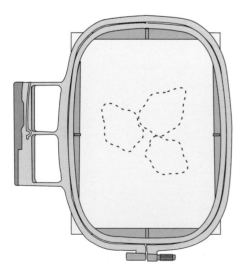

NUGGET OF INSPIRATION

If your machine has a thread sensor, you may need to "trick" the sensor to be able to stitch without thread. Thread your machine and tape the thread to the machine after the last thread guide. Do not thread the needle. It may not be nice to fool Mother Nature, but in this case, trickery is precisely what's needed.

- Remove cardstock from the hoop.

- Cut out the leaves using the needle holes as a guide. Use these leaf shapes to cut paper leaves for the picture.

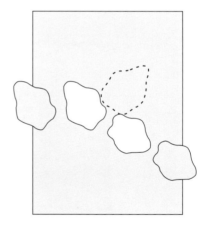

- Stitch the leaf veins and stem on sample cloth to make a template. Use that template to position the veins and stem on the paper leaves.

Expanding Your Vision

Stabilize

• Cut tear- or cut-away stabilizer large enough to tape to hoop back.

• Spray a small amount of adhesive to the back of the cutout paper leaves.

Hoop

• Place background paper, right side up, over stabilizer.

• Securely tape paper/stabilizer to the underside of the hoop, with background paper next to the hoop.

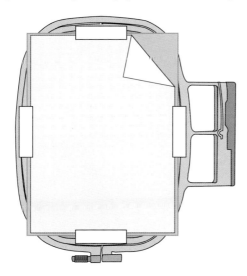

• Turn hoop right side up.

• Place leaves on background paper, sticky side down.

• Use the vein/stem template to position embroidery.

Embroider—Ready, Set, Stitch…Finish!

• Stitch the leaf veins and stem, using template to aid in positioning.

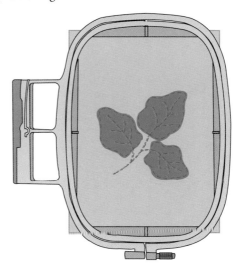

• Remove paper from the hoop.

• Trim background paper and stabilizer to desired size. There's no need to remove the stabilizer.

• Frame the embroidered design by gluing it to a larger paper background. Optional. Glue the leaf/background to another border for color enhancement.

Design used for Paper Leaf Appliqué picture:
Embroidery Machine Essentials—Appliqué Techniques,
    by Mary Mulari
Leaf design is on the CD included in the book.

Expanding Your Vision

Baby Belongings

*"Bye baby bunting"…
No more hunting! The
perfect embroidered
gifts for baby are
right here. Embroider,
appliqué and create
free-form 3-D designs
using your newfound
embroidery skills.*

Bunny Blanket

These bunnies are adorable, and they are easy because the plush appliqué on this flannel-backed blanket is done with your embroidery machine.

Position

- Cut waffle weave fabric to desired size. The pictured blanket is 32" square.

- Position and stitch the embroidery on the waffle weave fabric before adding the flannel backing.

- Make templates for the fence and a mirror imaged bunny following the instructions for templates on pages 48–49. We positioned the complete design in the bottom right hand corner, parallel with the bottom of the quilt rather than across the corner.

- Mark the center cross marks for each design.

Stabilize

- Use a tear-away stabilizer such as Cotton Soft by Madeira. This will give you firm support for the embroidery, and the excess can be torn away.

- Use a topper such as Clear Away Lite for the plush fabric appliqué so that the stitches don't sink into the fabric.

Hoop

- Place waffle weave over the tear-away stabilizer.

- Hoop both the fabric and the stabilizer.

Embroider—Ready, Set, Stitch…Finish!

- Set up the machine for embroidery as detailed in your instruction manual.

- Use the machine's arrow keys to position the needle at the center cross mark for the fence. Embroider the fence.

- Use the machine's arrow keys to position the needle at the center cross mark for the bunny. Embroider the tail and feet of the bunny using Dry Cover-Up™ as a topper.

- Stitch the next section of the design to provide a placement guide for positioning the plush fabric. After the stitching is completed, the machine stops for placing the fabric.

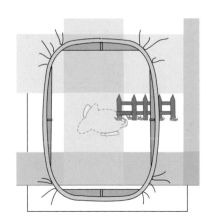

Expanding Your Vision

• Cut plush fabric a little larger than the sewn guideline and spray with adhesive such as KK2000™. Position the plush fabric wrong side down over sewn guideline covering it completely.

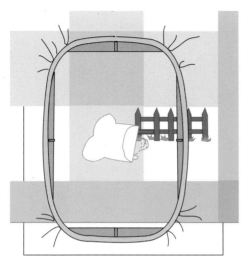

• Lightly spray a layer of Clear Away Lite with the spray adhesive and place it over the entire design in the hoop. Embroider the next portion of the design to tack down the plush fabric.

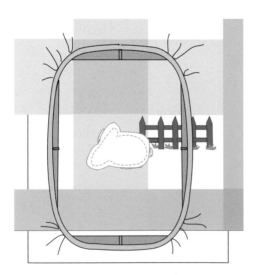

• Remove the hoop from the embroidery machine. **Do not remove the fabric from the hoop!**

• Carefully trim away all of the excess plush fabric in the hoop, getting as close to the tacked down stitching as possible.

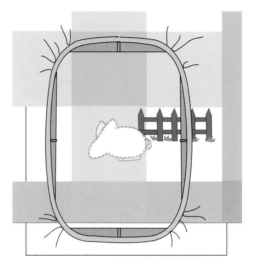

• Attach the embroidery hoop to the machine and finish remaining appliqué and embroidery stitching. Trim jump stitches, remove excess stabilizer.

• Complete blanket by adding a flannel backing and finishing edges.

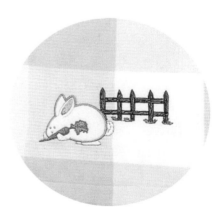

Design Collection used for Bunny Blanket:
Amazing Designs™ Sensational Series™ Plush Pals™ Bunnies
    Collection I
Designs #6427 and #6453

Expanding Your Vision

Baby's Name Wall Hanging

Personalize a special gift, or make a memento for your own little bundle of joy!

Position

• Cut the fabric about 2" larger on all sides than the frame opening .

• Mark the center of the wall hanging.

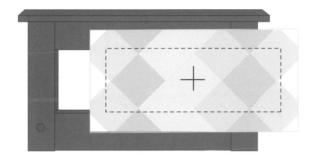

• Program letters for a name on your embroidery screen if you have this feature on your machine. If you are using a script font you may need to move the letters closer together using your positioning arrow keys.

• Combine bunnies with the floral grass designs if you are able to edit embroidery on your machine. If your machine doesn't have this feature, you can make a template for the grass as well as the bunny designs and position each separately.

• Stitch out templates for the lettering and bunny designs. (See pages 48–49.) The left design was mirror imaged so it faced the lettering. Mark center cross marks for each template.

• Save the name to the memory on your machine if your machine has this feature. Then it will be available when you're ready to embroider.

Expanding Your Vision

Stabilize

- Interface fabric with an iron-on interfacing such as Pellon® Sof-Shape®.

- Use a tear-away stabilizer.

- Use Dry Cover-Up™ as a topper when stitching the letters, bunny legs and tail to prevent the colors beneath from showing through.

- Use a topper such as Clear Away Lite for the appliqué.

Hoop

- Hoop the fabric and the stabilizer together.

- Center cross mark for lettering with center of hoop.

Embroider—Ready, Set, Stitch...Finish!

- Set up the machine for embroidery as detailed in your instruction manual.

- Use the machine's arrow keys to position the needle at the first design's starting point.

- Embroider the name.

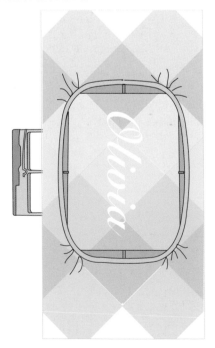

- Remove hoop. Reposition fabric as necessary for embroidering bunny designs.

- Position templates and mark center of bunny designs.

- Embroider bunnies and floral grass, using the appliqué technique featured in Bunny Blanket, pages 113–114, and as outlined in directions in the Plush Pals™ Bunnies Collection I, rehooping as necessary.

- Change colors on the bow and flowers to coordinate with the background fabric.

- Trim jump stitches, remove hoop.

- Add one layer of batting between the backing board for the frame and the embroidered fabric.

- Secure embroidered fabric to reverse side of backing board by taping in place.

- Frame and enjoy!

Design Collection used for Baby's Name Wall Hanging: Amazing Designs™ Plush Pals™ Bunnies Collection I (BMCS-PP4)
Designs #10886, #64537 and #64538

Lettering used is a built-in exclusive cursive font on the Baby Lock® ESG3

Organizer Hang-up for the Nursery

Use an organizer pattern of your choice; then embellish it with embroidery. A practical gift that's easy to make—what more could you ask for? Fill the pockets with baby essentials for an added sentiment. We used reinforced plastic for one of our pockets so you can see the contents at a glance.

Position

- Stitch out templates for each of the designs. (See pages 48–49.)

- Mark the center of the embroidery designs on the top pocket section within the plaid squares. Make sure to allow for a hem at the bottom of the pocket sections!

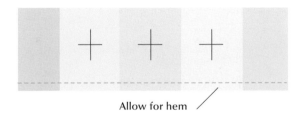

Allow for hem

- Mark the center of designs on bottom pocket also, keeping in mind that fabric is pleated between each design. On the pictured organizer, one square of the plaid is pleated to the inside between each pocket.

Pleat between pockets

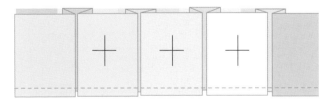

Stabilize

- Use a nonwoven cut-away stabilizer such as Pellon® Sof-Stitch™ or Mega Stay.

- Hoop stabilizer and spray with an adhesive such as KK2000™. Make a hoop bib (see page 58) to prevent your hoop from getting sticky.

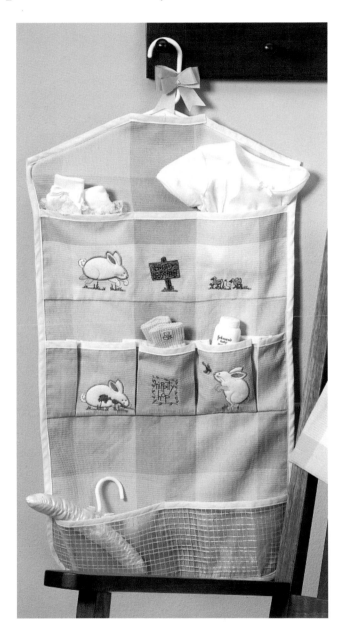

- Use Dry Cover-Up™ as a topper when stitching the bunny legs and tail to prevent the colors beneath from showing through.

- Use a topper such as Clear Away Lite for the appliqué.

Expanding Your Vision

Hoop

- Place the pocket on top of the hoop, gently smoothing the fabric to the sticky stabilizer.

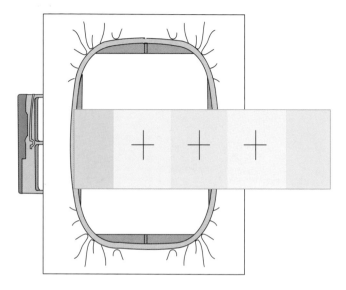

Embroider—Ready, Set, Stitch…Finish!

- Set up the machine for embroidery as detailed in your instruction manual.

- Use the machine's arrow keys to position the needle at the first design's starting point.

- Embroider all designs, rehooping as necessary. Embroider bunnies using appliqué techniques as featured in Bunny Blanket pages 113–114, and as outlined in directions in the Plush Pals™ Bunnies Collection I.

Motivating Memo

We added grass from another design (#64543) to several of the embroidered areas. Stitch the grass first. Then recenter the design for the bunny or duck. On the duck design, we skipped the water, embroidered the ducks and skipped the lettering. You could stitch the design "as is" for an easier variation.

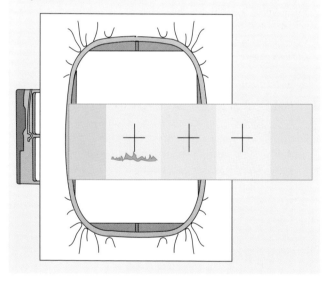

- Trim jump stitches and cut away excess stabilizer.

Design Collection used for the Organizer Hang-up:
Amazing Designs™ Sensational Series™ Plush Pals™ Bunnies
   Collection I
Designs #53336, #53337, #64536, #64540, #64541, #64542 and
   #64543 (grass only)

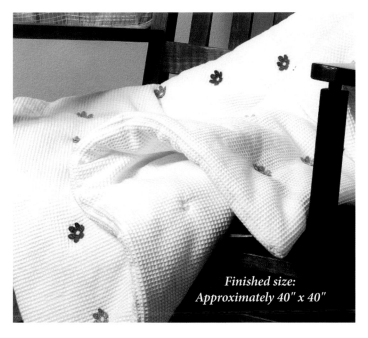

Daisy Tufted Baby Quilt

Daisies will tell you that this dainty 3-D floral quilt is fun to embroider and easy to sew. It's as fluffy as a featherbed! Two layers of high loft batting are sandwiched between two layers of white waffle weave fabric. It's a charming gift for a little bundle of joy!

Finished size: Approximately 40" x 40"

SUPPLIES NEEDED

- 2⅝ yards prewashed white waffle weave fabric
- 2½ yards batting
- ⅜ yard white polyester organza
- 2 yards wash-away stabilizer
- Ten colors of polyester embroidery thread (We used Madeira Polyneon colors 1816, 1712, 1817, 1951, 1645, 1702, 1911, 1831, 1932 and 1675.)

HELPFUL NOTIONS

- Sulky® KK2000™
- Stencil cutter tool
- 5" x 5" template or square ruler (5" or larger)
- 1½" curved basting pins
- 60 wt. clear monofilament thread

Embroidering the Daisies
Position

- Make a daisy template by stitching out one design on sample cloth. (See pages 48–49.)

- Use the template as a guide to position multiple daisies on stabilized polyester organza.

Stabilize

- Cut two pieces of wash-away and a piece of organza about 1" larger on all sides than the hoop.

- Make an "organza sandwich" by sandwiching the organza between the two layers of wash-away. Use a small amount of KK2000™ spray adhesive to temporarily adhere the organza and wash-away together. This makes hooping easier and prevents shifting.

Hoop

- Hoop the fused organza/wash-away together.

- If you use a large hoop, you can position several daisies in one hooping.

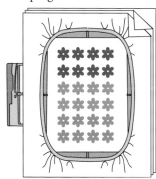

Sandwich organza between two sheets of wash-away

Embroider—Ready, Set, Stitch…Finish!

- Set up the machine for embroidery as detailed in your instruction manual.

- Use the machine's arrow keys to position the needle at the first design's starting point.

- Embroider daisies, changing colors for daisies as desired. Embroider at least six daisies of each thread color. Trim jump stitches and gently remove excess stabilizer.

- Rinse out remaining stabilizer; let organza dry.

- "Cut out" individual daisies from the organza using the stencil cutter tool. The stencil cutter efficiently melts away surrounding fabric from the embroidered designs for a neat, clean finish.

Expanding Your Vision

• Because the stencil cutter is designed to melt synthetic fibers like polyester organza, we usually use natural fiber threads such as cotton, rayon or silk for the embroidery because they tolerate higher temperatures. However, in this project the durability and color selection of the synthetic polyester thread are important. Just be careful when melting away the organza! You don't want to lose petals in the process.

◼ NUGGET OF INSPIRATION

Practice on one or two daisies first. You'll notice that the polyester organza melts more quickly than the thread. That's a good thing!

Constructing the Quilt

1 Prewash waffle weave fabric according to fabric care instructions.

2 Cut and layer fabrics.

• Cut batting into two 42" squares; stack one square on top of the other.

• Cut waffle weave fabric into two 41" squares.

• Place waffle weave fabric right sides together. Position it over the two batting layers.

• Pin all layers together.

3 Stitch ⅜" from cut edge of fabric around all four sides, wrapping corners, and leaving a 20" opening along one side.

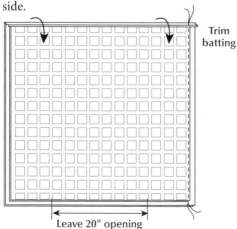

Trim batting

Leave 20" opening

Motivating Memo

Wrapped corners eliminate bulk and give smooth, professional looking results. Stitch one seam. Trim batting close to seam allowances to reduce bulk. Press or finger press the seam toward the underside of the quilt, folding the seam along the stitching line. Sew the second side of the corner, beginning at the fold of the fabric. Repeat on remaining corners.

4 Turn quilt right side out through opening, gently poking out corners. Hand stitch or machine stitch the opening shut.

5 Add daisy appliqués.

• Mark daisy positions using a water- or air-erasable fabric marking pen, and square ruler or template. Mark dots on quilt top, approximately 5" apart.

• Pin baste layers together with curved basting pins, centering pins between dots.

• Center one daisy over each dot, randomly arranging the colors. Pin in place.

- Securely machine stitch center of each daisy in place through all layers, using monofilament thread and a short stitch length.

- Use a drop of water on each marked dot to dissolve marking.

Design Collection used for daisies:
Amazing Designer Series™ Lace Vignettes Collection VII by Nancy Zieman
Design #28355

◼ NUGGET OF INSPIRATION

If marks are not removed from fabric they may "ghost" or reappear in the future. This quilt is much too lovely to have ghosts on it! What's even scarier is that they can become permanent if you press over them.

Fish Stories

As I tramped through the north woods I could feel the sun beating down on my head. Better get my cap on! Let's see, I brought enough clothes for 10 days (one shirt and one pair of jeans), my pillow, my blanket and my fishin' pole. I hung out the sign that said Gone Fishin' at the office. Now, I just need to catch Hugo, the fish that is so large he will probably break my line trying to reel him in…

Big Fish Denim Shirt

The big catch of the day!

Position

Make a cross mark for design position approximately 1½" above pocket, centered with middle of pocket.

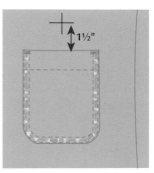

Stabilize

Stabilize area to be embroidered from wrong side with an iron-on fusible cut-away stabilizer such as Fusible No Show Mesh. This stabilizer won't stretch and distort stitches, and it is comfortable next to the skin.

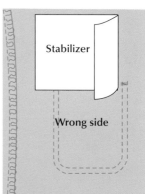

Hoop

Hoop shirt.

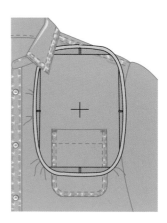

Embroider—Ready, Set, Stitch…Finish!

- Set up the machine for embroidery as detailed in your instruction manual.

- Use your arrow keys to position needle over cross marks of design before stitching.

- Embroider the design. If you plan to eliminate the lettering, remember **not** to stitch that portion.

- Trim jump stitches and remove stabilizer.

Design Collection used for Big Fish Denim Shirt:
Amazing Designs® Fishing I (ADC1405)
Design #64699

NUGGET OF INSPIRATION

If you want the shirt to be truly memorable you could use lettering that you may have on your machine to center and stitch "I caught Hugo!" under the fish.

Expanding Your Vision

Anchors Away Sweatshirt

Remember the time you threw the anchor over the side of the boat…
And, it didn't have the rope on it?

Position

Use a marking tool such as Embroider's Buddy or Perfect Placement Kit to mark the center placement cross mark on left chest of the sweatshirt. These tools use industry standards, so they take the guesswork out of design placement.

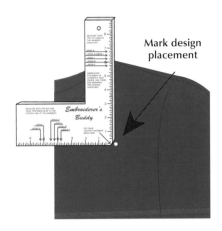

Mark design placement

Stabilize

Use a stabilizer that won't stretch and distort stitches on knits, such as tear-away Cotton Soft by Madeira. It works great on knits and is comfortable next to the skin. For heavier knits you may need to use more than one layer.

Hoop

• Turn sweatshirt "inside out" so that the right side of the shirt is on the inside. This makes hooping much easier.

• Cut stabilizer a little larger than the hoop.

• Hoop sweatshirt and stabilizer together, centering the placement position cross mark in the center of the hoop, aligning with marks on the hoop.

Embroider—Ready, Set, Stitch…Finish!

• Set up the machine for embroidery as detailed in your instruction manual.

• Use your arrow keys to position needle over cross marks of the design before stitching.

• Embroider the design, trim jump stitches and remove stabilizer.

Design Collection used for Anchors Away Sweatshirt:
Amazing Designer Series™ Memories by the Shore Collection IV
Design #29011

Expanding Your Vision

My Fishin' Gear Polo

Didn't catch any fish? Wear this new polo shirt to the fish fry downtown.

Position

Use a marking tool such as the Perfect Placement Kit or Embroiderer's Buddy to mark the center placement cross mark on left chest of the knit polo shirt. These tools use industry standards, so they take the guesswork out of design placement.

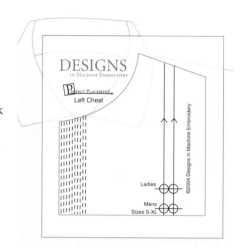

Stabilize

• Use a cut-away stabilizer such as Fusible No Show Mesh that won't stretch and distort stitches on knits. It is great on knits and comfortable next to the skin.

• Press the stabilizer to the wrong side of the polo, over the design area.

Motivating Memo

If you are not using one of the above tools, have the fisherman try on the garment to find a good placement for the design. Stitch design on sample cloth and move it around on the shirt until it looks good. Don't forget to make a cross mark on the shirt for centering the design in the hoop.

Hoop

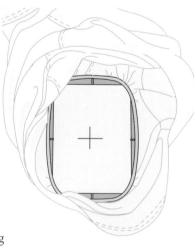

• Turn polo inside out so that the right side of the shirt is on the inside. This makes hooping much easier.

• Hoop shirt and stabilizer together, centering the placement position cross mark in the center of the hoop, aligning with marks on hoop.

Design Collection used for My Fishin' Gear Polo:
Amazing Designer Series™ Memories by the Shore Collection IV
Design #31032

Embroider—Ready, Set, Stitch…Finish!

• Set up the machine for embroidery as detailed in your instruction manual.

• Use your arrow keys to position needle over cross marks for the design before stitching.

• Embroider the design, trim jump stitches and cut away excess stabilizer.

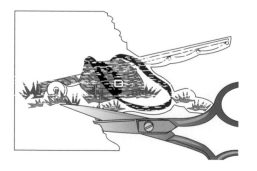

"A Luring" Fleece Pillowcase

Dream about the new lure that all the fish love!

When you're dreaming of the fish that got away, rest in comfort with an embroidered plush pillowcase. Add embroidery before stitching the side seams.

MATERIALS NEEDED
(makes one pillowcase)

- ⅔ yard fleece, 60" wide
- Three ¾–1" buttons
- Matching all-purpose thread
- Embroidery thread for fishing lures
- Embroidery bobbin thread

Preparing the Pillowcase:

- Cut one fleece rectangle 22" x 60".

- Turn under and stitch a 1" hem at one short end of the rectangle. Then turn under and stitch a ½" hem at the other short end.

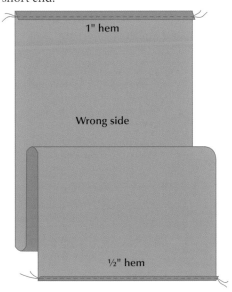

1" hem

Wrong side

½" hem

- Fold case in half, meeting lengthwise edges. Mark center of cuff.

Wrong side

Fold

- Mark buttonhole positions on the cuff (short end with the 1" hem).

- Fold lengthwise edges to the center pin. Mark each quarter mark with a pin.

• Cut four 1" x 2" pieces of cut-away stabilizer such as Mega Stay or Sulky® Cut-Away Plus™. Use three of the rectangles for stitching the buttonholes on the cuff of the pillowcase, and the fourth, for stitching a test buttonhole.

• Stitch the test buttonhole using the fourth stabilizer piece and a scrap of fleece.
Check that the length and width of the buttonhole stitching are correct for the selected buttons.

• After determining correct settings, stitch buttonholes, beginning each 1½" from the 1" hemmed edge. Open buttonholes using the Buttonhole Cutter Set.

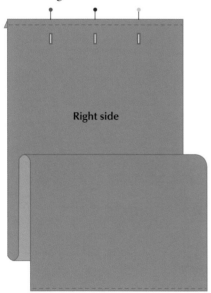

Right side

Adding Embroidery

Position

• Stitch out fishing lures on sample fabric so you can decide how much you want to rotate the design on the pillowcase.

• Mark the vertical and horizontal cross marks for the center of the design. Use this template and a fabric marking pen to position and transfer cross marks to the pillowcase.

Stabilize

Hoop the same type of cut-away stabilizer used for the buttonholes.

Hoop

• Hoop the stabilizer, rather than the fleece, to avoid unsightly hoop marks on the fleece.

• Spray the stabilizer with an adhesive spray such as Sulky® KK2000™, taking care not to get spray on the hoop. (See Hoop Bib, page 58.)

• Place the area to be embroidered over the sticky stabilizer, centering the cross marks, with wrong side of fleece toward the stabilizer.

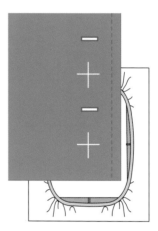

■ NUGGET OF INSPIRATION
OK, it's hard to spray adhesive on the stabilizer without getting it on your hoop, hands and maybe even your sewing table. To remove that "tacky touch" use a product such as DK5 Cleaning Agent. Say goodbye to gummy hoops!

Embroider—Ready, Set, Stitch…Finish!

• Set up the machine for embroidery as detailed in your instruction manual.

• Change the color order for each lure for interesting color combinations that coordinate.

• Use arrow keys to position the needle over the design cross marks.

• Embroider the design. Repeat, stitching each design.

• Trim jump stitches. Remove the fleece from the stabilizer and trim away excess stabilizer.

Completing the Pillowcase

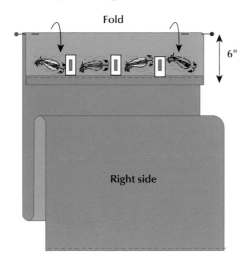

• Fold back 6" on the short end with the embroidery, meeting right sides. Mark fold with a pin.

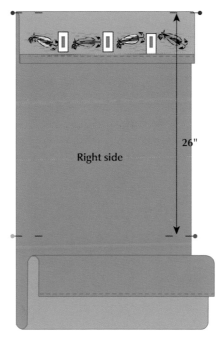

• Measure 26" from the fold; mark with pins.

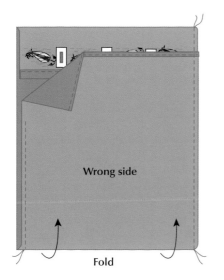

• Fold fleece at the pin marks, bringing the remaining hemmed edge up over the cuff. Pin and stitch side seams, guiding the right edge of the presser foot along the cut edge.

• Turn the pillowcase right side out.

• Turn cuff right side out, over the pillowcase. Mark corresponding button positions on the underlay. Stitch buttons to the underlay, adding a small square of cut-away stabilizer behind each button position to provide support and prevent the button from pulling out of the fleece.

Design Collection used for "A Luring" Fleece Pillowcase:
Amazing Designer Series™ Memories by the Shore Collection IV
Design #29015

Expanding Your Vision

Fleece Fishing Blanket

Warm enough to bundle up in after that spill into the lake!

Cut fleece to preferred size and hem edges as desired or use a purchased fleece blanket.

Position

• Use the Perfect Placement Kit and choose the placement template for an embroidery design in the corner of a blanket. Or, make your own template. (See pages 48–49.)

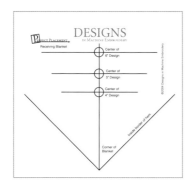

• Stitch out cattails and oars on sample fabric so that you can decide how close together you want to place them on the blanket. Mark the cross marks for centering each design on the sample. Use this template to position and make cross marks on the blanket. Use the Perfect Placement Kit to position the complete design in the corner of the blanket.

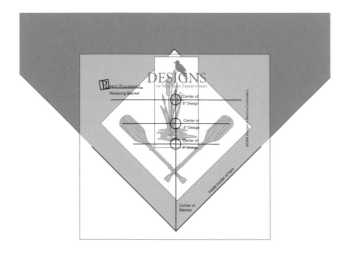

Stabilize

Use a sticky-backed stabilizer such as Filmoplast Stic Stabilizer in the embroidery hoop.

Hoop

• Hoop the stabilizer, rather than the fleece, and you won't have unsightly hoop marks on the fleece.

• Remove the paper covering within the hoop area to expose the adhesive. (Scoring the paper with a pin will make it easier to remove the paper.)

Embroider—Ready, Set, Stitch…Finish!

• Place the corner to be embroidered over the Filmoplast Stic with wrong side of fleece toward the adhesive.

• Set up the machine for embroidery as detailed in your instruction manual.

• Use your arrow keys to position needle over cross marks of the design before stitching.

• Embroider the design; trim jump stitches.

• Remove the fleece from the stabilizer and remove excess stabilizer.

Design Collection used for Fleece Fishing Blanket:
Amazing Designer Series™ Memories by the Shore Collection IV
Designs #29017 and #20136

Fishin' Hat

That's the kind of hat I'm talking about!

Position

- Select embroidery designs that fit in the various cap panels that you plan to embroider.

- Prepare a template for each design to aid in positioning on the hat. (See pages 48–49.) Make sure to mark centers of each design.

- Transfer the template markings directly to your hat with a washable fabric marker.

Stabilize

- Use a sticky stabilizer, such as Hydro-stick™.

Hoop

- Hoop the stabilizer with the shiny side up.

- Mark a placement line directly on the stabilizer and mark the center of the design.

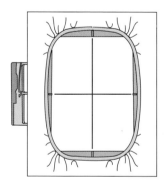

- Lightly and evenly moisten the adhesive with a sponge. Remember—a little water goes a long way!

- Position a crown panel on the stabilizer, matching center and placement marks. The adhesive stabilizer holds the crown in position and keeps it flat during embroidery. You can embroider the crown panels on the sides and back with this method.

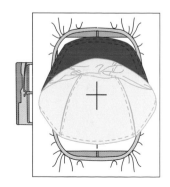

Embroider—Ready, Set, Stitch…Finish!

Motivating Memo

The easiest way to embroider a cap is using a cap hoop that fits your machine. Refer to the instructions for your model. It is next to impossible to embroider on the front of a cap without this special hoop. The cap hoop will hold the cap in place, and also hold the sweatband (inside the cap) out of the way so that you don't embroider through it.

- Another option for embroidering the front of a cap would be to make a free-form embroidered appliqué. (See Daisy Tufted Baby Quilt, pages 119–120.) Glue or sew the appliqué in position when the embroidery is complete.

- Set up the machine for embroidery as detailed in your instruction manual.

- *Optional:* Secure the cap hoop in position.

- Use your arrow keys to position needle over cross marks for the design before stitching.

- Embroider the design, trim jump stitches and remove stabilizer.

Design Collections used for Fishin' Hat:
Amazing Designs® North Woods Whimsy I (ADC1296)
Designs #90400, #90401, #90402 and #90403

Fishy Scrap Quilt

Nothing "fishy" about this lively colored quilt—except the embroidery! Make a scrap quilt using fabric from your stash and accent it with your favorite fish for under-the-sea allure. It will definitely be the catch of the day!

Stitch the embroidery before adding the backing, batting and binding to the quilt.

- Use the window technique with a sticky-backed stabilizer instead of hooping this quilt. (See pages 60–61.)
- Position Dry Cover-Up™ on top of the quilt before embroidering the fish. Embroidery colors will remain crisp and clear even over intense hues like those pictured on this quilt.

Design Collection used for Fishy Scrap Quilt: Amazing Designs™ Tropical Fish I (ADC1125)

Daisy Push Pins

Daisies are popping up as push pins! Brighten up your bulletin board with these embroidered delights. They're fun to make in 70s-inspired colors for your new millennium "flower child."

- Use a template to position several daisies on wash-away stabilizer.
- Stitch daisies on organza sandwiched between two layers of transparent wash-away stabilizer using the technique detailed on pages 119–120.
- Rinse to eliminate stabilizer. "Cut out" daisies from organza using the stencil cutter tool. (See page 120.)
- Glue daisies to the push pins.
- Add a pearl center using Hot-fix Pearls and the Hot-fix Applicator Wand.

The Dragonfly pictured on the bulletin board was embroidered using the same techniques as the daisies. Try different designs with this technique for 3-D accessories!

Design Collection used for Daisy Push Pins: Amazing Designer Series™ Lace Vignettes Collection VIII

Showcase

Fleece Bath Blanket

Rubber Duckies in billowing bubbles accent the corner of this cozy fleece blanket. Serge edges with variegated woolly nylon for a border that looks like luxurious binding.

- Make templates for duckies and bubbles. Combine, rotate and mirror bubble segments around duckies, marking centers as they are positioned.
- Use a soft tear-away stabilizer and spray adhesive to hold the blanket on the hoop.
- Lightly spray a layer of wash-away stabilizer with adhesive and place it over the fabric before embroidering to keep the stitches from sinking into the loft of the fleece.

Dcsign Collection used for Fleece Bath Blanket: Amazing Designs™ Elegant Nursery Collection I (AD1291)

Fleece Bunny Blanket

Soft fleece "blankie" with the beloved satin binding—brings back memories!

Combine multiple designs to obtain the ribbon and bows corner border, which highlights a single patchwork bunny.

- Make templates for bunny, ribbon and bow designs for ease in placement. Combine ribbon and bow design segments to create the corner border, mirror imaging the bow on the right.
- Use a soft tear-away stabilizer and spray adhesive to secure the corner of the blanket to the hoop, instead of hooping the fleece.
- Lightly spray a layer of wash-away stabilizer with adhesive and place it over the fabric before embroidering to keep the stitches from sinking into the loft of the fleece.

Design Collection used for Fleece Bunny Blanket: Amazing Designs™ Elegant Nursery Collection I (AD1291)

"Autumn in the Air" Design Embellishments

Looking for more fun blanks to embroider? Ready-made garments make the perfect palettes for embroidering these seasonal designs. There is something for everyone in the family! From Dad's necktie and Mom's jumper to children's playwear, small bits of embroidery set the tone for the season. Notice the little dress in the foreground—replace ordinary buttons with candy corn buttons, and embroider itsy-bitsy spiders between the buttonholes.

Design Collection used for the autumn
  embellishments:
Amazing Designer Series™ Autumn in the Air

4" Hoop (100 mm x 100 mm) Designs

You don't need a large hoop to add attractive accents. Each of these showcase pieces was embroidered on a machine with a 4" embroidery field. You're not as limited as you thought!

- Combine three designs as shown on the shirt. Simply stitch each one separately.
- Open the leg seam on a child's pair of jeans to stitch the giraffe; then restitch the seam after completing the embroidery.
- Sticky stabilizers and templates are a must when stitching on smaller items. Check out the various types of stabilizers on pages 28–35.

Designs in this photo are built-in designs from various machines. Use your favorite small design combinations to embellish your ready-to-wear garments.

Showcase

Oriental Floral Embellishment

Use embroidery to accent wardrobe classics. Tasteful embroidery strategically positioned transforms even a basic dress to rival a designer original.

Instead of embroidering one large flower, combine several sizes and colors. Form an embroidered floral swag to enhance even the simplest style. Templates are the secret to precise positioning. You don't need to be a florist to combine this arrangement!

Design Collection used for the Oriental Floral
    Embellishment:
Amazing Designer Series™ Accents for Style Collection
    XVI

Fireplace Mantle Scarf

Do you enjoy a bit of a challenge? Our mantle scarf delivers! Actually, it looks more complicated than it is. Templates are the secret to successfully placing the designs.

- Mirror image and/or rotate the poinsettia and holly motifs to fit exactly where you want them.
- Use additional templates to position and center the lettering in each scalloped section.

Design Collection used for the Fireplace Mantle
    Scarf designs:
Amazing Designer Series™ Christmas Splendor
    Collection XI

Floral Dresser Scarf

A profusion of embroidered flowers decorates this purchased dresser scarf—templates to the rescue!

• Rotate and mirror image the templates to create a pleasing arrangement on a paper pattern.
• Write down any notes regarding mirror imaging, rotation, exact design name or number, stabilizer and threads. These will be your "road map" to follow for accident free embroidery!

Design Collection used for the Floral Dresser Scarf designs:
Amazing Designer Series™ Blooming Elegance Collection X

Fence with Flowering Vines

Here's another scene reminiscent of a still life painting, created by combining fabrics with multiple embroidery designs. This embroidery features a fence and flowering vines in the foreground, as well as a window box, hanging basket and groups of potted plants. It is a great exercise in combining designs along with mirror imaging.

• Start by embroidering the window.
• Add the window box and hanging basket.
• Add trellis planter and tall pots.
• Stitch pots, embroidering those behind other pots first.
• Embroider the fence, mirror imaging the second half of the design.
• Embroider vines, again mirror imaging.

Design Collection used for the Fence with Flowering Vines designs:
Amazing Designer Series™ Water Color Garden Collection XIII

Showcase

Water Lily Keepsake Box

Use this exquisite Monet inspired keepsake box to store your cherished memorabilia. Regardless of the treasure stored inside the box, the outside embroidery is equally collectible.

Stitch background designs on the base fabric, using only individual portions of designs (for example, leaves, lilies, water). Then position sheer organza over the fabric and stitch complete designs in the foreground. The organza mutes the background and adds depth and dimension to the design.

- Use a sticky-backed stabilizer and the window hooping technique. (See pages 60–61.)
- Insert a new needle in your machine to minimize the chance of snagging the sheer fabric.

Design Collection used for Water Lily Keepsake Box: Amazing Designer Series™ Nature's Reflections

Snowy Trees Portrait

Combine several designs, arrange smaller designs in the border, add a sprinkling of crystal beads and you have a Showpiece! Arrange designs for a beautiful border by using templates for placement.

To keep the center embroidery as the focal point, stitch designs in the border area with threads that blend into the background.

Stitch the snowflake ornament and garland on organza, using the technique detailed for daisies, page 119–120.

Design Collection used for the Snowy Tree designs: Amazing Designer Series™ Enchanted Snowfall Collection XV

Shadows and Reflections

Fill stitches are the base of an embroidery design. When used alone, they look entirely different than the fully embroidered design. For example, create a shadow as on the scarecrow.

- Make a template of the fill stitch and the fully embroidered design to help determine where to effectively position the designs.
- Edit the design by rotating, stretching or resizing.
- Reduce the density of a design if the fully stitched design will overlap the fill stitches.
- Use shades of thread lighter or darker than the fully embroidered design to soften the look and allow the fill stitches to fade into the background.

Design Collections used for Shadows and Reflections: Amazing Designs™ Scarecrow I (ADC1386)

Home Decorating Ideas

Enhance your home décor with machine embroidery. The options are endless!

- Combine designs to frame as well as make a continuous border on a one of a kind curtain.
- Rotate and mirror designs as desired.
- Free form bugs and butterflies make the curtains come to life. Embroider them on organza sandwiched between two layers of transparent wash-away stabilizer using the technique detailed for daisies, pages 119–120.
- Rinse to eliminate stabilizer, and cut away organza using the stencil cutter tool. (See page 120.)
- Stitch or glue bug and butterfly bodies to the curtain leaving the wings free.

Design Collection used for Home Decorating Ideas: Amazing Designer Series™ Garden Friends
Collection V

Showcase

Holiday Message Board and Placemat

This novel holiday message board begins with a single rectangle of fabric.

- Mark positions for the smaller rectangle of chalkboard fabric as well as the binding.
- Center embroidery designs in the open border area between the markings.
- Use templates to position the designs, moving them around to achieve a pleasing composition.

Stitch a set of coordinating bound placemats as the perfect complement.

Design Collection used for Message Board and Placemat designs:
Amazing Designer Series™ Christmas Magic Collection VI

Tea Tray

The stunning embroidery on this tea tray can be as large or as small as you desire. "Paint" a lovely embroidered garden or vista with thread and your embroidery machine by combining a collection of embroidery designs. Remember to plan your picture before embroidering, and make cross marks to identify the center of each design.

- Stitch the background first (hills, clouds, shore-line).
- Stitch the midsection (tree trunk, leaves, middle grasses).
- Finish up with the foreground embroidery designs (flowers).

Using this stitching sequence adds depth and dimension to the scene.

Design Collection used for the Tea Tray designs:
Amazing Designer Series™ Four Seasons Landscape Collection IX

Troubleshooting

Stitching Problems

Bobbin thread is visible on the embroidery
- Check machine threading. Rethread the machine.
- Loosen the top tension.
- Use a different type of bobbin thread. Test a prewound bobbin or a heavier weight thread.
- Clean lint from the bobbin area.
- Use a different type of needle. Try a machine embroidery needle, or a metallic or titanium needle.

No bobbin thread is visible on back side of design
- Check thread tensions, both upper and lower.
- Check threading. Rethread if necessary.

Threads are tangled and twisted on the underside
- Check to ensure the presser foot is lowered.
- Check machine threading. Rethread if necessary.
- Remove the bobbin. Clean the area of thread or lint. Then rethread the bobbin.
- Adjust upper thread tension.
- Trim away tangles from the back side of the embroidery. If necessary, add new stabilizer. Back up the machine to the design area just before the problem. Then continue stitching.

Stitches skip
- Rethread the machine.
- Use the correct style of needle. For example, use a metallic needle for metallic threads.
- Check to ensure the needle is inserted correctly and that it is all the way up into the opening. Check the owner's manual for specific instructions.
- Insert a new needle.
- Use a smaller size needle.
- Clean lint and threads from the bobbin area.

Thread shreds
- Insert a new needle.
- Replace the needle with one with a larger eye. (Try a metallic or titanium needle.)
- Check for burrs on the throat plate. If you feel a burr, contact your dealer.

Top thread breaks
- Check that the thread hasn't looped around the spool pin or become caught on the thread spool.
- Check machine threading. Rethread both the needle and the bobbin.
- Check to ensure the needle is correctly inserted into the needle bar and that it is all the way up into the opening. Check the owner's manual for specific instructions.
- Use a needle designed for machine embroidery. An embroidery needle has a larger eye and a specially designed needle scarf which help reduce thread breakage, especially when stitching dense designs. Use a metallic needle for metallic threads. A metallic needle features a fine shaft and sharp point to eliminate thread breakage, a specialized scarf to prevent skipped stitches, and an elongated eye to prevent thread stripping.
- Be sure the presser foot is lowered into stitching position.
- Reduce the top tension.
- Insert a new needle.
- Change to a needle of a different size. Use a heavier needle (larger number) for heavier threads, and a smaller size for lightweight threads.
- Consider switching to another type of thread if necessary.
- Check that the fabric is securely hooped. Rehoop if necessary.
- Stitch more slowly if your machine has a variable speed setting.

Troubleshooting

Top thread appears to be threaded, but machine stops and indicates thread is broken
• Unthread and remove the top thread (floss tensions); rethread.
• Clean bobbin area from any dust, lint or threads.
• Check bobbin. If bobbin is nearly empty, change bobbins.

Design outline doesn't match with the design
• Change/add stabilizers. Design registration problems are often caused by inadequate stabilization. Prevention is the best solution.
• Check hooping. Incorrect hooping techniques sometimes cause registration problems.
• If the design is completely stitched, try these options for remedying the problem:
  - Fill in gaps with a fabric marker.
  - Hand embroider unfilled areas.
  - Use free-motion machine embroidery to fill the open areas.

Power was turned off in the middle of embroidery
• Turn machine back on. Advance machine to the portion of the design a few stitches before where stitching stopped, and resume stitching.
• If you moved your hoop before starting embroidery, do the same before restarting. Always write down the coordinates (for example, ↑ →). Keep a small notebook by the machine, just for that purpose.

Needle Problems

Needle breaks
• Check that the needle is securely screwed to the needle bar and that it is inserted according to machine instructions.
• Use a heavier needle, especially with heavy fabrics or dense designs.
• Use a lighter weight thread, especially with dense designs, or designs stitched over part of another design or over thick seams.
• Check to make sure the thread is not wound around the thread spindle.

Needle is gummy and sticky
• Clean the needle using alcohol or a cleaning agent. Thoroughly dry and wipe the needle clean before reinserting it.
• Stitch more slowly if your machine has a variable speed setting.
• Try a different adhesive-backed stabilizer.
• If inner works of the machine are sticky, contact dealer for cleaning and check-up.

Needle holes are visible
• When was the last time you changed your needle? Change the needle after a maximum of three hours of stitching.
• Check for burrs or imperfections on the needle. Insert a new needle if necessary.
• Use a smaller size needle.

Troubleshooting

Fabric Problems

Fabric is puckered around the embroidery
• Make sure the fabric is taut and secure in the hoop, but don't stretch the fabric.
• Try a different stabilizer. Test stitching on a fabric sample before stitching on the project.
• Reduce thread tensions.

Base fabric shows through the embroidery
• Use a different weight thread. For example, use 30 wt. thread rather than 40 wt. thread.
• Adjust the stitch density if your machine has this feature.
• Add a topper such as Dry Cover-Up™ on top of the fabric before embroidering.
• Place a clear stabilizer on top of the fabric before embroidering.

Underside of the embroidery is rough and scratchy
• Choose a different stabilizer. (For example, try Cotton Soft by Madeira, Fusible No Show Mesh, Simply Stable Polymesh, or Sulky® Cut-Away Soft 'n Sheer™.)
• Cut and fuse a layer of fusible tricot interfacing slightly larger than the embroidery and stabilizer to the underside of the embroidery.

Hoop Problems

Hoop is sticky
• Check for adhesive build-up. Use a cleaner designed for removing adhesive to clean the hoop; for example, DK5 Cleaning Agent.
• Use the "hoop bib" when spraying adhesive onto stabilizer to prevent overspray on the hoop or surrounding areas. (See page 58.)

Hoop marks are visible on the fabric
• Use the window hooping technique rather than hooping the fabric.(See pages 60–61.)
• Hoop only the stabilizer and secure the fabric by spraying a spray adhesive onto the stabilizer.
• Steam or launder the fabric (if consistent with fabric care instructions) to try to remove the marks.

Can't get fabric hooped
• Hoop is too tight. Loosen the tension screw and try again.
• Fabric is too thick. Use an alternate non-hooping method such as the Window Hooping Technique. See pages 60–61.
• Consider hooping aids such as Snappy. They help distribute pressure on all four sides of the hoop, making it easier to push in.
• Use Hoop Spreader Springs to help keep the outer hoop open to facilitate hooping.
• Use the window hooping technique for areas such as pockets that can't be hooped.

Stabilizer Problems

Stabilizer is difficult to remove
• With water-activated adhesives, remoisten the stabilizer. Then peel it off.
• With water-soluble stabilizers, immerse the embroidery in water. Rinse under running water while massaging the fabric.
• With tear-away stabilizers, position fingers of one hand firmly at outer edge of embroidery. With the other hand, gently tear away the stabilizer.

Stitches begin to pull and distort as stabilizer is removed
• Cut away excess stabilizer close to stitches, rather than tearing away the stabilizer.

Adhesive: a sticky surface, sometimes part of a wash-away, cut-away or tear-away stabilizer. Or, a spray which adds a sticky surface to the material on which it is sprayed. Adhesive allows fabric or other materials to adhere to the sticky surface.

Adhesive-backed stabilizer: a stabilizer that has a sticky surface. Ideal for fabric or garment sections too small to be hooped, or fabrics on which a hoop might leave an unsightly impression.

All-over design: a design that forms a continuous pattern over the entire area.

Appliqué Scissors: a specialty scissors designed for trimming close to fabric or an embroidered design. One blade of this scissors has a "bill" which lifts the section being trimmed without nicking the fabric underneath.

Appliqué: a section of fabric or embroidery cut into a specific shape and secured to another fabric by stitching or adhesive.

Backing: a stabilizer placed on the underside of a fabric during machine embroidery.

Baste. using long hand or sewing machine stitches to temporarily hold two or more layers of fabric together.

Bird's nest: twisted, looped, or snarled threads which sometimes accumulate on the underside of fabric during machine embroidery; usually the result of improper threading, tension, or hooping techniques.

Blank card: a medium used with reader/writer systems to save designs for use in a computerized embroidery machine. Cards are machine-specific and fit directly into the embroidery machine. Also known as a Flash Card.

Blanks: ready-made items such as garments, table linens, bed linens, accessories, and home décor that provide a palette for machine embroidery. The construction is already completed, so you can devote your energy to adding touches of embroidery to the item to make it one of a kind.

Bobbin: the spool or device that holds the lower thread that interlocks with the needle thread to form a stitch.

Burr: a rough spot or projection on a needle; often results in poor stitch quality or broken threads.

CD: a computer medium containing programmed designs that can be stitched on an embroidery machine. Using CD designs requires a separate IBM compatible home computer with a CD ROM drive, and in most cases, sewing machine software or a reader/writer system such as The Amazing Box™ II. CDs hold more information than disks.

Computerized embroidery: the ability to automatically stitch embroidery designs on a computerized embroidery machine.

Coordinates: numbers which identify the precise vertical and horizontal positions within an embroidery hoop.

Copyright: a legal term that prevents people other than the designer or artist who developed an embroidery design from unauthorized selling or profiting from that design.

Curved basting pins: curved nickel plated brass pins angled for easy insertion in quilting projects. These pins will not rust and can safely remain in fabric until the project is completed.

Curved embroidery scissors: a lightweight, easy to handle scissors designed specifically for trimming threads cleanly and closely following machine embroidery. The first curve of the scissors easily reaches over hand or machine hoops, while the second brings the blade tips close to the fabric to snip thread tails.

Customizing: changing an embroidery design in some way (for example, rotating, mirror imaging, resizing or adding lettering) to make the design unique for specific purposes.

Cut-away: a type of stabilizer removed by cutting with a scissors after embroidery is completed. A cut-away is appropriate for delicate fabrics and designs that might be distorted by tearing away the stabilizer.

Darning foot: a sewing machine presser foot used for free-motion stitching. This foot doesn't fit tightly against the fabric, so you can move the fabric around as you stitch.

Glossary

Density: how close together stitches are in a design; influenced by the number and type of stitches in a design.

Digitize: the process of converting artwork into computer-generated machine embroidery.

Dimensional embroidery: stitching designs onto a sheer fabric such as organza and cutting close to the outer edge of the design to make a free-standing motif or appliqué. A dimensional embroidery can be used independently, or it can be stitched or glued to another project.

Disk: a computer medium that stores programmed embroidery designs and/or software. Embroidery designs on disks require an IBM compatible computer with a floppy disk drive, and in most instances, sewing machine software or a reader/writer system such as The Amazing Box™ II. Also referred to as a 3½" floppy.

Download: the process of transferring a design from the Internet or a reader/writer box to a computer, or from the reader-writer box or computer to the embroidery machine.

Edit: using features built into an embroidery machine or computer software to modify a programmed embroidery design, for example, by eliminating part of a design, rotating, mirror imaging, etc.

Embroidery card: a small, flat medium containing programmed embroidery designs. An embroidery card usually fits directly into a special slot on an embroidery machine, where it can be read by the machine's computer.

Embroidery foot: a sewing machine presser foot used for free-motion stitching. This foot doesn't fit tightly against the fabric, so you can move the fabric around as you stitch.

Eye: the hole in the needle through which the needle is threaded.

Fill stitches: closely spaced machine embroidery stitches that are used to cover an area within an embroidery design.

Finishing: the final step in machine embroidery during which stabilizer is removed, jump stitches are trimmed away and the embroidered design is pressed or steamed.

Flash card: See Blank card.

Floppy disk: a computer medium containing programmed designs that can be stitched on an embroidery machine. Most machines require a separate IBM compatible computer with a floppy disk drive and in most instances, sewing machine software or a reader/writer system such as The Amazing Box™ II. Also referred to as a 3½" floppy.

Format: a computer language that can be read and interpreted by an embroidery machine. Each embroidery machine can read only formats specific to that machine. With embroidery designs, the letters following the period designate the machine format capable of reading that design. Examples of formats include PES, ART, SEW, EMD, JEF, PCS, PES, HUS and SHV.

Hardware: equipment such as an embroidery machine, a computer, or a reader/writer box that are used during the embroidery process.

Hoop: a tool that usually consists of inner and outer rings. A hoop is attached to the embroidery unit and used to secure the fabric and stabilizer during machine embroidery.

Hoop bib: a protective cardboard cutout positioned over the rings of the hoop when using spray adhesives to prevent adhesive build-up.

Hooping: the process of securing fabric and stabilizer in the embroidery hoop in preparation for machine embroidery.

Hooping aids: tools such as the Cap Hoop, Embroiderer's Buddy, and Perfect Placement Kit which make it easier to hoop unique garments or projects for machine embroidery.

Interfacing: an additional layer usually fused to the wrong side of fabric to add body and stability. Interfacing also prevents stabilizer from showing through the base fabric after embroidery is completed.

Iron-on stabilizer: a stabilizer with a surface that temporarily adheres to another fabric; especially suited for knits and loosely woven fabrics.

Jump stitches: the threads between the various portions of an embroidered design that are trimmed away after embroidery is completed.

Marking: using fabric marking pens or other devices to identify the starting point and vertical and horizontal center of an embroidery design.

Memory card: a medium containing programmed designs that can be read by a specific embroidery machine. A memory card fits directly into the embroidery machine. Always select the format required for your machine.

Memory: the area on a computerized embroidery machine where designs can be saved or stored for future use.

Monofilament thread: a lightweight transparent synthetic thread which blends easily with multiple colors. Often used as a bobbin thread during machine embroidery.

Monogram: embroidering one or more initials of a name.

Motif: a stitched embroidery design.

Napped fabric: a fabric that has a one-way texture. The pile or nap on the fabric reflects light differently when viewed from top to bottom than from bottom to top, so all sections of the fabric must be positioned in the same direction in a project.

Needle size: the higher the number, the heavier the needle. For example, a size 90/14 needle is heavier than a size 60/8 needle.

Open toe foot: a presser foot sometimes used during machine appliqué. The underside of this foot is grooved, allowing dense stitches to more easily pass through the machine. The opening at the front of the toe gives a clear view of where you're stitching.

Outline stitch: stitching which goes around the perimeter of an embroidery design; often stitched as the final color/stitching of the design. Also used to create a template of a design.

Pick 'n Choose: a technique in which only portions of an embroidery design are stitched.

Prewound bobbins: cardboard or plastic bobbins that are prewound with thread specially designed for the bobbins of embroidery machines.

Puckering: fabric that is drawn in and wrinkled around the edges of an embroidered design, rather than being smooth and flat. Often caused by inadequate hooping or stabilization, improper tension or a blunt, burred or incorrect needle.

Reader/writer box: hardware that makes it possible to read embroidery designs in one format and convert them into a different format which can be read by the embroidery machine or computer. Also offers the ability to save designs onto a card that can be inserted directly into the embroidery machine.

Registration: the alignment of various portions of a design to form the final embroidered design.

Sample cloth: prestiffened muslin often used to pretest an embroidery design's stitch density, colors and placement. Back the muslin with the same stabilizer you plan to use on your project.

Satin stitch: a closely spaced zigzag stitch sometimes used to fill or outline embroidery sections.

Scaling: changing the size of a design.

Glossary

Scarf: the indentation on the back of a needle, just above the eye, which holds the thread during stitch formation.

Software: computer programs, CDs, memory cards or disks used in the embroidery process.

Stabilizer: a material used to support the fabric and improve stitch quality during machine embroidery. Stabilizers are available in a variety of weights in cut-away, wash-away and tear-away forms, as well as in liquid form.

Stencil cutter tool: a heated tool, originally designed for cutting templates, that is useful for removing excess synthetic fabric from the outer edges of embroideries stitched onto a fabric such as organza or nylon tulle. A stencil cutter can be used to produce clean edges on an appliqué or three-dimensional embroidery.

Stitch count: the number of individual stitches in an embroidery design.

Stitch out: a design that has been embroidered onto a fabric as a test of the actual design.

Tear-away stabilizer: a stabilizer that can be removed from fabric by carefully tearing the stabilizer from around the design after embroidery is completed. Appropriate for dense stitching where tearing won't distort stitches or the fabric.

Templates: clear plastic, paper or fabric guides that include the outline of an embroidery design and are used to aid in positioning designs prior to embroidering them.

Tension: the tightness or looseness of the needle and bobbin threads during stitching or embroidery.

Topping: a stabilizer placed on the top of a fabric during machine embroidery, generally to prevent stitches from sinking into the base fabric.

Trace, or "walk-about": a machine feature that identifies the stitching area of the selected design within a hoop, as well as the center of the embroidery area.

Transfer: the ability to move an embroidery design from one piece of hardware or software to another using a cable, reader/writer box, computer software or the Internet.

Wash-away stabilizer: a stabilizer designed for washable fabrics. Can be easily removed by spraying or immersing in water, leaving no visible residue.

Water-activated adhesive stabilizer: a stabilizer that becomes sticky when a small amount of water is applied to its surface.

Window technique: Positioning an item for embroidery by positioning it on top of a hooped adhesive surface. Ideal for napped fabrics, fabrics on which hooping might leave an impression and items too small to hoop.

HANDKNITS
FOR BABY

HANDKNITS
FOR BABY

Over 30 Easy, Step-by-Step Patterns
for Newborn to 12 Months

TRAFALGAR SQUARE
North Pomfret, Vermont

First published in the United States of America
in 2017 by
Trafalgar Square Books
North Pomfret, Vermont 05053

Originally published in French as Layette facile.

Copyright © 2016 Éditions Marie Claire
English translation © 2017 Trafalgar Square Books

ISBN: 978-1-57076-805-7

Library of Congress Control Number: 2017950554

Editor: Thierry Lamarre
Concept design: Charlotte Rion
Creation: Frédérique Alexandre, for Phildar
Photography: Pierre Nicou
Styling: Kathrin Lezinsky
Retouching and digital work: Jean-Michel Boillot
Instructions, charts, knitting, and diagrams: Yolaine Fournie
Interior design: Either Studio
Technical editing: Véronique Blanc
Publishing liaison: Myriam Prez
Translation: Elizabeth Gray

Printed in China
10 9 8 7 6 5 4 3 2 1

Contents

Blankets..36, 119

Booties_____8, 36, 44, 111

Coats..45, 71

Cuddly friend..65, 119

Dress_____16

Hats...70, 113

Hoodie..99

Jackets, cardigans................8, 16, 37, 80, 104, 105

Mittens..70

Onesies and overalls.....................................29, 52

Poncho..112

Scarf..70

Shirts..8, 23, 53, 80

Short-sleeved shirt..90

Shorts..91

Sleep sack..64

Tunic..28

Wrap shirt..60

Introduction

This book is designed to make it fun and easy to follow pattern instructions. Plenty of diagrams, illustrations, and straightforward numbers are included to explain how to knit and assemble each garment, with color coding to help you keep track of sizing.

The pattern instructions in this book will include anywhere from one size to three sizes—the order in which sizes are listed at the beginning of the pattern is the order in which the numbers that apply to them will be listed throughout that pattern. We've made it as simple as possible to find and read the instructions for the specific size you're looking for.

Under the **Materials** heading, the yarn brand, amounts, and colors that are listed first correspond to what was used to knit the sample garment in any accompanying photos.

Under the **Stitches used** heading, you'll find a list of all the knitting stitches used in the pattern plus a quick explanation of how to work them.

Drawings or diagrams that accompany the instructions show the "right side" of the work. "Casting on" will always be the first step in the instructions; each step after that is numbered, and all you have to do is follow them, one after the other.

Arrows will indicate where you should be in the knitting at the point where you perform a particular step (often where you need to decrease, increase, or switch to a different kind of stitch).

Instructions between asterisks (*) are steps that will need to be repeated; you'll be told exactly how many times to do this.

For **assembly and finishing** instructions, different colors on drawings and diagrams correspond to different seams (side seams, sleeve attachments, etc.) so you can see which parts of each piece will be joined, and will also indicate where to attach or seam hoods, add pockets, place buttonholes, or embroider.

2. Shirt

Worked in stripes with finishing in garter stitch, using Partner 3,5 and U.S. size 2.5 / 3 mm needles, U.S. size 4 / 3.5 mm needles.

1. Booties

Worked in garter stitch in two colors, using Partner 3,5 and U.S. size 2.5 / 3 mm needles.

3. Cardigan

Worked in garter stitch in two colors, using Partner 3,5 and U.S. size 2.5 / 3 mm needles.

1. Booties

One size

Newborn/3 months

Materials

◊ CYCA #2 (sport/baby) Phildar Partner 3,5 (50% polyamide, 25% combed wool, 25% acrylic; 137 yd / 125 m / 50 g): 1 skein Acier; 1 skein of Soufre or Grenadine or Piscine (see gauges, page 15)
◊ U.S. size 2-3 / 3 mm needles

Stitches used

◊ **Garter stitch**
Row 1 (right side of work): Knit.
Row 2: Knit.
Repeat Rows 1 and 2.
The instructions given here match the sample pictured in most of the photographs. If you'd like to make a different version (see alternate color options, page 15), choose one of the other colors suggested—or use a different yarn, larger or smaller needles, or any other colors you like.

Pattern

4¾ in / 12 cm

1½ in / 4 cm
1½ in / 4 cm
2¾ in / 7 cm

6 in / 15 cm

6¾ in / 17 cm

Instructions

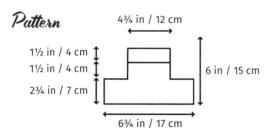

5) When work measures 6 in / 15 cm, bind off the remaining 29 sts.

4) When work measures 4¼ in / 11 cm, cut yarn and switch from Acier to Soufre; keep working in garter stitch.

3) Bind off 7 sts at start of next row; complete row.

1) With Acier, cast on 43 sts. Work in garter stitch.

2) When work measures 2¾ in / 7 cm, bind off 7 sts at start of row; complete row.

Assembly and finishing

Fold the bootie in half.

Seam across the bottom of the sole, and seam the instep at the top of the foot.

Fold the section worked in Soufre down over the part worked in Acier.

Weave a strand of Acier through the stitches at the toe opening, and then pull tight to draw the toe closed. Poke ends through to inside of bootie.

Weave in ends neatly on wrong side.

2. Shirt

Sizes

3 months (6 months, 12 months)

The instructions include all 3 sizes; the order above corresponds to the order in which instructions will be given for each size throughout. For example: for the 6-month size, always look for the first of two numbers in parentheses—in the materials list, the written instructions, and all the diagram labels showing size or length measurements.

Materials

◊ CYCA #2 (sport/baby) Phildar Partner 3,5 (50% polyamide, 25% combed wool and 25% acrylic; 137 yd / 125 m / 50 g): 2 (2, 3) skeins Acier; 1 (1, 1) skein of Soufre or Grenadine or Piscine (see gauges, page 15)
◊ U.S. size 2.5 / 3 mm needles and U.S. size 4 / 3.5 mm needles
◊ 4 buttons in a matching color

The instructions given here match the sample pictured in most of the photographs. If you'd like to make a different version (see alternate color options, page 15), choose one of the other colors suggested—or use a different yarn, larger or smaller needles, or any other colors you like.

Stitches used

◊ **Garter stitch**
  Row 1 (right side of work): Knit.
  Row 2: Knit.
  Repeat Rows 1 and 2.
◊ **Stockinette**
  Row 1 (right side of work): Knit.
  Row 2: Purl.
  Repeat Rows 1 and 2.
◊ **Stockinette stripes**
  4 rows in Acier, *2 rows in Soufre or Grenadine or Piscine, 6 rows in Acier*; repeat from * to * 3 more times and end with 2 rows in Soufre or Grenadine or Piscine.

Gauges

23 sts and 30 rows in stockinette using larger needles = 4 x 4 in / 10 x 10 cm.
23 sts and 45 rows in garter stitch using smaller needles = 4 x 4 in / 10 x 10 cm.
Adjust needle sizes to obtain correct gauge if necessary.

Pattern

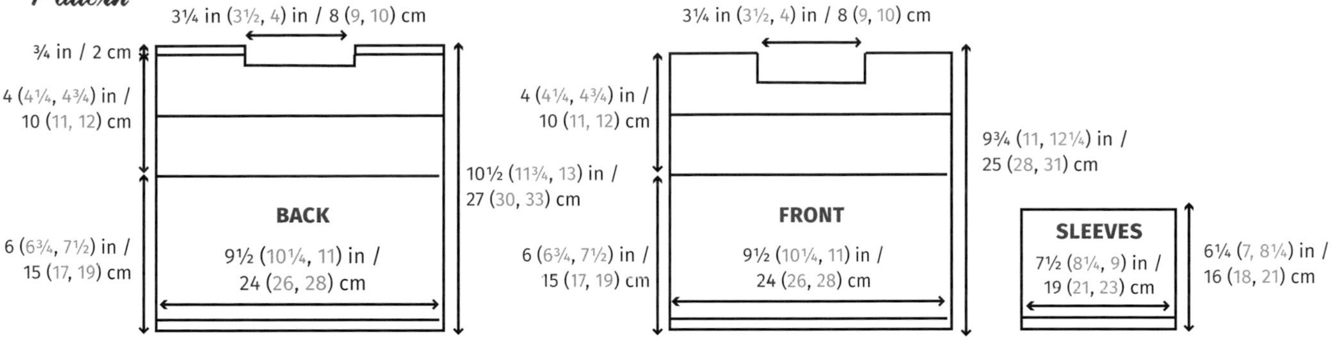

BACK

¾ in / 2 cm

3¼ in (3½, 4) in / 8 (9, 10) cm

4 (4¼, 4¾) in / 10 (11, 12) cm

10½ (11¾, 13) in / 27 (30, 33) cm

6 (6¾, 7½) in / 15 (17, 19) cm

9½ (10¼, 11) in / 24 (26, 28) cm

FRONT

3¼ in (3½, 4) in / 8 (9, 10) cm

4 (4¼, 4¾) in / 10 (11, 12) cm

9¾ (11, 12¼) in / 25 (28, 31) cm

6 (6¾, 7½) in / 15 (17, 19) cm

9½ (10¼, 11) in / 24 (26, 28) cm

SLEEVES

7½ (8¼, 9) in / 19 (21, 23) cm

6¼ (7, 8¼) in / 16 (18, 21) cm

Instructions

BACK

11) With smaller needles and Acier, pick up the **19 (20, 22)** sts you set aside at right and begin working in garter stitch.

13) When work measures 10½ (11¾, 13) in / 27 (30, 33) cm, bind off all sts for the shoulder.

10) When work measures **10½ (11¾, 13)** in / 27 (30, 33) cm, bind off all sts for the shoulder.

12) When work measures **9¾ (11, 12¼)** in / 25 (28, 31) cm, tie a little contrast-color yarn or place a marker at the outer edge to mark the right button band.

9) When work measures **9¾ (11, 12¼)** in / **25 (28, 31)** cm, tie a little contrast-color yarn or place a marker at the outer edge to mark the left button band.

6) When work measures **8 (8¾, 9½)** in / **20 (22, 24)** cm, switch to smaller needles and garter stitch (still using Acier).

7) When work measures **9½ (10½, 11¾)** in / **24 (27, 30)** cm, knit the first **19 (20, 22)** sts of row; bind off next **19 (21, 23)** sts for neck; knit remaining **19 (20, 22)** sts. Move first **19 (20, 22)** sts to a holder and set aside.

8) Continue working the **19 (20, 22)** sts at left in garter stitch.

5) Continue working stockinette with Acier.

4) On the same row, tie a little contrast-color yarn or place a marker at the last stitch (outer edge) to mark armhole.

2) Switch to larger needles and stockinette. Work 4 more rows in Acier, and then *2 rows in Soufre, 6 rows in Acier*; repeat from * to * 3 more times, and end with 2 rows in Soufre.

3) When work measures **6 (6¾, 7½)** in / **15 (17, 19)** cm, tie a little contrast-color yarn or place a marker at the first stitch (outer edge) to mark armhole.

1) With smaller needles and Acier, cast on **57 (61, 67)** sts. Work 4 rows in garter stitch = 2 "ridges".

SLEEVES
MAKE 2 ALIKE

2) Switch to larger needles and stockinette. Work 4 more rows in Acier, and then *2 rows in Soufre, 6 rows in Acier*; repeat from * to * once more.

1) With smaller needles and Acier, cast on **46 (50, 54)** sts. Work 4 rows in garter stitch.

3) When sleeve measures **6¼ (7, 8¼)** in / **16 (18, 21)** cm, bind off all stitches.

Instructions

FRONT

10) With smaller needles and Acier, pick up the **19 (20, 22)** sts you set aside at right and begin working in garter stitch.

9) When work measures **9¾ (11, 12¼)** in / **25 (28, 31)** cm, bind off all sts for the shoulder.

8) Continue working the **14 (15, 17)** sts at left in garter stitch.

4) On the same row, tie a little contrast-color yarn or place a marker at the last stitch (outer edge) to mark armhole.

6) When work measures **8 (8¾, 9½)** in / **19 (20, 22)** cm, switch to smaller needles and garter stitch (still using Acier).

5) Continue working in stockinette with Acier.

2) Switch to larger needles and stockinette. Work 4 more rows in Acier, and then *2 rows in Soufre, 6 rows in Acier*; repeat from * to * 3 more times, and end with 2 rows in Soufre.

11) When work measures **9¾ (11, 12¼)** in / **25 (28, 31)** cm, bind off all sts for the shoulder.

7) When work measures **8¾ (9¾, 10½)** in / **22 (25, 27)** cm, knit the first **19 (20, 22)** sts of row; bind off next **19 (21, 23)** sts for neck; knit remaining **19 (20, 22)** sts. Move first **19 (20, 22)** sts to a holder and set aside.

3) When work measures **6 (6¾, 7½)** in / **15 (17, 19)** cm, tie a little contrast-color yarn or place a marker at the first stitch (outer edge) to mark armhole.

1) With smaller needles and Acier, cast on **57 (61, 67)** sts. Work 4 rows in garter stitch = 2 "ridges".

Assembly and finishing

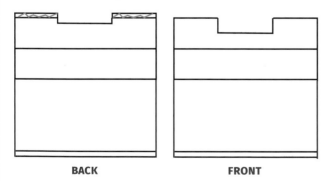

BACK   **FRONT**   **FRONT**

— Seam sides.

〰 Fold the button bands on the back to the inside, so they lie beneath the front shoulders.

— Attach sleeves to armholes.

— Seam sleeves

● Make 2 buttonholes on the front of each shoulder (the knitting should be elastic enough for you to push a pencil or knitting needle between a couple stitches and gently widen a hole). Sew 2 buttons in position on the button bands, opposite the buttonholes.

Weave in ends neatly on wrong side.

3. Cardigan

Sizes

3 months (6 months, 12 months)

The instructions include all 3 sizes; the order above corresponds to the order in which instructions will be given for each size throughout. For example: for the 6-month size, always look for the first of two numbers in parentheses—in the materials list, the written instructions, and all the diagram labels showing size or length measurements.

Materials

◊ CYCA #2 (sport/baby) Phildar Partner 3,5 (50% polyamide, 25% combed wool and 25% acrylic; 137 yd / 125 m / 150 g): 2 (3, 4) skeins of Acier; 1 (1, 1) skein of Soufre or Grenadine or Piscine (see gauges, page 15)
◊ U.S. size 2.5 / 3 mm needles
◊ 5 buttons

Stitches used

◊ **Garter stitch**
  Row 1 (right side of work): Knit.
  Row 2: Knit.
  Repeat Rows 1 and 2.

Gauge

23 sts and 45 rows in garter stitch = 4 x 4 in / 10 x 10 cm.
Adjust needle sizes to obtain correct gauge if necessary.

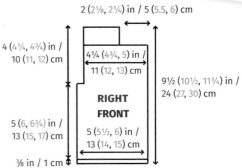

Pattern

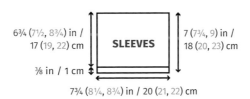

6¾ (7½, 8¾) in / 17 (19, 22) cm

SLEEVES

7 (7¾, 9) in / 18 (20, 23) cm

⅜ in / 1 cm

7¾ (8¼, 8¾) in / 20 (21, 22) cm

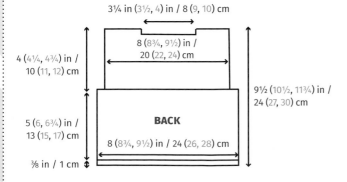

3¼ in (3½, 4) in / 8 (9, 10) cm

8 (8¾, 9½) in / 20 (22, 24) cm

4 (4¼, 4¾) in / 10 (11, 12) cm

9½ (10½, 11¾) in / 24 (27, 30) cm

BACK

5 (6, 6¾) in / 13 (15, 17) cm

8 (8¾, 9½) in / 24 (26, 28) cm

⅜ in / 1 cm

2 (2⅛, 2¼) in / 5 (5.5, 6) cm

4 (4¼, 4¾) in / 10 (11, 12) cm

4¼ (4¾, 5) in / 11 (12, 13) cm

9½ (10½, 11¾) in / 24 (27, 30) cm

RIGHT FRONT

5 (6, 6¾) in / 13 (15, 17) cm

5 (5½, 6) in / 13 (14, 15) cm

⅜ in / 1 cm

Instructions

BACK

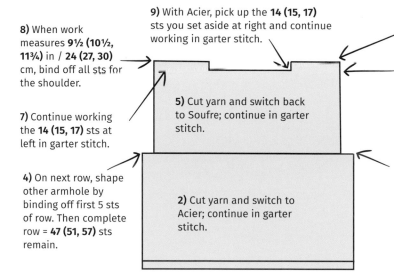

8) When work measures **9½ (10½, 11¾)** in / **24 (27, 30)** cm, bind off all sts for the shoulder.

9) With Acier, pick up the **14 (15, 17)** sts you set aside at right and continue working in garter stitch.

10) When work measures **9½ (10½, 11¾)** in / **24 (27, 30)** cm, bind off all sts for the shoulder.

7) Continue working the **14 (15, 17)** sts at left in garter stitch.

5) Cut yarn and switch back to Soufre; continue in garter stitch.

6) When work measures **9 (10¼, 11½)** in / **23 (26, 29)** cm, knit first **14 (15, 17)** sts of row; bind off next **19 (21, 23)** sts for neck; knit remaining **14 (15, 17)**. Move first **14 (15, 17)** sts to a holder and set aside.

4) On next row, shape other armhole by binding off first 5 sts of row. Then complete row = **47 (51, 57)** sts remain.

2) Cut yarn and switch to Acier; continue in garter stitch.

3) When work measures **5½ (6¼, 7)** in / **14 (16, 18)** cm, shape armhole by binding off first 5 sts of row. Then complete row = **52 (56, 62)** sts remain.

1) With Soufre, cast on **57 (61, 67)** sts. Work in garter stitch for ⅜ in / 1 cm.

RIGHT FRONT

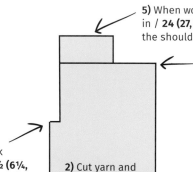

5) When work measures **9½ (10½, 11¾)** in / **24 (27, 30)** cm, bind off all sts for the shoulder.

4) When work measures **7¾ (9, 9¾)** in / **20 (23, 25)** cm, bind off **12 (13, 14)** sts for neck at inner edge; cut yarn and switch to Soufre to continue working the remaining **14 (15, 17)** sts.

3) When work measures **5½ (6¼, 7)** in / **14 (16, 18)** cm, shape armhole by binding off 5 sts at outer edge. **26 (28, 31)** sts remain.

2) Cut yarn and switch to Acier; continue in garter stitch.

1) With Soufre, cast on **31 (33, 36)** sts. Work in garter stitch for ⅜ in / 1 cm.

SLEEVES
MAKE 2 ALIKE

3) When work measures **7 (7¾, 9)** in / **18 (20, 23)** cm, bind off all sts.

2) Cut yarn and switch to Acier; continue in garter stitch.

1) With Soufre, cast on **46 (50, 54)** sts. Work in garter stitch for ⅜ in / 1 cm.

LEFT FRONT

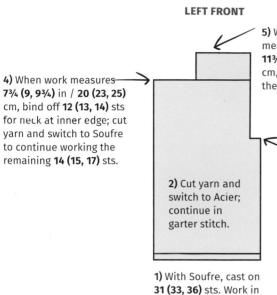

4) When work measures **7¾ (9, 9¾)** in / **20 (23, 25)** cm, bind off **12 (13, 14)** sts for neck at inner edge; cut yarn and switch to Soufre to continue working the remaining **14 (15, 17)** sts.

5) When work measures **9½ (10½, 11¾)** in / **24 (27, 30)** cm, bind off all sts for the shoulder.

2) Cut yarn and switch to Acier; continue in garter stitch.

3) When work measures **5½ (6¼, 7)** in / **14 (16, 18)** cm, shape armhole by binding off 5 sts at outer edge. **26 (28, 31)** sts remain.

1) With Soufre, cast on **31 (33, 36)** sts. Work in garter stitch for ⅜ in / 1 cm.

Phildar Partner 3,5 in Acier and Grenadine or Piscine instead of Soufre, in garter stitch and striped stockinette, showing suggested color variations for the projects pictured on page 8.

Assembly and finishing

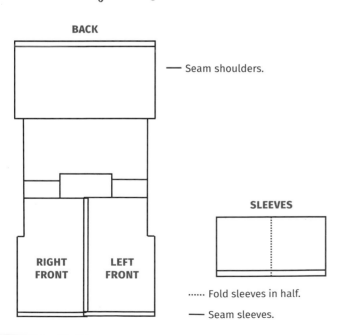

BACK

— Seam shoulders.

RIGHT FRONT   **LEFT FRONT**

SLEEVES

····· Fold sleeves in half.

— Seam sleeves.

FRONT

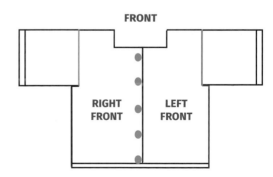

RIGHT FRONT   **LEFT FRONT**

— Attach sleeves to armholes.

— Seam sides.

● Make 5 buttonholes along edge of right front (the knitting should be elastic enough for you to push a pencil or knitting needle between a couple stitches and gently widen a hole), about 3 sts in from edge, with the lowest buttonhole at the edge of the ⅜ in / 1 cm of Soufre at bottom edge, the highest ⅜ in / 1 cm below neck edge, and the rest spaced evenly between.

— Sew buttons in position, opposite buttonholes.

Weave in ends neatly on wrong side.

4. Cardigan

Worked in stockinette with finishing in garter stitch and duplicate stitch, using Phil Coton 4 and U.S. size 6 / 4 mm needles.

5. Dress

Worked in stockinette with finishing in garter stitch and duplicate stitch, using Phil Coton 4 and U.S. size 6 / 4 mm needles.

4. Cardigan

Sizes

3 months (6 months, 12 months)

The instructions include all 3 sizes; the order above corresponds to the order in which instructions will be given for each size throughout. For example: for the 6-month size, always look for the first of two numbers in parentheses—in the materials list, the written instructions, and all the diagram labels showing size or length measurements.

Materials

◊ CYCA #3 (DK/light worsted) Phildar Phil Coton 4 (100% cotton; 74 yd / 68 m / 50 g): 3 (3, 4) skeins of Guimauve; 1 (1, 1) skein of Silver
◊ U.S. size 6 / 4 mm needles
◊ U.S. size C-2 or D-3 / 3 mm crochet hook

Stitches used

◊ **Garter stitch**
   Row 1 (right side of work): Knit.
   Row 2: Knit.
   Repeat Rows 1 and 2.
◊ **Stockinette stitch**
   Row 1 (right side of work): Knit.
   Row 2: Purl.
   Repeat Rows 1 and 2.
◊ **Chain stitch**
◊ **Slip stitch:** insert crochet hook into one st, yarn around hook and pull through st and through loop on hook.
◊ **Embroidery, duplicate stitch:** see diagram and key.

Gauge

22 sts and 28 rows in stockinette = 4 x 4 in / 10 x 10 cm. Adjust needle sizes to obtain correct gauge if necessary.

EMBROIDERY CHART

7 sts

☐ = 1 st and 1 row in Guimauve
+ = 1 st and 1 row in Silver

Patterns

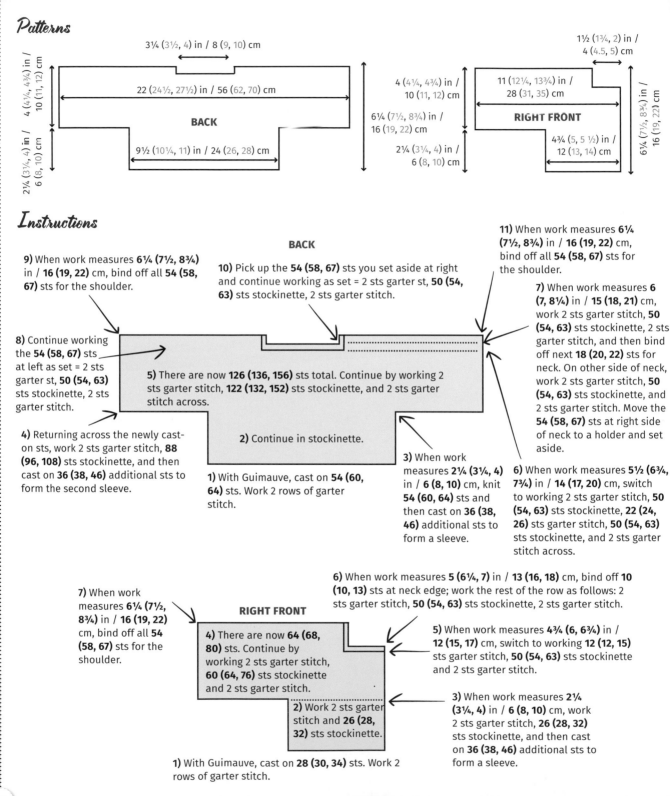

3¼ (3½, 4) in / 8 (9, 10) cm

22 (24½, 27½) in / 56 (62, 70) cm

4 (4¼, 4¾) in / 10 (11, 12) cm

2¼ (3¼, 4) in / 6 (8, 10) cm

BACK

9½ (10¼, 11) in / 24 (26, 28) cm

4 (4¼, 4¾) in / 10 (11, 12) cm

6¼ (7½, 8¾) in / 16 (19, 22) cm

2¼ (3¼, 4) in / 6 (8, 10) cm

1½ (1¾, 2) in / 4 (4.5, 5) cm

11 (12¼, 13¾) in / 28 (31, 35) cm

RIGHT FRONT

4¾ (5, 5 ½) in / 12 (13, 14) cm

6¼ (7½, 8¾) in / 16 (19, 22) cm

Instructions

BACK

9) When work measures 6¼ (7½, 8¾) in / 16 (19, 22) cm, bind off all **54 (58, 67)** sts for the shoulder.

10) Pick up the **54 (58, 67)** sts you set aside at right and continue working as set = 2 sts garter st, **50 (54, 63)** sts stockinette, 2 sts garter stitch.

8) Continue working the **54 (58, 67)** sts at left as set = 2 sts garter st, **50 (54, 63)** sts stockinette, 2 sts garter stitch.

5) There are now **126 (136, 156)** sts total. Continue by working 2 sts garter stitch, **122 (132, 152)** sts stockinette, and 2 sts garter stitch across.

4) Returning across the newly cast-on sts, work 2 sts garter stitch, **88 (96, 108)** sts stockinette, and then cast on **36 (38, 46)** additional sts to form the second sleeve.

2) Continue in stockinette.

1) With Guimauve, cast on **54 (60, 64)** sts. Work 2 rows of garter stitch.

3) When work measures 2¼ (3¼, 4) in / 6 (8, 10) cm, knit **54 (60, 64)** sts and then cast on **36 (38, 46)** additional sts to form a sleeve.

11) When work measures 6¼ (7½, 8¾) in / 16 (19, 22) cm, bind off all **54 (58, 67)** sts for the shoulder.

7) When work measures 6 (7, 8¼) in / 15 (18, 21) cm, work 2 sts garter stitch, **50 (54, 63)** sts stockinette, 2 sts garter stitch, and then bind off next **18 (20, 22)** sts for neck. On other side of neck, work 2 sts garter stitch, **50 (54, 63)** sts stockinette, and 2 sts garter stitch. Move the **54 (58, 67)** sts at right side of neck to a holder and set aside.

6) When work measures 5½ (6¾, 7¾) in / 14 (17, 20) cm, switch to working 2 sts garter stitch, **50 (54, 63)** sts stockinette, 22 (24, 26) sts garter stitch, **50 (54, 63)** sts stockinette, and 2 sts garter stitch across.

RIGHT FRONT

7) When work measures 6¼ (7½, 8¾) in / 16 (19, 22) cm, bind off all **54 (58, 67)** sts for the shoulder.

4) There are now **64 (68, 80)** sts. Continue by working 2 sts garter stitch, **60 (64, 76)** sts stockinette and 2 sts garter stitch.

2) Work 2 sts garter stitch and **26 (28, 32)** sts stockinette.

1) With Guimauve, cast on **28 (30, 34)** sts. Work 2 rows of garter stitch.

6) When work measures 5 (6¼, 7) in / 13 (16, 18) cm, bind off **10 (10, 13)** sts at neck edge; work the rest of the row as follows: 2 sts garter stitch, **50 (54, 63)** sts stockinette, 2 sts garter stitch.

5) When work measures 4¾ (6, 6¾) in / 12 (15, 17) cm, switch to working 12 (12, 15) sts garter stitch, **50 (54, 63)** sts stockinette and 2 sts garter stitch.

3) When work measures 2¼ (3¼, 4) in / 6 (8, 10) cm, work 2 sts garter stitch, **26 (28, 32)** sts stockinette, and then cast on **36 (38, 46)** additional sts to form a sleeve.

6) When work measures **5 (6¼, 7)** in / **13 (16, 18)** cm, bind off **10 (10, 13)** sts at next edge; work the rest of the row as follows: 2 sts garter stitch, **50 (54, 63)** sts stockinette, and 2 sts garter stitch.

5) When work measures **4¾ (6, 6¾)** in / **12 (15, 17)** cm, work **12 (12, 15)** sts garter stitch, **50 (54, 63)** sts stockinette, and 2 sts garter stitch.

3) When work measures **2¼ (3¼, 4)** in / **6 (8, 10)** cm, work 2 sts garter stitch, **26 (28, 30)** sts stockinette, and then cast on **36 (38, 46)** sts to form sleeve.

LEFT FRONT

4) There are now **64 (68, 80)** sts. Continue by working 2 sts garter stitch, **60 (64, 76)** sts stockinette, and 2 sts garter stitch.

2) Switch to working **26 (28, 32)** sts stockinette and 2 sts garter stitch.

1) With Guimauve, cast on **28 (30, 34)** sts. Work 2 rows of garter stitch.

7) When work measures **6¼ (7½, 8¾)** in / **16 (19, 22)** cm, bind off all **54 (58, 67)** sts for the shoulder.

Assembly and finishing

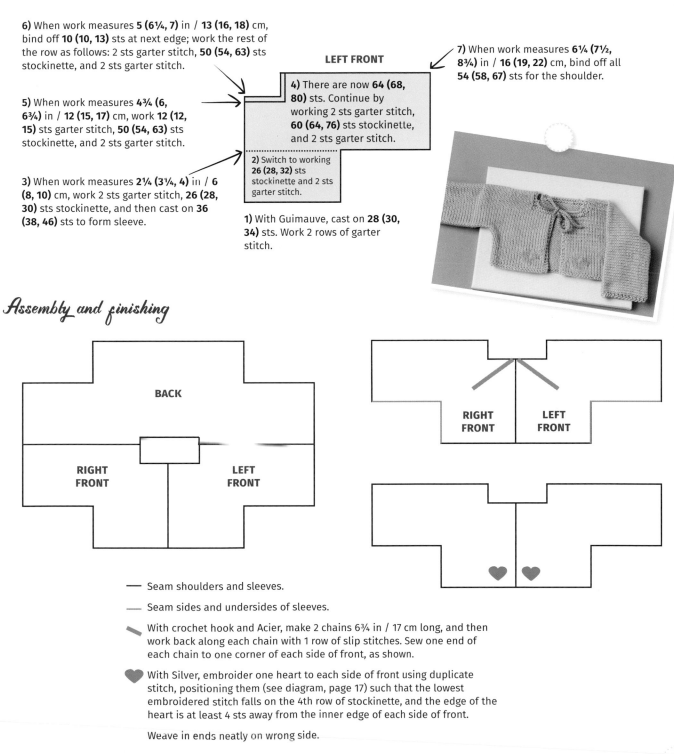

BACK

RIGHT FRONT

LEFT FRONT

RIGHT FRONT

LEFT FRONT

— Seam shoulders and sleeves.

— Seam sides and undersides of sleeves.

With crochet hook and Acier, make 2 chains 6¾ in / 17 cm long, and then work back along each chain with 1 row of slip stitches. Sew one end of each chain to one corner of each side of front, as shown.

With Silver, embroider one heart to each side of front using duplicate stitch, positioning them (see diagram, page 17) such that the lowest embroidered stitch falls on the 4th row of stockinette, and the edge of the heart is at least 4 sts away from the inner edge of each side of front.

Weave in ends neatly on wrong side.

5. Dress

Sizes

3 months (6 months, 12 months)

The instructions include all 3 sizes; the order above corresponds to the order in which instructions will be given for each size throughout. For example: for the 6-month size, always look for the first of two numbers in parentheses—in the materials list, the written instructions, and all the diagram labels showing size or length measurements.

Materials

◊ CYCA #3 (DK/light worsted) Phildar Phil Coton 4 (100% cotton; 74 yd / 68 m / 50 g): 3 (3, 4) skeins of Silver; 1 (1, 1) skein of Guimauve
◊ U.S. size 6 / 4 mm needles
◊ U.S. size C-2 or D-3 / 3 mm hook

Stitches used

◊ **Garter stitch**
  Row 1 (right side of work): Knit.
  Row 2: Knit.
  Repeat Rows 1 and 2.
◊ **Stockinette stitch**
  Row 1 (right side of work): Knit.
  Row 2: Purl.
  Repeat Rows 1 and 2.
◊ **Chain stitch**
◊ **Slip stitch:** insert crochet hook into one st, yarn around hook and pull through st and through loop on hook.
◊ **Embroidery, duplicate stitch:** see diagram and key.

Gauge

22 sts and 28 rows in stockinette = 4 x 4 in / 10 x 10 cm. Adjust needle sizes to obtain correct gauge if necessary.

Pattern

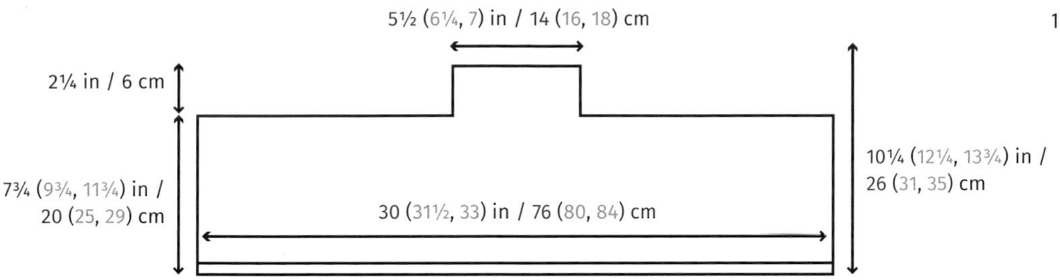

5½ (6¼, 7) in / 14 (16, 18) cm

2¼ in / 6 cm

7¾ (9¾, 11¾) in / 20 (25, 29) cm

30 (31½, 33) in / 76 (80, 84) cm

10¼ (12¼, 13¾) in / 26 (31, 35) cm

EMBROIDERY CHART

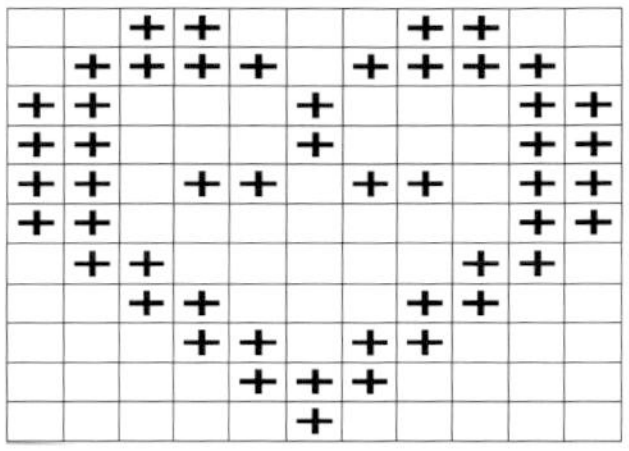

11

	+	+					+	+		
+	+	+	+			+	+	+	+	
+	+			+			+		+	+
+	+			+			+		+	+
+	+		+			+		+	+	
+	+							+	+	
	+	+					+	+		
		+	+			+	+			
			+	+	+	+				
				+						

1

11 stitches

☐ = 1 st and 1 row in Silver

+ = 1 st and 1 row in Guimauve

Instructions

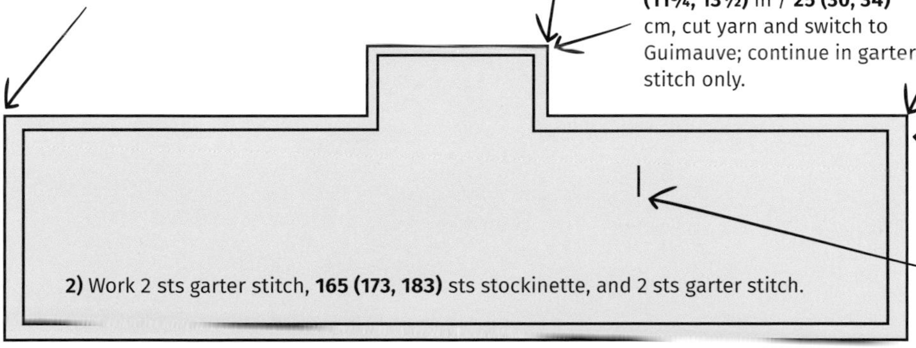

6) On next row, bind off the first **68 (71, 73)** sts garter stitch on this side; then work 2 sts garter stitch, **29 (31, 37)** sts stockinette, and 2 sts garter stitch.

8) When work measures **10¼ (12¼, 13¾)** in / **26 (31, 35)** cm, bind off all sts.

7) When work measures **9¾ (11¾, 13½)** in / **25 (30, 34)** cm, cut yarn and switch to Guimauve; continue in garter stitch only.

5) When work measures **7¾ (9¾, 11½)** in / **20 (25, 29)** cm, bind off the first **68 (71, 73)** sts garter stitch; then work 2 sts garter stitch, **29 (31, 37)** sts stockinette, and **70 (73, 75)** sts garter stitch.

4) When work measures **7½ (9½, 11)** in / **19 (24, 28)** cm, switch to working **70 (73, 75)** sts garter stitch, **29 (31, 37)** sts stockinette, and **70 (73, 75)** sts garter stitch.

3) When work measures **6¾ (8¾, 10¼)** in / **17 (22, 26)** cm, work 2 sts garter stitch, **51 (53, 57)** sts stockinette, 1 yarnover, knit 2 sts together (to form a small opening where the belt will be threaded through), **112 (118, 124)** sts stockinette, and 2 sts garter stitch. Then continue as before.

2) Work 2 sts garter stitch, **165 (173, 183)** sts stockinette, and 2 sts garter stitch.

1) With Silver, cast on **169 (177, 187)** sts. Work 2 rows of garter stitch.

Finishing

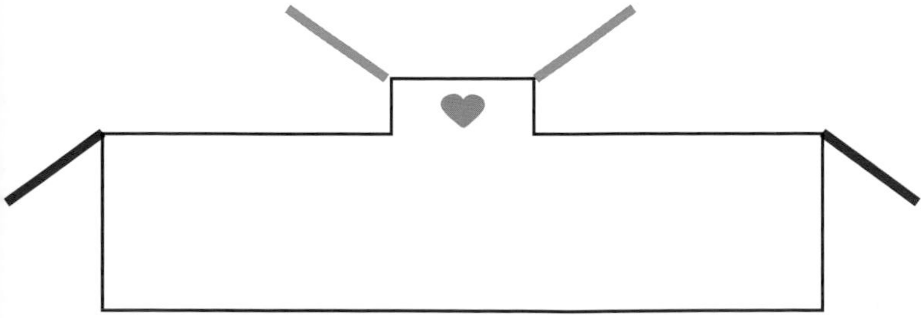

♥ With Guimauve, embroider a heart using duplicate stitch in the middle of the top of the dress, as shown.

— With the crochet hook and Guimauve, make 2 chains 10¼ in / 26 cm long, and then work back along each chain with 1 row of slip stitch. Sew one end of each chain to each of the top corners of the dress, as shown.

— With the crochet hook and Guimauve, make 2 chains 13¾ in / 35 cm long, and then work back along each chain with 1 row of slip stitch. Sew one end of each chain to each of the middle corners of the dress, as shown. (The dress will then wrap and can be tied, with these two chains forming a belt that can be threaded through the yarnover for extra security.)

Weave in ends neatly on wrong side.

6. Shirt

Worked in stockinette with finishing in garter stitch, using Partner 3,5 and U.S. size 4 / 3.5 mm needles.

6. Shirt

Sizes

3 months (6 months, 12 months)

The instructions include all 3 sizes; the order above corresponds to the order in which instructions will be given for each size throughout. For example: for the 6-month size, always look for the first of two numbers in parentheses—in the materials list, the written instructions, and all the diagram labels showing size or length measurements.

Materials

- ◊ CYCA #2 (sport/baby) Phildar Partner 3,5 (50% polyamide, 25% combed wool and 25% acrylic; 137 yd / 125 m / 50 g): 2 (3, 3) skeins of Brume; 1 (1, 1) skein of Grenadine or Piscine
- ◊ Or go for a classic variation: CYCA #2 (sport/baby) Phildar Partner 3,5 (50% polyamide, 25% combed wool and 25% acrylic; 137 yd / 125 m / 50 g): 2 (3, 3) skeins of Rose or Ciel; 1 (1, 1) skein of Acier
- ◊ U.S. size 4 / 3.5 mm needles
- ◊ 1 snap or 1 button

Stitches used

- ◊ **Garter stitch**
  Row 1 (right side of work): Knit.
  Row 2: Knit.
  Repeat Rows 1 and 2.
- ◊ **Stockinette**
  Row 1 (right side of work): Knit.
  Row 2: Purl.
  Repeat Rows 1 and 2.

Gauge

23 sts and 30 rows in stockinette = 4 x 4 in / 10 x 10 cm. Adjust needle sizes to obtain correct gauge if necessary.

Patterns

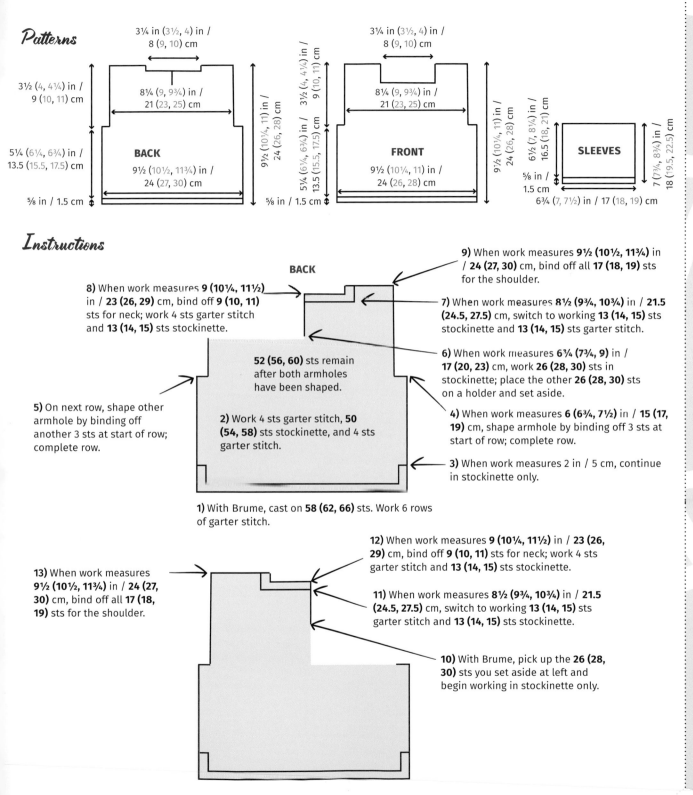

BACK

3¼ in (3½, 4) in / 8 (9, 10) cm

3½ (4, 4¼) in / 9 (10, 11) cm

8¼ (9, 9¾) in / 21 (23, 25) cm

5¼ (6¼, 6¾) in / 13.5 (15.5, 17.5) cm

BACK

9½ (10½, 11¾) in / 24 (27, 30) cm

9½ (10¼, 11) in / 24 (26, 28) cm

⅝ in / 1.5 cm

FRONT

3¼ in (3½, 4) in / 8 (9, 10) cm

3½ (4, 4¼) in / 9 (10, 11) cm

8¼ (9, 9¾) in / 21 (23, 25) cm

5¼ (6¼, 6¾) in / 13.5 (15.5, 17.5) cm

FRONT

9½ (10¼, 11) in / 24 (26, 28) cm

9½ (10¼, 11) in / 24 (26, 28) cm

⅝ in / 1.5 cm

SLEEVES

6½ (7, 8¼) in / 16.5 (18, 21) cm

SLEEVES

7 (7¾, 8¾) in / 18 (19.5, 22.5) cm

⅝ in / 1.5 cm

6¾ (7, 7½) in / 17 (18, 19) cm

Instructions

BACK

8) When work measures **9 (10¼, 11½)** in / **23 (26, 29)** cm, bind off **9 (10, 11)** sts for neck; work 4 sts garter stitch and **13 (14, 15)** sts stockinette.

9) When work measures 9½ (10½, 11¾) in / **24 (27, 30)** cm, bind off all **17 (18, 19)** sts for the shoulder.

7) When work measures **8½ (9¾, 10¾)** in / **21.5 (24.5, 27.5)** cm, switch to working **13 (14, 15)** sts stockinette and **13 (14, 15)** sts garter stitch.

6) When work measures **6¾ (7¾, 9)** in / **17 (20, 23)** cm, work **26 (28, 30)** sts in stockinette; place the other **26 (28, 30)** sts on a holder and set aside.

5) On next row, shape other armhole by binding off another 3 sts at start of row; complete row.

52 (56, 60) sts remain after both armholes have been shaped.

2) Work 4 sts garter stitch, **50 (54, 58)** sts stockinette, and 4 sts garter stitch.

4) When work measures **6 (6¾, 7½)** in / **15 (17, 19)** cm, shape armhole by binding off 3 sts at start of row; complete row.

3) When work measures 2 in / 5 cm, continue in stockinette only.

1) With Brume, cast on **58 (62, 66)** sts. Work 6 rows of garter stitch.

12) When work measures **9 (10¼, 11½)** in / **23 (26, 29)** cm, bind off **9 (10, 11)** sts for neck; work 4 sts garter stitch and **13 (14, 15)** sts stockinette.

13) When work measures 9½ (10½, 11¾) in / **24 (27, 30)** cm, bind off all **17 (18, 19)** sts for the shoulder.

11) When work measures **8½ (9¾, 10¾)** in / **21.5 (24.5, 27.5)** cm, switch to working **13 (14, 15)** sts garter stitch and **13 (14, 15)** sts stockinette.

10) With Brume, pick up the **26 (28, 30)** sts you set aside at left and begin working in stockinette only.

Instructions

BOWS
MAKE 1-4 ALIKE, AS DESIRED

1) With Grenadine or Piscine (or any other color you prefer), cast on 14 sts. Work 8 rows of stockinette and then bind off all sts.

SLEEVES
MAKE 2 ALIKE

2) Continue in stockinette.

3) When work measures **7 (7¾, 8¾)** in / **18 (19.5, 22.5)** cm, bind off all sts.

1) With Brume, cast on **41 (43, 45)** sts. Work 6 rows of garter stitch.

Partner 3,5 in Ciel, Rose, and Acier, garter stitch and stockinette, showing suggested color variations for this project.

FRONT

9) When work measures **9½ (10½, 11¾)** in / **24 (27, 30)** cm, bind off all **17 (18, 19)** sts for the shoulder.

8) Continue working **17 (18, 19)** sts at right as set: garter stitch over garter stitch and stockinette over stockinette.

5) On next row, shape other armhole by binding off another 3 sts at start of row; complete row.

10) With Brume, pick up the **17 (18, 19)** sts you set aside at right and continue as set: garter stitch over garter stitch and stockinette over stockinette.

52 (56, 60) sts remain after both armholes have been shaped.

2) Work 4 sts garter stitch, **50 (54, 58)** sts stockinette, and 4 sts garter stitch.

1) With Brume, cast on **58 (62, 66)** sts. Work 6 rows of garter stitch.

11) When work measures **9½ (10½, 11¾)** in / **24 (27, 30)** cm, bind off all **17 (18, 19)** sts for the shoulder.

7) When work measures **8¼ (9½, 10¼)** in / **21 (24, 26)** cm, work **13 (14, 15)** sts stockinette, 4 sts garter stitch, bind off **18 (20, 22)** sts for neck, and then work another 4 sts garter stitch and **13 (14, 15)** sts stockinette. Move **17 (18, 19)** sts at right to a holder and set aside.

6) When work measures **7¾ (8¾, 9¾)** in / **19.5 (22.5, 24.5)** cm, switch to working **13 (14, 15)** sts stockinette, **26 (28, 30)** sts garter stitch, and **13 (14, 15)** sts stockinette.

4) When work measures **6 (6¾, 7½)** in / **15 (17, 19)** cm, shape armhole by binding off 3 sts at start of row; complete row.

3) When work measures 2 in / 5 cm, switch to working in stockinette only.

Assembly and finishing

BACK

FRONT

SLEEVES

BOWS

—— Seam shoulders.

····· Fold sleeves in half.

—— Seam sleeves.

····· Wrap a piece of yarn around bow and secure tightly.

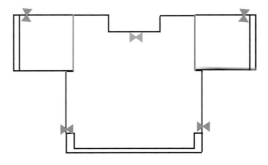

—— Attach sleeves to armholes.

—— Seam sides down to start of garter stitch at bottom edge.

▶◀ If you made multiple bows, they can be attached at sleeves and/or sides.

▶◀ If you made 1 bow, consider attaching at the front of the neck.

—— At split in back neck, pick up one side and knit or crochet buttonhole band or button strap, as desired; sew a button in position opposite the strap, or sew half of snap to strap and half to other side of back neck.

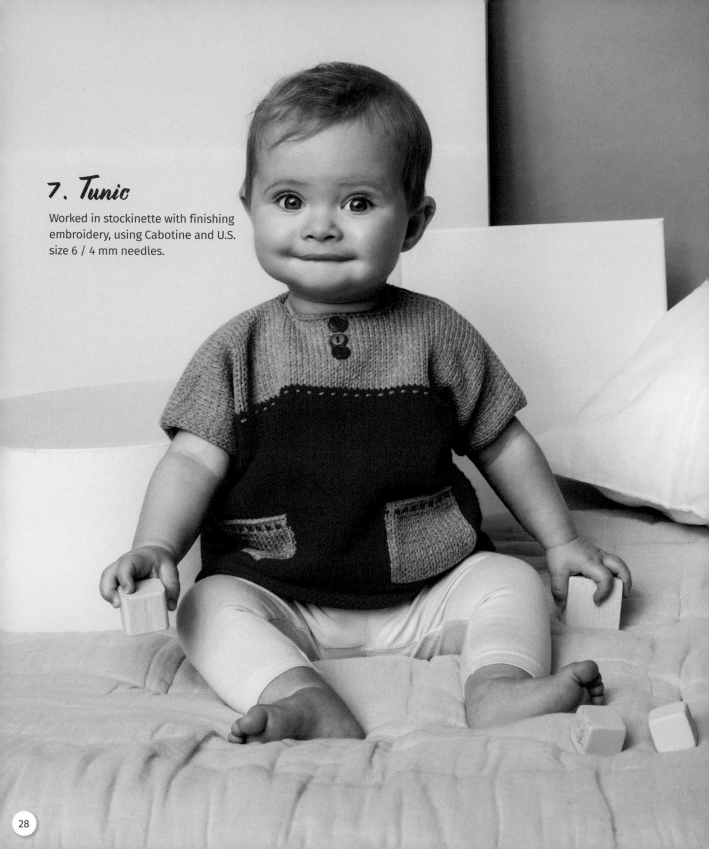

7. Tunic

Worked in stockinette with finishing embroidery, using Cabotine and U.S. size 6 / 4 mm needles.

8. Onesie

Worked in stockinette with finishing embroidery, using Cabotine and U.S. size 4 / 3.5 mm needles.

7. Tunic

Sizes

3 months (6 months, 12 months)

The instructions include all 3 sizes; the order above corresponds to the order in which instructions will be given for each size throughout. For example: for the 6-month size, always look for the first of two numbers in parentheses—in the materials list, the written instructions, and all the diagram labels showing size or length measurements.

Materials

◊ CYCA #3 (DK/light worsted) Phildar Cabotine (55% cotton, 45% acrylic; 136 yd / 124 m / 50 g): 2 (2, 2) skeins of Bengale; 1 (1, 1) skein of Œillet
◊ U.S. size 6 / 4 mm needles
◊ 7 buttons

Stitches used

◊ **Garter stitch**
   Row 1 (right side of work): Knit.
   Row 2: Knit.
   Repeat Rows 1 and 2.
◊ **Stockinette**
   Row 1 (right side of work): Knit.
   Row 2: Purl.
   Repeat Rows 1 and 2.
◊ **Embroidery, backstitch**

Gauge

22 sts and 28 rows in stockinette = 4 x 4 in / 10 x 10 cm. Adjust needle sizes to obtain correct gauge if necessary.

Patterns

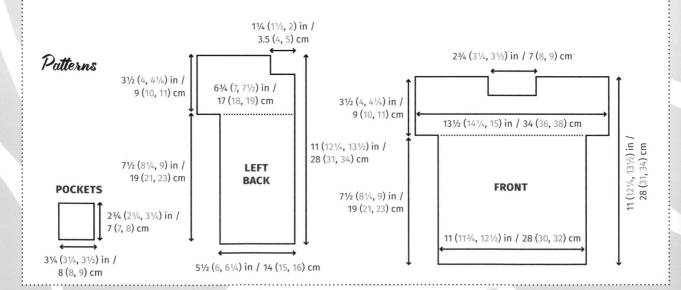

Instructions

6) When work measures **11 (12¼, 13½)** in / **28 (31, 34)** cm, bind off all **30 (31, 32)** sts for the shoulder.

5) Continue working the **30 (31, 32)** sts at left in stockinette.

3) Returning across the newly cast-on sts, work stockinette and then at end of row, cast on 7 additional sts to form the second sleeve. Continue in stockinette.

POCKETS
MAKE 2 ALIKE

2) When work measures **2¾ (2¾, 3¼)** in / **7 (7, 8)** cm, bind off all sts.

1) With Œillet, cast on **18 (18, 20)** sts. Work in stockinette.

FRONT

7) With Œillet, pick up the **30 (31, 32)** sts you set aside at right and work in stockinette.

8) When work measures **11 (12¼, 13½)** in / **28 (31, 34)** cm, bind off all **30 (31, 32)** sts for the shoulder.

4) When work measures **9¾ (11, 11¾)** in / **25 (28, 30)** cm, work first **30 (31, 32)** sts, bind off **14 (16, 18)** sts for neck, and then work last **30 (31, 32)** sts. Move first **30 (31, 32)** sts to a holder and set aside.

You'll have **74 (78, 82)** sts total once both sleeves have been shaped.

2) When work measures **7½ (8¼, 9)** in / **19 (21, 23)** cm, cut yarn and switch to Œillet; continue in stockinette and then cast on 7 additional sts at end of row to form a sleeve = **67 (71, 75)** sts.

1) With Bengale, cast on **60 (64, 68)** sts. Work in stockinette.

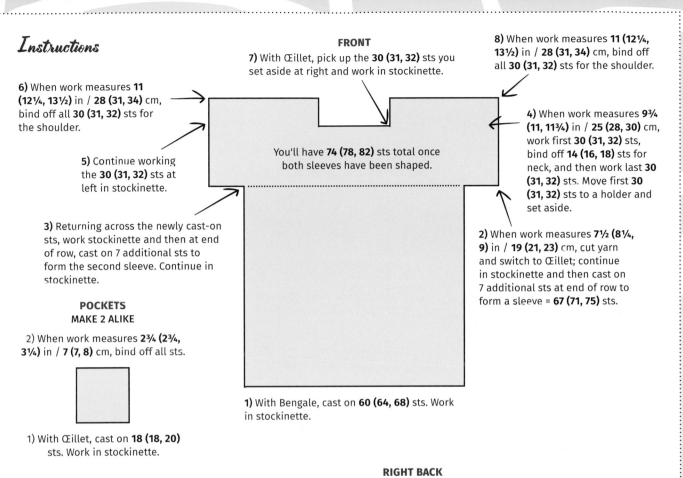

RIGHT BACK

3) When work measures **10½ (11¾, 13)** in / **27 (30, 33)** cm, bind off **7 (8, 9)** sts at inner edge for neck.

4) When work measures **11 (12¼, 13½)** in / **28 (31, 34)** cm, bind off all **30 (31, 32)** sts for the shoulder.

You'll have **37 (39, 41)** sts total once sleeve has been shaped.

2) When work measures **7½ (8¼, 9)** in / **19 (21, 23)** cm, cut yarn and switch to Œillet; continue in stockinette and then cast on 7 additional sts at outer edge to form a sleeve.

1) With Bengale, cast on **30 (32, 34)** sts. Work in stockinette.

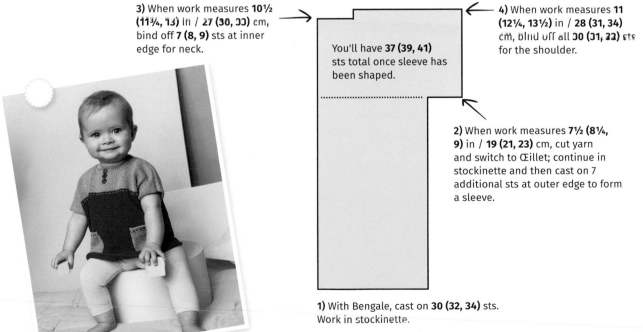

Instructions

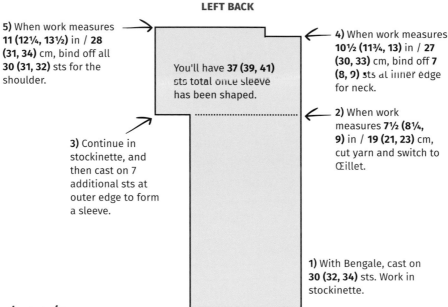

LEFT BACK

5) When work measures **11 (12¼, 13½)** in / **28 (31, 34)** cm, bind off all **30 (31, 32)** sts for the shoulder.

You'll have **37 (39, 41)** sts total once sleeve has been shaped.

4) When work measures **10½ (11¾, 13)** in / **27 (30, 33)** cm, bind off **7 (8, 9)** sts at inner edge for neck.

3) Continue in stockinette, and then cast on 7 additional sts at outer edge to form a sleeve.

2) When work measures **7½ (8¼, 9)** in / **19 (21, 23)** cm, cut yarn and switch to Œillet.

1) With Bengale, cast on **30 (32, 34)** sts. Work in stockinette.

Assembly and finishing

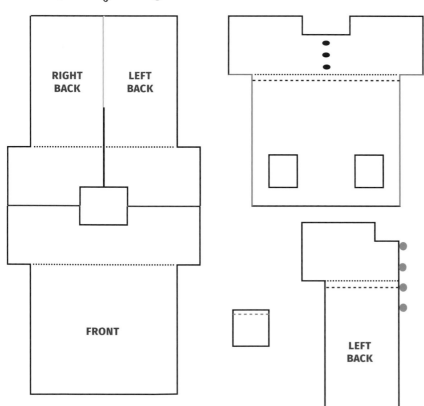

RIGHT BACK

LEFT BACK

FRONT

LEFT BACK

Join sides of back with a seam 5½ (6¾, 7¾) in / 14 (17, 20) cm long, starting at bottom edge (it will NOT join sides of back all the way up to back neck).

— Seam shoulders.

--- With Bengale, embroider a line of backstitch across second-to-last row of each pocket. (Embroidered stitches should cross a stitch and then skip a stitch; see photo, page 28.)

— Seam sides of tunic and undersides of sleeves.

--- With Œillet, embroider a line of backstitch 1 row below the change to Œillet. (Embroidered stitches should cross a stitch and then skip a stitch; see photo, page 28.)

— Sew pockets in position.

● Sew decorative buttons to front.

At top of left back, make 4 buttonholes, evenly spaced (the knitting should be elastic enough for you to push a pencil or knitting needle between a couple stitches and gently widen a hole). Sew buttons in position on top of right back, opposite buttonholes.

Weave in ends neatly on wrong side.

8. Onesie

Sizes

3 months (6 months, 12 months)

The instructions include all 3 sizes; the order above corresponds to the order in which instructions will be given for each size throughout. For example: for the 6-month size, always look for the first of two numbers in parentheses—in the materials list, the written instructions, and all the diagram labels showing size or length measurements.

Materials

◊ CYCA #3 (DK/light worsted) Phildar Cabotine (55% cotton and 45% acrylic; 136 yd / 124 m / 50 g): 2 (2, 2) skeins of Outremer; 1 (2, 2) skeins of Faïence
◊ U.S. size 4 / 3.5 mm needles
◊ 6 buttons

Stitches used

◊ **Stockinette**
  Row 1 (right side of work): Knit.
  Row 2: Purl.
  Repeat Rows 1 and 2.
◊ **Embroidery, backstitch**

Gauge

21 sts and 30 rows in stockinette = 4 x 4 in / 10 x 10 cm. Adjust needle sizes to obtain correct gauge if necessary.

Patterns

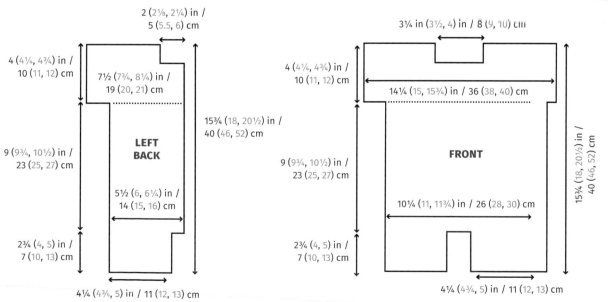

LEFT BACK

2 (2⅛, 2¼) in / 5 (5.5, 6) cm

4 (4¼, 4¾) in / 10 (11, 12) cm

7½ (7¾, 8¼) in / 19 (20, 21) cm

15¾ (18, 20½) in / 40 (46, 52) cm

9 (9¾, 10½) in / 23 (25, 27) cm

5½ (6, 6¼) in / 14 (15, 16) cm

2¾ (4, 5) in / 7 (10, 13) cm

4¼ (4¾, 5) in / 11 (12, 13) cm

FRONT

3¼ in (3½, 4) in / 8 (9, 10) cm

4 (4¼, 4¾) in / 10 (11, 12) cm

14¼ (15, 15¾) in / 36 (38, 40) cm

9 (9¾, 10½) in / 23 (25, 27) cm

10¼ (11, 11¾) in / 26 (28, 30) cm

15¾ (18, 20½) in / 40 (46, 52) cm

2¾ (4, 5) in / 7 (10, 13) cm

4¼ (4¾, 5) in / 11 (12, 13) cm

Instructions

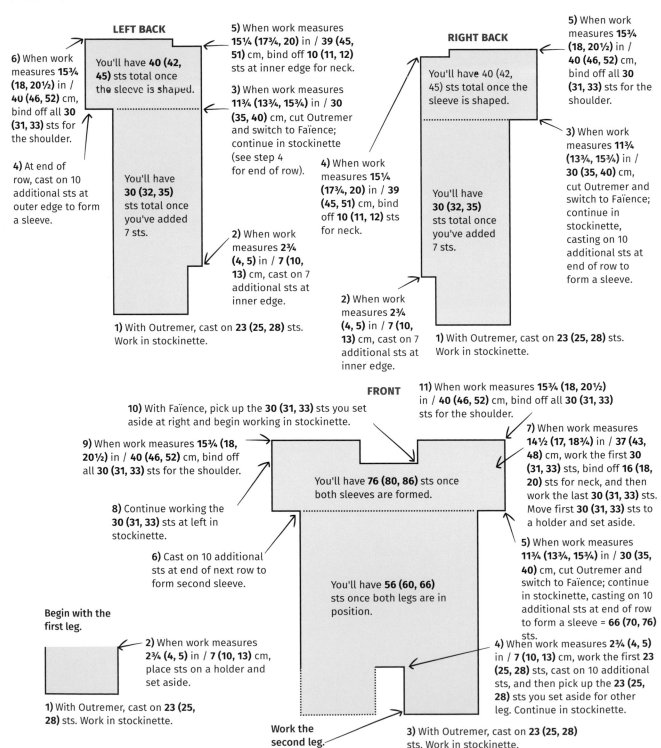

LEFT BACK

6) When work measures **15¾ (18, 20½)** in / **40 (46, 52)** cm, bind off all **30 (31, 33)** sts for the shoulder.

You'll have **40 (42, 45)** sts total once the sleeve is shaped.

4) At end of row, cast on 10 additional sts at outer edge to form a sleeve.

You'll have **30 (32, 35)** sts total once you've added 7 sts.

5) When work measures **15¼ (17¾, 20)** in / **39 (45, 51)** cm, bind off **10 (11, 12)** sts at inner edge for neck.

3) When work measures **11¾ (13¾, 15¾)** in / **30 (35, 40)** cm, cut Outremer and switch to Faïence; continue in stockinette (see step 4 for end of row).

4) When work measures **15¼ (17¾, 20)** in / **39 (45, 51)** cm, bind off **10 (11, 12)** sts for neck.

2) When work measures **2¾ (4, 5)** in / **7 (10, 13)** cm, cast on 7 additional sts at inner edge.

1) With Outremer, cast on **23 (25, 28)** sts. Work in stockinette.

RIGHT BACK

5) When work measures **15¾ (18, 20½)** in / **40 (46, 52)** cm, bind off all **30 (31, 33)** sts for the shoulder.

You'll have 40 (42, 45) sts total once the sleeve is shaped.

3) When work measures **11¾ (13¾, 15¾)** in / **30 (35, 40)** cm, cut Outremer and switch to Faïence; continue in stockinette, casting on 10 additional sts at end of row to form a sleeve.

You'll have **30 (32, 35)** sts total once you've added 7 sts.

2) When work measures **2¾ (4, 5)** in / **7 (10, 13)** cm, cast on 7 additional sts at inner edge.

1) With Outremer, cast on **23 (25, 28)** sts. Work in stockinette.

FRONT

10) With Faïence, pick up the **30 (31, 33)** sts you set aside at right and begin working in stockinette.

9) When work measures **15¾ (18, 20½)** in / **40 (46, 52)** cm, bind off all **30 (31, 33)** sts for the shoulder.

8) Continue working the **30 (31, 33)** sts at left in stockinette.

6) Cast on 10 additional sts at end of next row to form second sleeve.

You'll have **76 (80, 86)** sts once both sleeves are formed.

You'll have **56 (60, 66)** sts once both legs are in position.

Begin with the first leg.

2) When work measures **2¾ (4, 5)** in / **7 (10, 13)** cm, place sts on a holder and set aside.

1) With Outremer, cast on **23 (25, 28)** sts. Work in stockinette.

Work the second leg.

11) When work measures **15¾ (18, 20½)** in / **40 (46, 52)** cm, bind off all **30 (31, 33)** sts for the shoulder.

7) When work measures **14½ (17, 18¾)** in / **37 (43, 48)** cm, work the first **30 (31, 33)** sts, bind off **16 (18, 20)** sts for neck, and then work the last **30 (31, 33)** sts. Move first **30 (31, 33)** sts to a holder and set aside.

5) When work measures **11¾ (13¾, 15¾)** in / **30 (35, 40)** cm, cut Outremer and switch to Faïence; continue in stockinette, casting on 10 additional sts at end of row to form a sleeve = **66 (70, 76)** sts.

4) When work measures **2¾ (4, 5)** in / **7 (10, 13)** cm, work the first **23 (25, 28)** sts, cast on 10 additional sts, and then pick up the **23 (25, 28)** sts you set aside for other leg. Continue in stockinette.

3) With Outremer, cast on **23 (25, 28)** sts. Work in stockinette.

Assembly and finishing

RIGHT BACK   **LEFT BACK**

FRONT

— Seam shoulders.

LEFT BACK

— Seam sides of onesie and undersides of sleeves.

— Seam inseam of legs.

- - - With Faïence, embroider a line of backstitch one row below the change to Faïence. (Embroidered stitches should cross a stitch and then skip a stitch; see photo, page 29.)

● On right back, make 6 buttonholes, evenly spaced (the knitting should be elastic enough for you to push a pencil or knitting needle between a couple stitches and gently widen a hole). Sew buttons in position on right back, opposite buttonholes.

Weave in ends neatly on wrong side.

9. Blanket

Worked in stockinette and reverse stockinette with finishing embroidery, using Nébuleuse and U.S. size 10½-11 / 7 mm needles.

11. Booties

Worked in garter stitch and welt stitch, using Partner 3,5 and U.S. size 2.5 / 3 mm needles.

10. Cardigan

Worked in welt stitch, using Partner 3,5 and U.S. size 4 / 3.5 mm needles

9. Blanket

Dimensions

23½ x 28¼ in / 60 x 72 cm

Materials

◊ CYCA #5 (chunky/craft/rug) Phildar Nébuleuse (41% wool, 41% acrylic, 18% polyamide; 56 yd / 51 m / 50 g): 6 skeins of Jeans
◊ CYCA #2 (sport baby) Phildar Phil Diamant (55% polyester, 45% acrylic; 306 yd / 280 m / 50 g): 1 skein of Argent
◊ U.S. size 10½-11 / 7 mm needles

Stitches used

◊ **Stockinette**
  Row 1 (right side of work): Knit.
  Row 2: Purl.
  Repeat Rows 1 and 2.
◊ **Reverse stockinette**
  Row 1 (right side of work): Purl.
  Row 2: Knit.
  Repeat Rows 1 and 2.
◊ **Embroidery, straight stitch and blanket stitch**

Gauge

12 sts and 17 rows in stockinette or reverse stockinette = 4 x 4 in / 10 x 10 cm.
Adjust needle sizes to obtain correct gauge if necessary.

Pattern

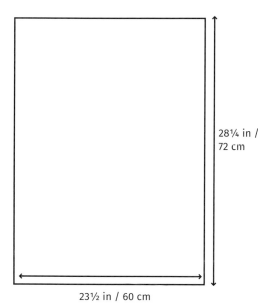

28¼ in / 72 cm

23½ in / 60 cm

Instructions

7) When work measures 28¼ in / 72 cm, bind off all sts.

15 sts of stockinette	15 sts of reverse stockinette	15 sts of stockinette	15 sts of reverse stockinette	15 sts of stockinette
15 sts of reverse stockinette	15 sts of stockinette	15 sts of reverse stockinette	15 sts of stockinette	15 sts of reverse stockinette
15 sts of stockinette	15 sts of reverse stockinette	15 sts of stockinette	15 sts of reverse stockinette	15 sts of stockinette
15 sts of reverse stockinette	15 sts of stockinette	15 sts of reverse stockinette	15 sts of stockinette	15 sts of reverse stockinette
15 sts of stockinette	15 sts of reverse stockinette	15 sts of stockinette	15 sts of reverse stockinette	15 sts of stockinette
15 sts of reverse stockinette	15 sts of stockinette	15 sts of reverse stockinette	15 sts of stockinette	15 sts of reverse stockinette

6) When work measures 23½ in / 60 cm, reverse blocks again.

5) When work measures 18¾ in / 48 cm, reverse blocks again.

4) When work measures 14¼ in / 36 cm, reverse blocks again.

3) When work measures 9½ in / 24 cm, reverse blocks again.

2) When work measures 4¾ in / 12 cm, reverse blocks of stockinette and reverse stockinette, as shown.

1) With Nébuleuse, cast on 75 sts. Work across in alternating groups of 15 sts stockinette, 15 sts reverse stockinette, as shown.

Finishing

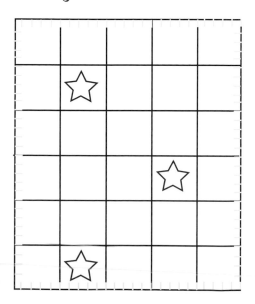

⭐ With Argent (held double), embroider stars with straight stitch in the marked stockinette squares.

With Argent (held double), embroider blanket stitch all the way around the edge of the blanket.

Weave in ends neatly on wrong side.

10. Cardigan

Sizes

Newborn (3 months, 6 months)

The instructions include all 3 sizes; the order above corresponds to the order in which instructions will be given for each size throughout. For example: for the 3-month size, always look for the first of two numbers in parentheses—in the materials list, the written instructions, and all the diagram labels showing size or length measurements.

Materials

◊ CYCA #2 (sport/baby) Phildar Partner 3,5 (50% polyamide, 25% combed wool and 25% acrylic; 137 yd / 125 m / 50 g):
   3 (3, 4) skeins of Acier
◊ U.S. size 4 / 3.5 mm needles
◊ 3 buttons
◊ 1 additional needle

Stitches used

◊ **Welt stitch (2x2)**
   Row 1: Knit.
   Row 2: Purl.
   Row 3: Purl.
   Row 4: Knit.
   Repeat Rows 1-4.

Gauge

53 sts and 48 rows in 2x2 welt stitch = 8 x 4 in / 20 x 10 cm.
Adjust needle sizes to obtain correct gauge if necessary.

Pattern

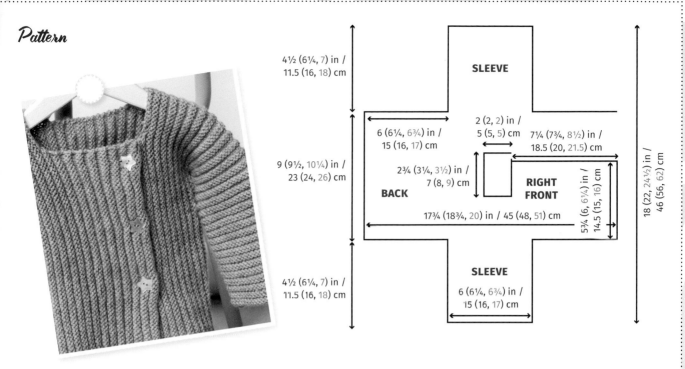

4½ (6¼, 7) in /
11.5 (16, 18) cm

SLEEVE

6 (6¼, 6¾) in /
15 (16, 17) cm

2 (2, 2) in /
5 (5, 5) cm

7¼ (7¾, 8½) in /
18.5 (20, 21.5) cm

9 (9½, 10¼) in /
23 (24, 26) cm

2¾ (3¼, 3½) in /
7 (8, 9) cm

BACK

RIGHT FRONT

5¾ (6, 6¼) in /
14.5 (15, 16) cm

18 (22, 24½) in /
46 (56, 62) cm

17¾ (18¾, 20) in / 45 (48, 51) cm

SLEEVE

4½ (6¼, 7) in /
11.5 (16, 18) cm

6 (6¼, 6¾) in /
15 (16, 17) cm

Instructions

1ST PART
Instructions for right sleeve, right front, and half of back

6) When work measures **10½ (12½, 14)** in / **26.5 (32, 35.5)** cm, place sts on a holder and set aside.

7) Pick up the **50 (54, 58)** sts you set aside earlier for right front and begin working in welt stitch.

8) When work measures **10¼ (12¼, 13½)** in / **26 (31, 34)** cm, bind off sts for right front. The right front is now complete.

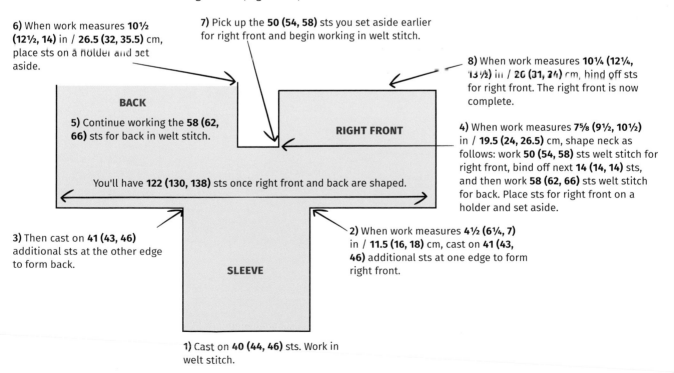

BACK

5) Continue working the **58 (62, 66)** sts for back in welt stitch.

RIGHT FRONT

4) When work measures **7⅝ (9½, 10½)** in / **19.5 (24, 26.5)** cm, shape neck as follows: work **50 (54, 58)** sts welt stitch for right front, bind off next **14 (14, 14)** sts, and then work **58 (62, 66)** sts welt stitch for back. Place sts for right front on a holder and set aside.

You'll have **122 (130, 138)** sts once right front and back are shaped.

3) Then cast on **41 (43, 46)** additional sts at the other edge to form back.

SLEEVE

2) When work measures **4½ (6¼, 7)** in / **11.5 (16, 18)** cm, cast on **41 (43, 46)** additional sts at one edge to form right front.

1) Cast on **40 (44, 46)** sts. Work in welt stitch.

Instructions

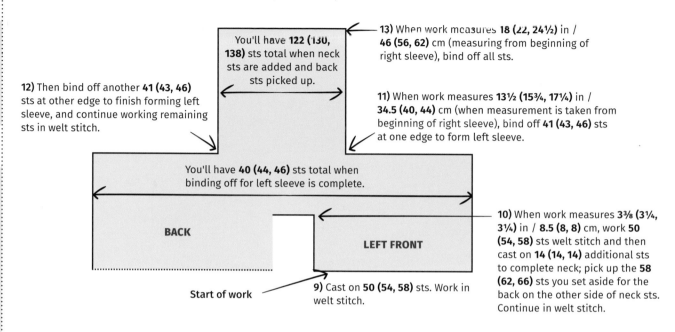

2ᴺᴰ PART
Instructions for left front, rest of back, and left sleeve

You'll have **122 (130, 138)** sts total when neck sts are added and back sts picked up.

13) When work measures **18 (22, 24½)** in / **46 (56, 62)** cm (measuring from beginning of right sleeve), bind off all sts.

12) Then bind off another **41 (43, 46)** sts at other edge to finish forming left sleeve, and continue working remaining sts in welt stitch.

11) When work measures **13½ (15¾, 17¼)** in / **34.5 (40, 44)** cm (when measurement is taken from beginning of right sleeve), bind off **41 (43, 46)** sts at one edge to form left sleeve.

You'll have **40 (44, 46)** sts total when binding off for left sleeve is complete.

BACK

LEFT FRONT

10) When work measures **3⅜ (3¼, 3¼)** in / **8.5 (8, 8)** cm, work **50 (54, 58)** sts welt stitch and then cast on **14 (14, 14)** additional sts to complete neck; pick up the **58 (62, 66)** sts you set aside for the back on the other side of neck sts. Continue in welt stitch.

Start of work

9) Cast on **50 (54, 58)** sts. Work in welt stitch.

Assembly and finishing

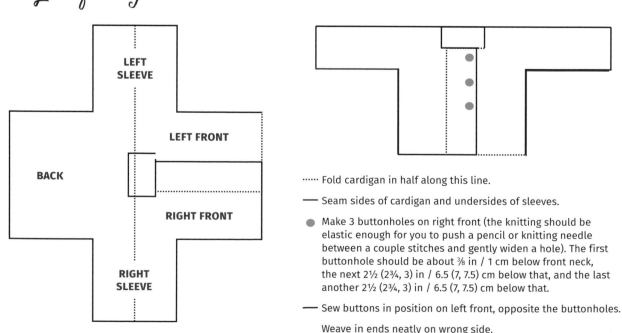

LEFT SLEEVE

LEFT FRONT

BACK

RIGHT FRONT

RIGHT SLEEVE

······ Fold cardigan in half along this line.

—— Seam sides of cardigan and undersides of sleeves.

● Make 3 buttonholes on right front (the knitting should be elastic enough for you to push a pencil or knitting needle between a couple stitches and gently widen a hole). The first buttonhole should be about ⅜ in / 1 cm below front neck, the next 2½ (2¾, 3) in / 6.5 (7, 7.5) cm below that, and the last another 2½ (2¾, 3) in / 6.5 (7, 7.5) cm below that.

—— Sew buttons in position on left front, opposite the buttonholes.

Weave in ends neatly on wrong side.

11. Booties

One size

Newborn-3 months

Materials

◊ CYCA #2 (sport/baby) Phildar Partner 3,5 (50% polyamide, 25% combed wool and 25% acrylic; 137 yd / 125 m / 50 g): 1 skein of Acier
◊ U.S. size 2-3 / 3 mm needles
◊ 2 buttons

Stitches used

◊ **Garter stitch**
  Row 1: Knit.
  Row 2: Knit.
  Repeat Rows 1 and 2.
◊ **Welt stitch (2x2)**
  Row 1: Knit.
  Row 2: Purl.
  Row 3: Purl.
  Row 4: Knit.
  Repeat Rows 1-4.

Pattern

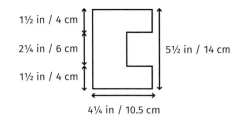

1½ in / 4 cm
2¼ in / 6 cm
1½ in / 4 cm
5½ in / 14 cm
4¼ in / 10.5 cm

Instructions

BOOTIE
MAKE 2 ALIKE

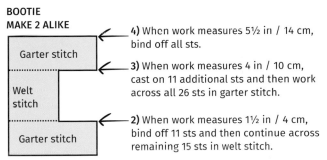

Garter stitch

Welt stitch

Garter stitch

4) When work measures 5½ in / 14 cm, bind off all sts.

3) When work measures 4 in / 10 cm, cast on 11 additional sts and then work across all 26 sts in garter stitch.

2) When work measures 1½ in / 4 cm, bind off 11 sts and then continue across remaining 15 sts in welt stitch.

1) Cast on 26 sts. Work in garter stitch.

Assembly and finishing

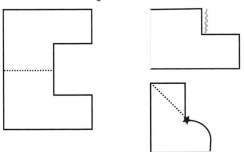

...... Fold bootie.

— Seam back and ankle of bootie.

Seam sole.

〜〜 Weave a strand of Acier through the stitches along instep, and then pull tight to gather and secure.

★ Sew a button to front top of bootie.

— Fold edges of front ankle to outside along this line, and secure in place with a couple stitches.

Weave in ends neatly on wrong side.

13. Booties

Worked in garter stitch, using Partner 6 and Phil Douce, and U.S. size 8 / 5 mm and U.S. size 9 / 5.5 mm needles.

12. Coat with hood

Worked in garter stitch and reverse stockinette, using Partner 6 and Phil Douce, and U.S. size 8 / 5 mm and U.S. size 9 / 5.5 mm needles.

12. Coat with hood

Sizes

3 months (6 months, 12 months)

The instructions include all 3 sizes; the order above corresponds to the order in which instructions will be given for each size throughout. For example: for the 6-month size, always look for the first of two numbers in parentheses—in the materials list, the written instructions, and all the diagram labels showing size or length measurements.

Materials

◊ CYCA #5 (chunky, craft, rug) Phildar Partner 6 (50% polyamide, 25% combed wool and 25% acrylic; 71 yd / 65 m / 50 g): 4 (5, 6) skeins of Naval
◊ CYCA #5 (chunky, craft, rug) Phildar Phil Douce (100% polyester; 94 yd / 86 m / 50 g): 2 (2, 2) skeins of Indigo
◊ U.S. size 8 / 5 mm and U.S. size 9 / 5.5 mm needles
◊ 3 buttons

Stitches used

◊ **Garter stitch**
  Row 1 (right side of work): Knit.
  Row 2: Knit.
  Repeat Rows 1 and 2.
◊ **Reverse stockinette**
  Row 1 (right side of work): Purl.
  Row 2: Knit.
  Repeat Rows 1 and 2.

Gauge

17 sts and 67 rows in garter stitch using larger needles and Partner 6 = 4 x 8 in / 10 x 20 cm.
Adjust needle sizes to obtain correct gauge if necessary.

Patterns

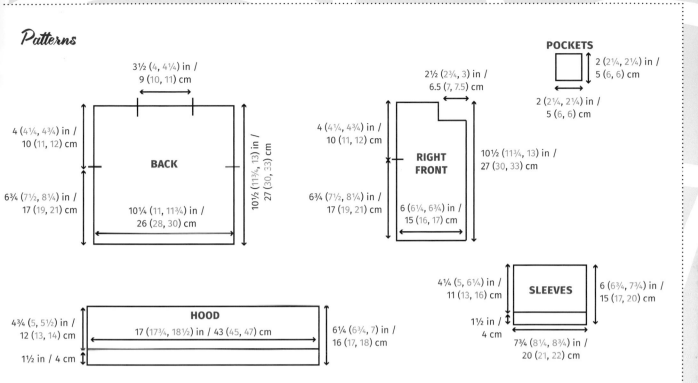

BACK

3½ (4, 4¼) in / 9 (10, 11) cm

4 (4¼, 4¾) in / 10 (11, 12) cm

6¾ (7½, 8¼) in / 17 (19, 21) cm

10½ (11¾, 13) in / 27 (30, 33) cm

10¼ (11, 11¾) in / 26 (28, 30) cm

RIGHT FRONT

2½ (2¾, 3) in / 6.5 (7, 7.5) cm

4 (4¼, 4¾) in / 10 (11, 12) cm

6¾ (7½, 8¼) in / 17 (19, 21) cm

10½ (11¾, 13) in / 27 (30, 33) cm

6 (6¼, 6¾) in / 15 (16, 17) cm

POCKETS

2 (2¼, 2¼) in / 5 (6, 6) cm

2 (2¼, 2¼) in / 5 (6, 6) cm

SLEEVES

4¼ (5, 6¼) in / 11 (13, 16) cm

1½ in / 4 cm

6 (6¾, 7¾) in / 15 (17, 20) cm

7¾ (8¼, 8¾) in / 20 (21, 22) cm

HOOD

17 (17¾, 18½) in / 43 (45, 47) cm

4¾ (5, 5½) in / 12 (13, 14) cm

1½ in / 4 cm

6¼ (6¾, 7) in / 16 (17, 18) cm

Instructions

BACK

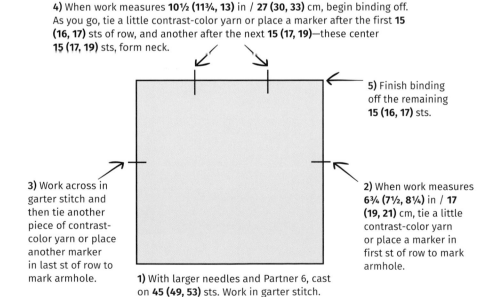

4) When work measures **10½ (11¾, 13)** in / **27 (30, 33)** cm, begin binding off. As you go, tie a little contrast-color yarn or place a marker after the first **15 (16, 17)** sts of row, and another after the next **15 (17, 19)**—these center **15 (17, 19)** sts, form neck.

5) Finish binding off the remaining **15 (16, 17)** sts.

3) Work across in garter stitch and then tie another piece of contrast-color yarn or place another marker in last st of row to mark armhole.

2) When work measures **6¾ (7½, 8¼)** in / **17 (19, 21)** cm, tie a little contrast-color yarn or place a marker in first st of row to mark armhole.

1) With larger needles and Partner 6, cast on **45 (49, 53)** sts. Work in garter stitch.

SLEEVES
MAKE 2 ALIKE

3) When work measures **6 (6¾, 7¾)** in / **15 (17, 20)** cm, bind off all sts.

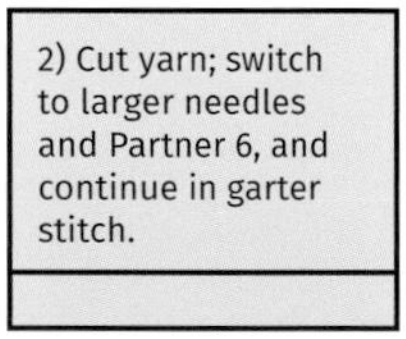

2) Cut yarn; switch to larger needles and Partner 6, and continue in garter stitch.

1) With smaller needles and Phil Douce, cast on **35 (37, 39)** sts. Work 1½ in / 4 cm in reverse stockinette.

Instructions

RIGHT FRONT

4) When work measures **10½ (11¾, 13)** in / **27 (30, 33)** cm, bind off the remaining **15 (16, 17)** sts.

2) When work measures **6¾ (7½, 8¼)** in / **17 (19, 21)** cm, tie a little contrast-color yarn or place a marker at outer edge to mark armhole.

3) When work measures **9 (10¼, 11)** in / **23 (26, 28)** cm, bind off **12 (13, 14)** sts at inner edge for neck.

1) With larger needles and Partner 6, cast on **27 (29, 31)** sts. Work in garter stitch.

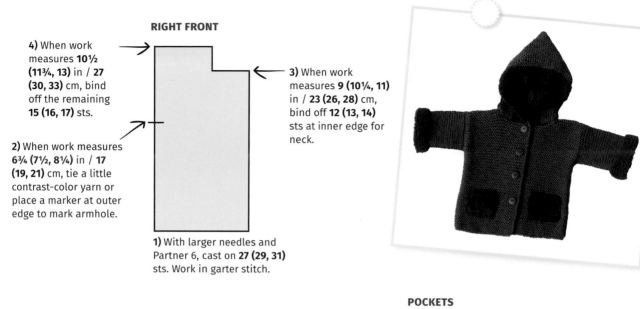

HOOD

3) When work measures **6¼ (6¾, 7)** in / **16 (17, 18)** cm, bind off all sts.

2) Cut yarn; switch to larger needles and Partner 6, and continue in garter stitch.

1) With smaller needles and Phil Douce, cast on **74 (78, 82)** sts. Work 1½ in / 4 cm in reverse stockinette.

POCKETS
MAKE 2 ALIKE

2) When work measures **2 (2¼, 2¼)** in / **5 (6, 6)** cm, bind off all sts.

1) With smaller needles and Phil Douce, cast on **9 (13, 13)** sts. Work in reverse stockinette.

LEFT FRONT

3) When work measures **9 (10¼, 11)** in / **23 (26, 28)** cm, bind off **12 (13, 14)** sts at inner edge for neck.

4) When work measures **10½ (11¾, 13)** in / **27 (30, 33)** cm, bind off the remaining **15 (16, 17)** sts.

2) When work measures **6¾ (7½, 8¼)** in / **17 (19, 21)** cm, tie a little contrast-color yarn or place a marker at outer edge to mark armhole.

1) With larger needles and Partner 6, cast on **27 (29, 31)** sts. Work in garter stitch.

Assembly and finishing

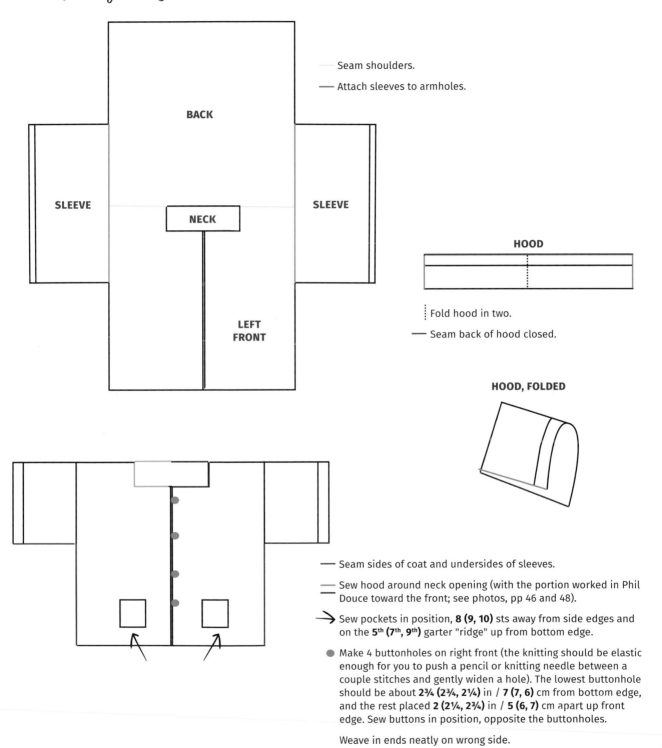

Seam shoulders.

Attach sleeves to armholes.

BACK

SLEEVE

SLEEVE

NECK

LEFT FRONT

HOOD

Fold hood in two.

Seam back of hood closed.

HOOD, FOLDED

Seam sides of coat and undersides of sleeves.

Sew hood around neck opening (with the portion worked in Phil Douce toward the front; see photos, pp 46 and 48).

→ Sew pockets in position, **8 (9, 10)** sts away from side edges and on the **5th (7th, 9th)** garter "ridge" up from bottom edge.

● Make 4 buttonholes on right front (the knitting should be elastic enough for you to push a pencil or knitting needle between a couple stitches and gently widen a hole). The lowest buttonhole should be about **2¾ (2¾, 2¼)** in / **7 (7, 6)** cm from bottom edge, and the rest placed **2 (2¼, 2¾)** in / **5 (6, 7)** cm apart up front edge. Sew buttons in position, opposite the buttonholes.

Weave in ends neatly on wrong side.

13. Booties

One size

Suitable for 3-6 months

Materials

◊ CYCA #5 (chunky, craft, rug) Phildar Phil Douce (100% polyester; 94 yd / 86 m / 50 g): 1 skein of Indigo
◊ CYCA #5 (chunky, craft, rug) Phildar Partner 6 (50% polyamide, 25% combed wool, 25% acrylic; 71 yd / 65 m / 50 g): 1 skein of Naval
◊ U.S. size 8 / 5 mm and U.S. size 9 / 5.5 mm needles

Stitches used

◊ **Garter stitch**
   Row 1 (right side of work): Knit.
   Row 2: Knit.
   Repeat Rows 1 and 2.
◊ **Stockinette**
   Row 1 (right side of work): Knit.
   Row 2: Purl.
   Repeat Rows 1 and 2.

Pattern

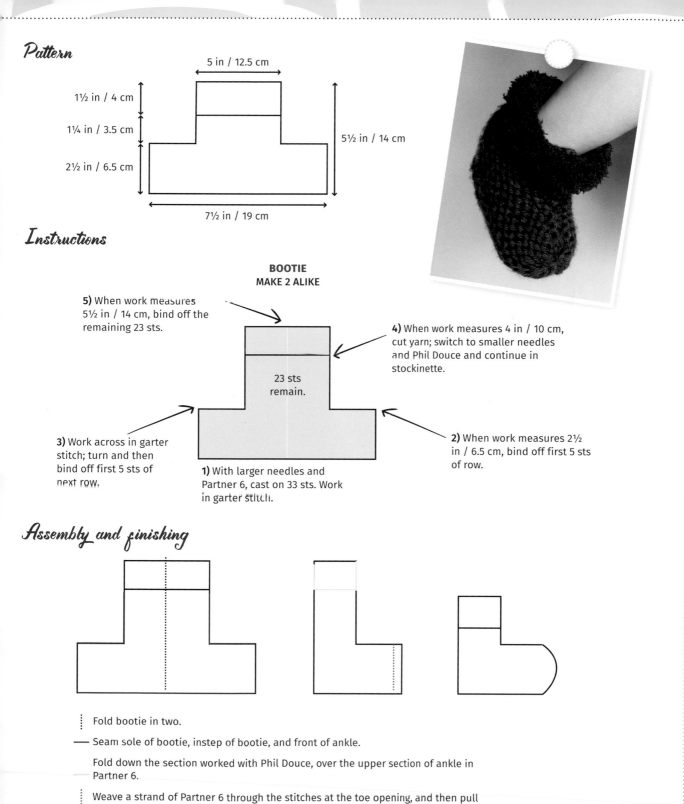

5 in / 12.5 cm

1½ in / 4 cm

1¼ in / 3.5 cm

5½ in / 14 cm

2½ in / 6.5 cm

7½ in / 19 cm

Instructions

BOOTIE
MAKE 2 ALIKE

5) When work measures 5½ in / 14 cm, bind off the remaining 23 sts.

4) When work measures 4 in / 10 cm, cut yarn; switch to smaller needles and Phil Douce and continue in stockinette.

23 sts remain.

3) Work across in garter stitch; turn and then bind off first 5 sts of next row.

1) With larger needles and Partner 6, cast on 33 sts. Work in garter stitch.

2) When work measures 2½ in / 6.5 cm, bind off first 5 sts of row.

Assembly and finishing

Fold bootie in two.

Seam sole of bootie, instep of bootie, and front of ankle.

Fold down the section worked with Phil Douce, over the upper section of ankle in Partner 6.

Weave a strand of Partner 6 through the stitches at the toe opening, and then pull tight to draw the toe closed. Poke ends through to inside of bootie and weave in.

14. Overalls

Worked in stockinette and garter stitch, using Phil Thalassa and U.S. size 4 / 3.5 mm and U.S. size 6 / 4 mm needles.

15. Shirt

Worked in welt stitch (1x3) with finishing in garter stitch, using Phil Thalassa and U.S. size 6 / 4 mm needles.

14. Overalls

Sizes

3 months (6 months, 12 months)

The instructions include all 3 sizes; the order above corresponds to the order in which instructions will be given for each size throughout. For example: for the 6-month size, always look for the first of two numbers in parentheses—in the materials list, the written instructions, and all the diagram labels showing size or length measurements.

Materials

◊ CYCA #4 (worsted/afghan/aran) Phildar Phil Thalassa (75% cotton, 25% tencel; 89 yd / 81 m / 50 g): 3 (4, 4) skeins of Indigo
◊ U.S. size 4 / 3.5 mm and U.S. size 6 / 4 mm needles
◊ 2 buttons

Stitches used

◊ **Garter stitch**
  Row 1 (right side of work): Knit.
  Row 2: Knit.
  Repeat Rows 1 and 2.
◊ **Stockinette**
  Row 1 (right side of work): Knit.
  Row 2: Purl.
  Repeat Rows 1 and 2.

Gauges

20 sts and 28 rows in stockinette using larger needles = 4 x 4 in / 10 x 10 cm.
21 sts and 42 rows in garter stitch using smaller needles = 4 x 4 in / 10 x 10 cm.
Adjust needle sizes to obtain correct gauge if necessary.

Patterns

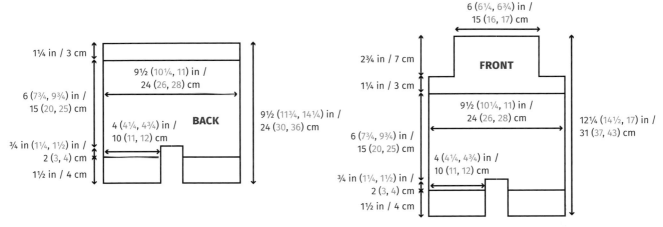

Instructions

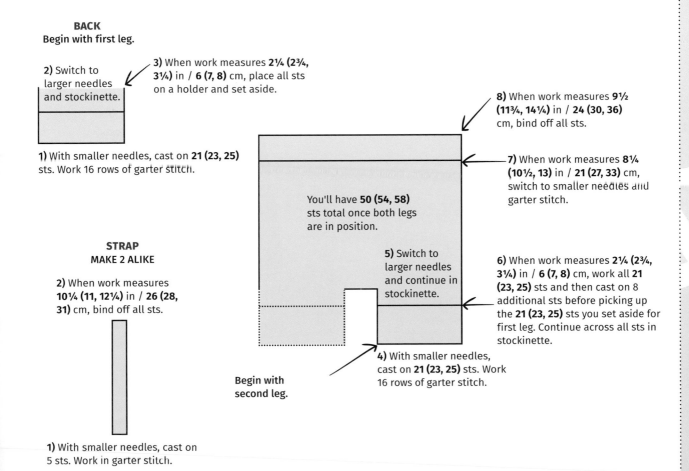

BACK
Begin with first leg.

2) Switch to larger needles and stockinette.

3) When work measures **2¼ (2¾, 3¼)** in / **6 (7, 8)** cm, place all sts on a holder and set aside.

1) With smaller needles, cast on **21 (23, 25)** sts. Work 16 rows of garter stitch.

STRAP
MAKE 2 ALIKE

2) When work measures **10¼ (11, 12¼)** in / **26 (28, 31)** cm, bind off all sts.

1) With smaller needles, cast on 5 sts. Work in garter stitch.

You'll have **50 (54, 58)** sts total once both legs are in position.

5) Switch to larger needles and continue in stockinette.

Begin with second leg.

4) With smaller needles, cast on **21 (23, 25)** sts. Work 16 rows of garter stitch.

8) When work measures **9½ (11¾, 14¼)** in / **24 (30, 36)** cm, bind off all sts.

7) When work measures **8¼ (10½, 13)** in / **21 (27, 33)** cm, switch to smaller needles and garter stitch.

6) When work measures **2¼ (2¾, 3¼)** in / **6 (7, 8)** cm, work all 21 **(23, 25)** sts and then cast on 8 additional sts before picking up the **21 (23, 25)** sts you set aside for first leg. Continue across all sts in stockinette.

Instructions

FRONT

10) When work measures **12¼ (14½, 17)** in / **31 (37, 43)** cm, bind off all sts.

9) On next row, bind off another **0 (9, 10)** sts at other edge. Continue across the remaining **34 (36, 38)** sts in garter stitch.

8) When work measures **9½ (11¾, 14¼)** in / **24 (30, 36)** cm, bind off **8 (9, 10)** sts at edge and continue across the remaining **42 (45, 48)** sts.

7) When work measures **8¼ (10½, 13)** in / **21 (27, 33)** cm, switch to smaller needles and garter stitch.

You'll have **50 (54, 58)** sts total once both legs are in position.

Begin with first leg.

2) Switch to larger needles and stockinette.

3) When work measures **2¼ (2¾, 3¼)** in / **6 (7, 8)** cm, place all sts on a holder and set aside.

5) Switch to larger needles and stockinette.

6) When work measures **2¼ (2¾, 3¼)** in / **6 (7, 8)** cm, work all **21 (23, 25)** sts and then cast on 8 additional sts before picking up the **21 (23, 25)** sts you set aside for first leg. Continue across all sts in stockinette.

1) With smaller needles, cast on **21 (23, 25)** sts. Work 16 rows of garter stitch.

Begin with second leg.

4) With smaller needle, cast on **21 (23, 25)** sts.

Assembly and finishing

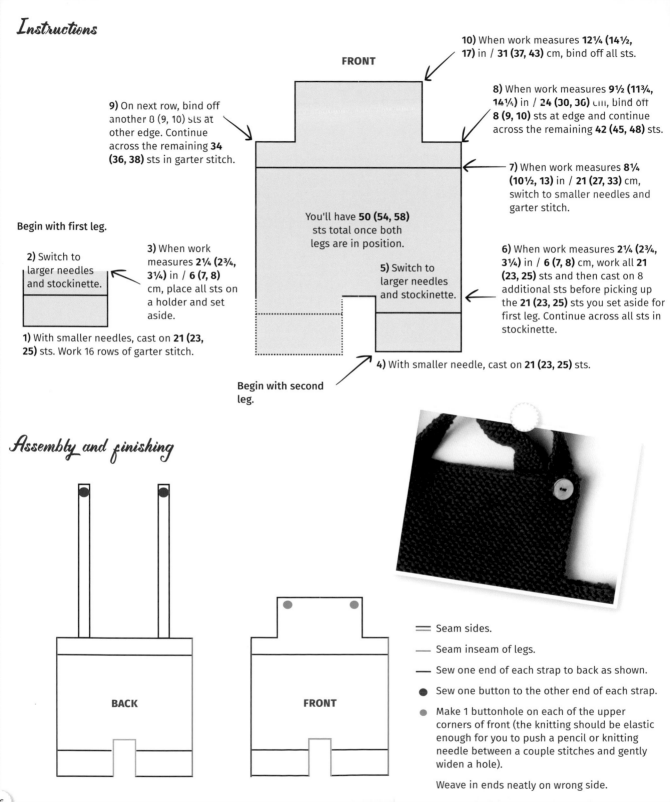

BACK

FRONT

= Seam sides.

— Seam inseam of legs.

— Sew one end of each strap to back as shown.

● Sew one button to the other end of each strap.

● Make 1 buttonhole on each of the upper corners of front (the knitting should be elastic enough for you to push a pencil or knitting needle between a couple stitches and gently widen a hole).

Weave in ends neatly on wrong side.

15. Shirt

Sizes

3 months (6 months, 12 months)

The instructions include all 3 sizes; the order above corresponds to the order in which instructions will be given for each size throughout. For example: for the 6-month size, always look for the first of two numbers in parentheses—in the materials list, the written instructions, and all the diagram labels showing size or length measurements.

Materials

◊ CYCA #4 (worsted/afghan/aran) Phildar Phil Thalassa (75% cotton, 25% tencel; 89 yd / 81 m / 50 g): 3 (4, 5) skeins of Ardoise
◊ U.S. size 6 / 4 mm needles
◊ 4 buttons

Stitches used

◊ **Garter stitch**
  Row 1 (right side of work): Knit.
  Row 2: Knit.
  Repeat Rows 1 and 2.
◊ **Stockinette**
  Row 1 (right side of work): Knit.
  Row 2: Purl.
  Repeat Rows 1 and 2.
◊ **Welt stitch (1x3)**
  Row 1 (right side of work): Knit.
  Row 2: Purl.
  Rows 3-4: Knit.
  Repeat Rows 1-4.

Gauge

20 sts and 31 rows in 1x3 welt stitch = 4 x 4 in / 10 x 10 cm.
Adjust needle sizes to obtain correct gauge if necessary.

Patterns

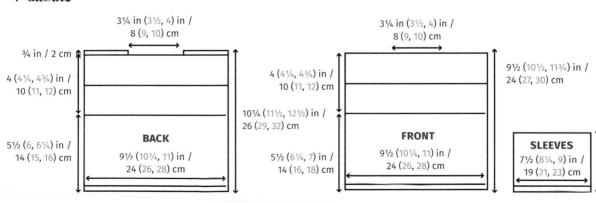

3¼ in (3½, 4) in / 8 (9, 10) cm

¾ in / 2 cm

4 (4¼, 4¾) in / 10 (11, 12) cm

5½ (6, 6¼) in / 14 (15, 16) cm

BACK

9½ (10¼, 11) in / 24 (26, 28) cm

3¼ in (3½, 4) in / 8 (9, 10) cm

4 (4¼, 4¾) in / 10 (11, 12) cm

10¼ (11½, 12½) in / 26 (29, 32) cm

5½ (6¼, 7) in / 14 (16, 18) cm

FRONT

9½ (10¼, 11) in / 24 (26, 28) cm

9½ (10½, 11¾) in / 24 (27, 30) cm

SLEEVES

7½ (8¼, 9) in / 19 (21, 23) cm

6¼ (7, 8¼) in / 16 (18, 21) cm

Instructions

7) When work measures **10¼ (11½, 12½)** in / **26 (29, 32)** cm, bind off all sts at left.

BACK

8) Pick up the **17 (18, 19)** sts you set aside at right and work second button band.

9) When work measures **10¼ (11½, 12½)** in / **26 (29, 32)** cm, bind off all sts.

6) Continue working sts at left for button band.

5) When work measures **9½ (10½, 11¾)** in / **24 (27, 30)** cm, work first **17 (18, 19)** sts, bind off next **16 (18, 20)** sts for neck, and then work the remaining **17 (18, 19)** sts. Move first **17 (18, 19)** sts to a holder and set aside.

4) Work across and then tie another piece of contrast-color yarn or place another marker in last st of row to mark armhole.

3) When work measures **5½ (6¼, 7)** in / **14 (16, 18)** cm, tie a little contrast-color yarn or place a marker in first st of row to mark armhole.

2) Continue in 1x3 welt stitch (see "Stitches used" for instructions).

1) Cast on **50 (54, 58)** sts. Work 4 rows of garter stitch.

SLEEVE
MAKE 2 ALIKE

3) When work measures **6¼ (7, 8¼)** in / **16 (18, 21)** cm, bind off all sts.

2) Continue in 1x3 welt stitch (see "Stitches used" for instructions).

1) Cast on **40 (44, 48)** sts. Work 4 rows of garter stitch.

FRONT

5) When work measures **7½ (8¾, 9¾)** in / **19 (22, 25)** cm, switch to stockinette.

7) When work measures **9½ (10½, 11¾)** in / **24 (27, 30)** cm, bind off all sts.

6) When work measures **9 (10¼, 11½)** in / **23 (26, 29)** cm, work 2 rows of garter stitch.

4) Work across and then tie another piece of contrast-color yarn or place another marker in last st of row to mark armhole.

3) When work measures **5½ (6¼, 7)** in / **14 (16, 18)** cm, tie a little contrast-color yarn or place a marker in first st of row to mark armhole.

2) Continue in 1x3 welt stitch (see "Stitches used" for instructions).

1) Cast on **50 (54, 58)** sts. Work 4 rows of garter stitch.

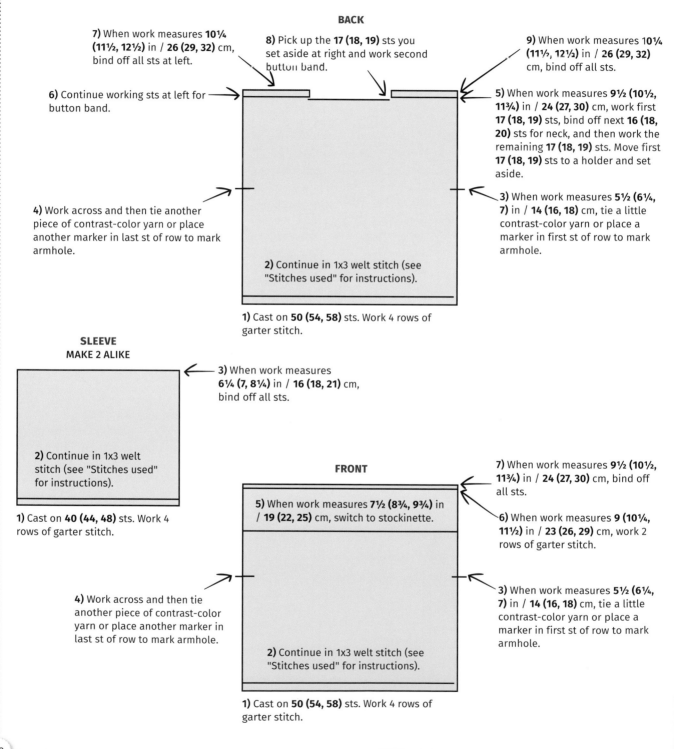

Assembly and finishing

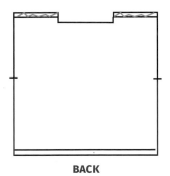 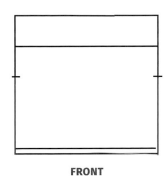

BACK   **FRONT**

—— Seam sides.

〜 Fold button bands to inside.

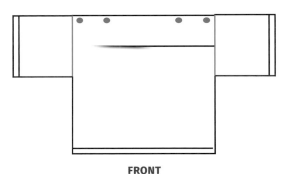

FRONT

—— Sew sleeves to armholes.

—— Seam undersides of sleeves.

● Make 2 buttonholes in each shoulder of front (the knitting should be elastic enough for you to push a pencil or knitting needle between a couple stitches and gently widen a hole). Sew buttons in position on button bands of back, opposite buttonholes.

Weave in ends neatly on wrong side.

16. Wrap shirt

Worked in reverse stockinette with finishing in stockinette, using Cabotine and U.S. size 4 / 3.5 mm needles.

16. Wrap shirt

Sizes

3 months (6 months, 12 months)

The instructions include all 3 sizes; the order above corresponds to the order in which instructions will be given for each size throughout. For example: for the 6-month size, always look for the first of two numbers in parentheses—in the materials list, the written instructions, and all the diagram labels showing size or length measurements.

Materials

◊ CYCA #3 (DK/light worsted) Phildar Cabotine (55% cotton, 45% acrylic; 136 yd / 124 m / 50 g): 3 (3, 4) skeins of Peau
◊ U.S. size 4 / 3.5 mm needles
◊ 2 buttons

Stitches used

◊ **Stockinette**
Row 1 (right side of work): Knit.
Row 2: Purl.
Repeat Rows 1 and 2.
◊ **Reverse stockinette**
Row 1 (right side of work): Purl.
Row 2: Knit.
Repeat Rows 1 and 2.

Gauge

21 sts and 30 rows in stockinette or reverse stockinette = 4 x 4 in / 10 x 10 cm.
Adjust needle sizes to obtain correct gauge if necessary.

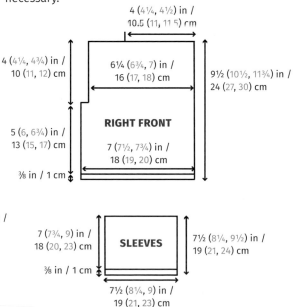

4 (4¼, 4½) in / 10.5 (11, 11.5) cm

4 (4¼, 4¾) in / 10 (11, 12) cm

6¼ (6¾, 7) in / 16 (17, 18) cm

9½ (10½, 11¾) in / 24 (27, 30) cm

RIGHT FRONT

5 (6, 6¾) in / 13 (15, 17) cm

7 (7½, 7¾) in / 18 (19, 20) cm

⅜ in / 1 cm

7 (7¾, 9) in / 18 (20, 23) cm

SLEEVES

7½ (8¼, 9½) in / 19 (21, 24) cm

⅜ in / 1 cm

7½ (8¼, 9) in / 19 (21, 24) cm

Patterns

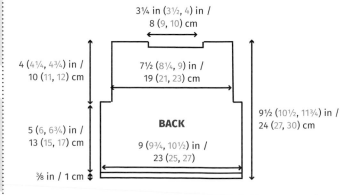

3¼ in (3½, 4) in / 8 (9, 10) cm

4 (4¼, 4¾) in / 10 (11, 12) cm

7½ (8¼, 9) in / 19 (21, 23) cm

9½ (10½, 11¾) in / 24 (27, 30) cm

5 (6, 6¾) in / 13 (15, 17) cm

BACK

9 (9¾, 10½) in / 23 (25, 27)

⅜ in / 1 cm

Instructions

BACK

7) When work measures **9½ (10½, 11¾)** in / **24 (27, 30)** cm, bind off these sts for the shoulder.

8) Pick up the **13 (14, 15)** sts you set aside at right and work in reverse stockinette.

9) When work measures **9½ (10½, 11¾)** in / **24 (27, 30)** cm, bind off these sts for the shoulder

6) Continue working sts at left in reverse stockinette.

5) When work measures **9 (10¼, 11½)** in / **23 (26, 29)** cm, work first **13 (14, 15)** sts, bind off next **16 (18, 20)** sts for neck, and then work the remaining **13 (14, 15)** sts. Move first **13 (14, 15)** sts to a holder and set aside.

4) Then bind off another 4 sts at start of next row to shape other armhole; complete row.

You'll have **42 (46, 50)** sts total once both armholes have been shaped.

2) Switch to reverse stockinette.

3) When work measures **5½ (6¼, 7)** in / **14 (16, 18)** cm, bind off 4 sts at start of row to shape armhole; complete row.

1) Cast on **50 (54, 58)** sts. Work 3 rows of stockinette.

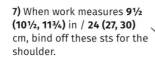

SLEEVE
MAKE 2 ALIKE

2) Switch to reverse stockinette.

3) When work measures **7½ (8¼, 9½)** in / **19 (21, 24)** cm, bind off all sts.

1) Cast on **42 (46, 50)** sts. Work 3 rows of stockinette.

RIGHT FRONT

4) When work measures **9½ (10½, 11¾)** in / **24 (27, 30)** cm, bind off all sts.

You'll have **36 (38, 40)** sts total after binding off for armhole.

2) Switch to reverse stockinette.

3) When work measures **5½ (6¼, 7)** in / **14 (16, 18)** cm, bind off 4 sts at outer edge to shape armhole.

1) Cast on **40 (42, 44)** sts. Work 3 rows of stockinette.

LEFT FRONT

4) When work measures **9½ (10½, 11¾)** in / **24 (27, 30)** cm, bind off all sts.

You'll have 36 **(38, 40)** sts total after binding off for armhole.

2) Switch to reverse stockinette.

3) When work measures **5½ (6¼, 7)** in / **14 (16, 18)** cm, bind off 4 sts at outer edge to shape armhole.

1) Cast on **40 (42, 44)** sts. Work 3 rows of stockinette.

Assembly and finishing

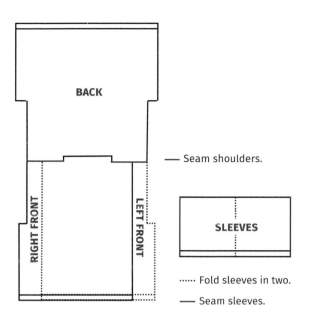

— Seam shoulders.

— Fold sleeves in two.

— Seam sleeves.

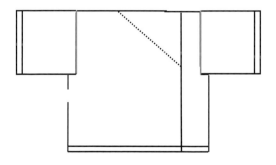

— Sew sleeves to armholes.

— Seam sides, leaving an opening of ⅜ **in / 1 cm** for cord beneath right armhole, as shown.

⋯⋯ Fold upper corners of left and right front to outside (see pp 60 and 62).

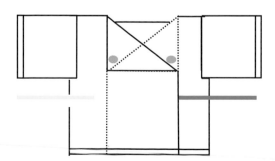

● Sew buttons in position over folded corners to secure them in place.

▬ Make a cord from 4 lengths of yarn folded in two, with a final length of about **8¾ (10½, 12½)** in / **22 (27, 32)** cm, and sew end firmly to outer edge of right front, level with hole in side seam.

▬ Make a cord from 4 lengths of yarn folded in two, with a final length of about **16½ (18½, 20½)** in / **42 (47, 52)** cm, and sew end firmly to outer edge of left front; pass cord through hole in right side seam so cords can be tied at outside of back as shown.

Weave in ends neatly on wrong side.

17. Sleep sack

Worked in stockinette and garter
stitch, using Frimas and Partner 6,
and U.S. size 10 / 6 mm needles.

18. Cuddly friend

Worked in stockinette and reverse stockinette with finishing embroidery, using Partner 3,5 and U.S. size 2.5 / 3 mm needles.

17. Sleep sack

One size

Materials

- ◊ CYCA #5 (chunky, craft, rug) Phildar Frimas (50% wool, 50% cotton; 86 yd / 79 m / 50 g): 7 skeins of Églantine
- ◊ CYCA #5 (chunky, craft, rug) Phildar Partner 6 (50% polyamide, 25% combed wool, 25% acrylic; 71 yd / 65 m / 50 g): 1 skein of Écru
- ◊ U.S. size 10 / 6 mm needles
- ◊ 4 snaps, 21 mm in diameter

Stitches used

- ◊ **Garter stitch**
  Row 1 (right side of work): Knit.
  Row 2: Knit.
  Repeat Rows 1 and 2.
- ◊ **Stockinette**
  Row 1 (right side of work): Knit.
  Row 2: Purl.
  Repeat Rows 1 and 2.

Gauge

29 sts and 22 rows in stockinette = 8 x 4 in / 20 x 10 cm. Adjust needle sizes to obtain correct gauge if necessary.

Pattern

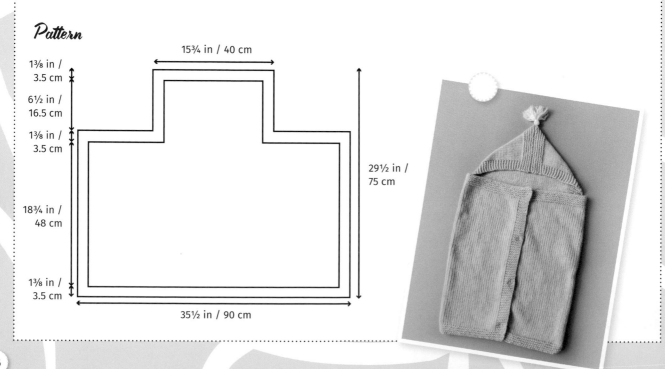

15¾ in / 40 cm

1⅜ in / 3.5 cm

6½ in / 16.5 cm

1⅜ in / 3.5 cm

18¾ in / 48 cm

1⅜ in / 3.5 cm

29½ in / 75 cm

35½ in / 90 cm

Instructions

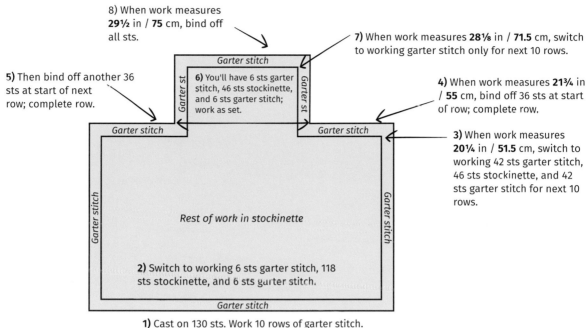

8) When work measures **29½ in / 75 cm**, bind off all sts.

7) When work measures **28⅛ in / 71.5 cm**, switch to working garter stitch only for next 10 rows.

5) Then bind off another 36 sts at start of next row; complete row.

6) You'll have 6 sts garter stitch, 46 sts stockinette, and 6 sts garter stitch; work as set.

Garter st

Garter st

Garter stitch

Garter stitch

4) When work measures **21¾ in / 55 cm**, bind off 36 sts at start of row; complete row.

3) When work measures **20¼ in / 51.5 cm**, switch to working 42 sts garter stitch, 46 sts stockinette, and 42 sts garter stitch for next 10 rows.

Garter stitch

Garter stitch

Rest of work in stockinette

2) Switch to working 6 sts garter stitch, 118 sts stockinette, and 6 sts garter stitch.

Garter stitch

1) Cast on 130 sts. Work 10 rows of garter stitch.

Assembly and finishing

····· Fold the sleep sack along dotted lines as shown (folding inner section first, so outer section, when folded, will overlap it to the outside).

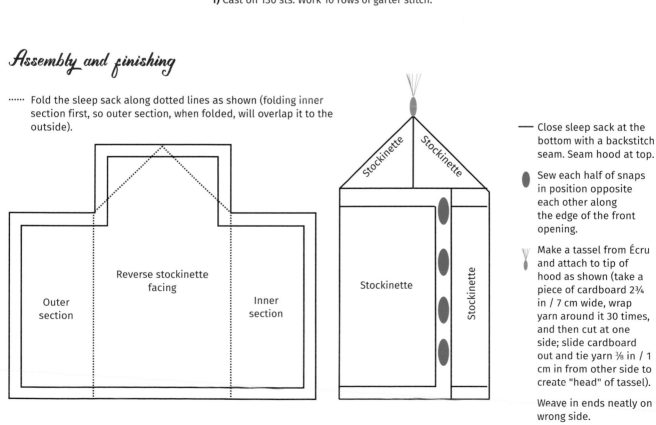

Outer section

Reverse stockinette facing

Inner section

Stockinette

Stockinette

Stockinette

Stockinette

— Close sleep sack at the bottom with a backstitch seam. Seam hood at top.

● Sew each half of snaps in position opposite each other along the edge of the front opening.

Make a tassel from Écru and attach to tip of hood as shown (take a piece of cardboard 2¾ in / 7 cm wide, wrap yarn around it 30 times, and then cut at one side; slide cardboard out and tie yarn ⅜ in / 1 cm in from other side to create "head" of tassel).

Weave in ends neatly on wrong side.

18. Cuddly friend

Dimensions

Approx. 9 in / 23 cm long

Materials

◊ CYCA #2 (sport/baby) Phildar Partner 3,5 (50%
  polyamide, 25% combed wool, and 25% acrylic;
  137 yd / 125 m / 50 g): 1 skein of Acier; 1 skein of
  Écru; 1 skein of Rose; 1 skein of Grenadine
◊ U.S. size 2.5 / 3 mm needles
◊ Fiberfill

Stitches used

◊ **Stockinette**
  Row 1 (right side of work): Knit.
  Row 2: Purl.
  Repeat Rows 1 and 2.
◊ **Reverse stockinette**
  Row 1 (right side of work): Purl.
  Row 2: Knit.
  Repeat Rows 1 and 2.
◊ **Embroidery:** straight stitch, stem stitch, and cross
  stitch

Instructions

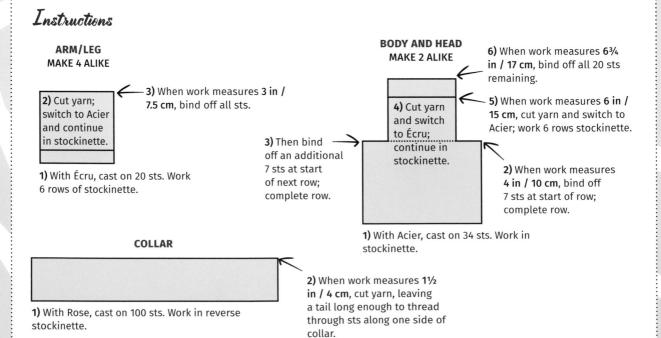

**ARM/LEG
MAKE 4 ALIKE**

2) Cut yarn;
switch to Acier
and continue
in stockinette.

3) When work measures **3 in /
7.5 cm**, bind off all sts.

1) With Écru, cast on 20 sts. Work
6 rows of stockinette.

**BODY AND HEAD
MAKE 2 ALIKE**

6) When work measures **6¾
in / 17 cm**, bind off all 20 sts
remaining.

5) When work measures **6 in /
15 cm**, cut yarn and switch to
Acier; work 6 rows stockinette.

4) Cut yarn
and switch
to Écru;
continue in
stockinette.

3) Then bind
off an additional
7 sts at start
of next row;
complete row.

2) When work measures
4 in / 10 cm, bind off
7 sts at start of row;
complete row.

1) With Acier, cast on 34 sts. Work in
stockinette.

COLLAR

1) With Rose, cast on 100 sts. Work in reverse
stockinette.

2) When work measures **1½
in / 4 cm**, cut yarn, leaving
a tail long enough to thread
through sts along one side of
collar.

Assembly and finishing

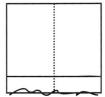

..... Fold leg in two.

—— Seam sides.

〰 Weave a strand of Écru through sts of cast-on row and pull to draw bottom of leg closed.

Stuff with fiberfill. Finish the other leg the same way.

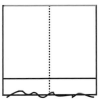

..... Fold arm in two.

—— Seam sides.

〰 Weave a strand of Écru through sts of cast-on row and pull to draw end of arm closed.

—— After stuffing, close other end of arm with a fine seam.

Stuff with fiberfill. Finish the other arm the same way.

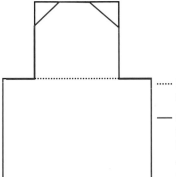

..... Line the two body-and-head pieces up against each other, right sides facing in.

—— Seam sides, shoulders, and head, working at an angle across corners of head to round it off.

Turn right side out and stuff with fiberfill.

..... Fold collar in half.

—— Seam ends of collar together carefully with matching thread.

—— Slide collar into place over head; the side of the collar with yarn woven along it should be inward, so when you pull the yarn, it gathers against the neck. Tighten, secure, and then weave in end.

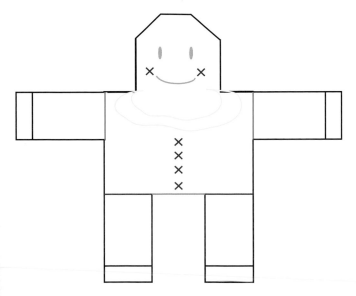

❘ Embroider eyes with Acier and straight stitch.

⌣ Embroider mouth with Rose and stem stitch.

✕ Embroider cheeks and "buttons" with Grenadine and cross stitch.

—— Sew one arm to either side of the body.

—— Sew one leg to either end of the underside of the body.

—— Make any final adjustments to stuffing of body.

—— Seam inseam between legs carefully.

Weave in ends neatly on wrong side.

19. Hat

Worked in stockinette with finishing embroidery, using Phil Douce and U.S. size 8 / 5 mm needles.

20. Mittens

Worked in stockinette with finishing embroidery, using Phil Douce and U.S. size 8 / 5 mm needles.

21. Scarf

Worked in stockinette stripes, using Partner 6 and Phil Douce, and U.S. size 8 / 5 mm needles.

22. Jacket

Worked in garter stitch, using Partner 6 and Phil Douce, and U.S. size 8 / 5 mm and U.S. size 9 / 5.5 mm needles.

19. Hat

Sizes

3-6 months (12 months)

The instructions include both sizes; the order above corresponds to the order in which instructions will be given for each size throughout. If you want to make the 3-6-month size, always look for the first number, outside the parentheses—in the materials list, the written instructions, and all the diagram labels showing size or length measurements. If you want to make the 12-month size, look inside the parentheses instead.

Materials

◊ CYCA #5 (chunky, craft, rug) Phildar Phil Douce (100% polyester; 94 yd / 86 m / 50 g): 1 (1) skein of Écru
◊ CYCA #5 (chunky, craft, rug) Phildar Partner 6 (50% polyamide, 25% combed wool, 25% acrylic; 71 yd / 65 m / 50 g): 1 (1) skein of Renne
◊ U.S. size 8 / 5 mm needles

Stitches used

◊ Stockinette
  Row 1 (right side of work): Knit.
  Row 2: Purl.
  Repeat Rows 1 and 2.
◊ Embroidery, straight stitch

Gauge

18 sts and 20 rows in stockinette using Phil Douce = 4 x 4 in / 10 x 10 cm.
Adjust needle sizes to obtain correct gauge if necessary.

Pattern

7½ (8) in /
19 (20.5) cm

6¾ (7) in /
17 (18) cm

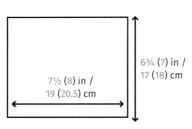

Instructions

HAT SECTION
MAKE 2 ALIKE

2) When work measures **6¾ (7)** in / **17 (18)** cm, bind off all sts.

1) With Phil Douce, cast on **35 (39)** sts. Work in stockinette.

Assembly and finishing

— Line up sections of hat and seam sides and top.

— Work front stitch at an angle across corners of hat as shown; gather as shown to form ears, and then wrap yarn tightly around bases of ears to secure.

— With Renne, embroider eyes, nose, and mouth with straight stitch.

Weave in ends neatly on wrong side.

20. Mittens

Sizes

3-6 months (12 months)

The instructions include both sizes; the order above corresponds to the order in which instructions will be given for each size throughout. If you want to make the 3-6-month size, always look for the first number, outside the parentheses—in the materials list, the written instructions, and all the diagram labels showing size or length measurements. If you want to make the 12-month size, look inside the parentheses instead.

Stitches used

◊ **Stockinette**
Row 1 (right side of work): Knit.
Row 2: Purl.
Repeat Rows 1 and 2.
◊ **Embroidery, straight stitch**

Materials

◊ CYCA #5 (chunky, craft, rug) Phildar Phil Douce (100% polyester; 94 yd / 86 m / 50 g): 1 (1) skein of Écru
◊ CYCA #5 (chunky, craft, rug) Phildar Partner 6 (50% polyamide, 25% combed wool, 25% acrylic; 71 yd / 65 m / 50 g): 1 (1) skein of Renne
◊ U.S. size 8 / 5 mm needles
◊ Elastic cord (lastex)

Gauge

18 sts and 20 rows in stockinette using Phil Douce = 4 x 4 in / 10 x 10 cm.
Adjust needle sizes to obtain correct gauge if necessary.

Pattern

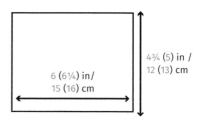

6 (6¼) in/ 15 (16) cm

4¾ (5) in / 12 (13) cm

Instructions

MITTEN
MAKE 2 ALIKE

2) When work measures 4¾ **(5)** in /
12 (13) cm, bind off all sts.

1) With Phil Douce, cast on **29 (31)** sts.
Work in stockinette.

Assembly and finishing

⋮ Assembly and finishing

— Fold mittens in half.

Seam sides and top of each mitten.

— Work front stitch at an angle across
corners of mittens as shown; gather as
shown to form ears, and then wrap yarn
tightly around bases of ears to secure.

— With Renne, embroider eyes, nose, and
mouth with straight stitch.

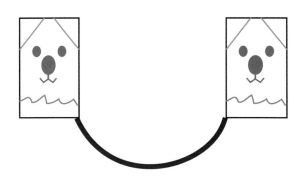

〰 Weave elastic cord through wrists of mittens
and sew securely into a loop.

⌣ Make a cord with 2 lengths of yarn folded in
two, with a final length of about 19¾ in / 50 cm,
and attach one end to each mitten.

Weave in ends neatly on wrong side.

21. Scarf

One size

Materials

◊ CYCA #5 (chunky, craft, rug) Phildar Phil Douce
   (100% polyester; 94 yd / 86 m / 50 g): 1 skein
   of Écru
◊ CYCA #5 (chunky, craft, rug) Phildar Partner 6
   (50% polyamide, 25% combed wool, 25% acrylic;
   71 yd / 65 m / 50 g): 1 skein of Écru
◊ U.S. size 8 / 5 mm needles

Stitches used

◊ **Stockinette**
   Row 1 (right side of work): Knit.
   Row 2: Purl.
   Repeat Rows 1 and 2.
◊ **Stockinette stripes**
   *10 rows of stockinette using Phil Douce, 10 rows
   of stockinette using Partner 6*; repeat from * to *
   5 more times, and end with 10 rows Phil Douce.

Gauge

35 sts and 21 rows in stockinette stripes = 8 x 4 in /
20 x 10 cm.
Adjust needle sizes to obtain correct gauge if
necessary.

Pattern

24½ in /
62 cm

3½ in / 9 cm

Instructions

2) When work measures **24½ in /
62 cm**, bind off all sts.

10 rows of Phil Douce
10 rows of Partner 6
10 rows of Phil Douce
10 rows of Partner 6
10 rows of Phil Douce
10 rows of Partner 6
10 rows of Phil Douce
10 rows of Partner 6
10 rows of Phil Douce
10 rows of Partner 6
10 rows of Phil Douce
10 rows of Partner 6
10 rows of Phil Douce

1) With Phil Douce, cast on 16 sts.
Work in stockinette stripes.

22. Jacket

Sizes

3 months (6 months, 12 months)

The instructions include all 3 sizes; the order above corresponds to the order in which instructions will be given for each size throughout. For example: for the 6-month size, always look for the first of two numbers in parentheses—in the materials list, the written instructions, and all the diagram labels showing size or length measurements.

Materials

◊ CYCA #5 (chunky, craft, rug) Phildar Partner 6 (50% polyamide, 25% combed wool, 25% acrylic; 71 yd / 65 m / 50 g): 4 (5, 5) skeins of Écru
◊ CYCA #5 (chunky, craft, rug) Phildar Phil Douce (100% polyester; 94 yd / 86 m / 50 g): 1 (1, 2) skeins of Écru
◊ U.S. size 0 / 5 mm and U.S. size 9 / 5.5 mm needles
◊ 6 buttons

Stitches used

◊ Garter stitch
   Row 1 (right side of work): Knit.
   Row 2: Knit.
   Repeat Rows 1 and 2.

Gauges

17 sts and 67 rows in garter stitch using larger needles and Partner 6 = 4 x 8 in / 10 x 20 cm.
18 sts and 41 rows in garter stitch using smaller needles and Phil Douce = 4 x 8 in / 10 x 20 cm.
Adjust needle sizes to obtain correct gauge if necessary.

Patrons

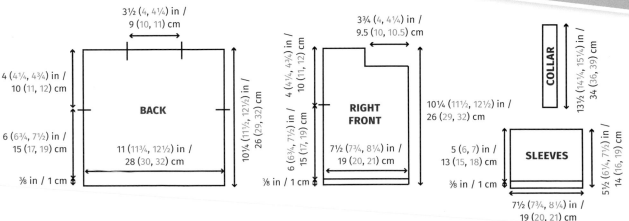

BACK
3½ (4, 4¼) in / 9 (10, 11) cm
4 (4¼, 4¾) in / 10 (11, 12) cm
6 (6¾, 7½) in / 15 (17, 19) cm
⅜ in / 1 cm
11 (11¾, 12½) in / 28 (30, 32) cm
10¼ (11½, 12½) in / 26 (29, 32) cm

RIGHT FRONT
3¾ (4, 4¼) in / 9.5 (10, 10.5) cm
4 (4¼, 4¾) in / 10 (11, 12) cm
6 (6¾, 7½) in / 15 (17, 19) cm
7½ (7¾, 8¼) in / 19 (20, 21) cm
⅜ in / 1 cm
10¼ (11½, 12½) in / 26 (29, 32) cm

COLLAR
13½ (14¼, 15¼) in / 34 (36, 39) cm

SLEEVES
5 (6, 7) in / 13 (15, 18) cm
5½ (6¼, 7½) in / 14 (16, 19) cm
⅜ in / 1 cm
7½ (7¾, 8¼) in / 19 (20, 21) cm

Instructions

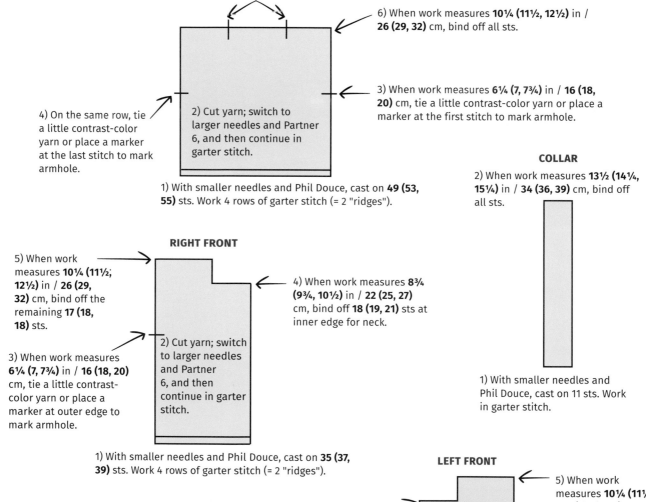

BACK

5) When work measures **10¼ (11½, 12½)** in / **26 (29, 32)** cm, tie a little contrast-color yarn to either side of the center **15 (17, 19)** sts of row to mark neck.

6) When work measures **10¼ (11½, 12½)** in / **26 (29, 32)** cm, bind off all sts.

3) When work measures **6¼ (7, 7¾)** in / **16 (18, 20)** cm, tie a little contrast-color yarn or place a marker at the first stitch to mark armhole.

4) On the same row, tie a little contrast-color yarn or place a marker at the last stitch to mark armhole.

2) Cut yarn; switch to larger needles and Partner 6, and then continue in garter stitch.

1) With smaller needles and Phil Douce, cast on **49 (53, 55)** sts. Work 4 rows of garter stitch (= 2 "ridges").

COLLAR

2) When work measures **13½ (14¼, 15¼)** in / **34 (36, 39)** cm, bind off all sts.

1) With smaller needles and Phil Douce, cast on 11 sts. Work in garter stitch.

RIGHT FRONT

5) When work measures **10¼ (11½; 12½)** in / **26 (29, 32)** cm, bind off the remaining **17 (18, 18)** sts.

4) When work measures **8¾ (9¾, 10½)** in / **22 (25, 27)** cm, bind off **18 (19, 21)** sts at inner edge for neck.

3) When work measures **6¼ (7, 7¾)** in / **16 (18, 20)** cm, tie a little contrast-color yarn or place a marker at outer edge to mark armhole.

2) Cut yarn; switch to larger needles and Partner 6, and then continue in garter stitch.

1) With smaller needles and Phil Douce, cast on **35 (37, 39)** sts. Work 4 rows of garter stitch (= 2 "ridges").

LEFT FRONT

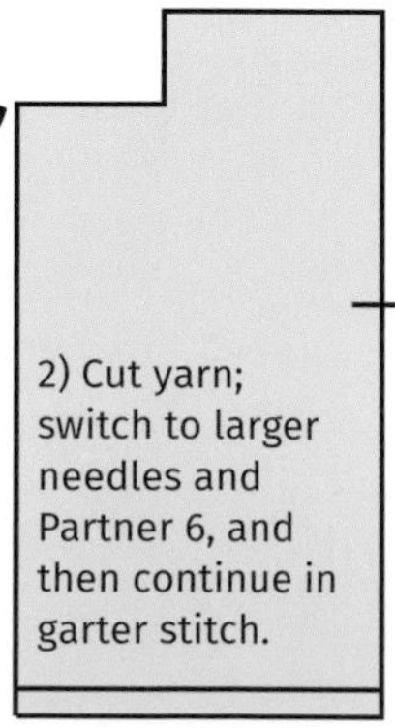

5) When work measures **10¼ (11½, 12½)** in / **26 (29, 32)** cm, bind off all sts.

4) When work measures **8¾ (9¾, 10½)** in / **22 (25, 27)** cm, bind off **18 (19, 21)** sts at inner edge for neck.

3) When work measures **6¼ (7, 7¾)** in / **16 (18, 20)** cm, tie a little contrast-color yarn or place a marker at outer edge to mark armhole.

2) Cut yarn; switch to larger needles and Partner 6, and then continue in garter stitch.

1) With smaller needles and Phil Douce, cast on **35 (37, 39)** sts. Work 4 rows of garter stitch (= 2 "ridges").

SLEEVE
MAKE 2 ALIKE

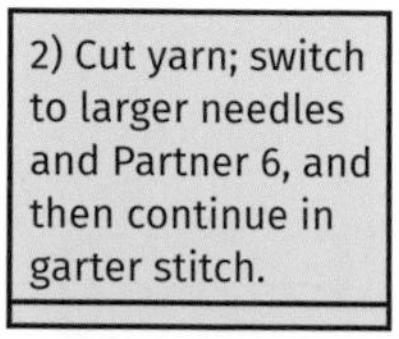

3) When work measures **5½ (6¼, 7½)** in / **14 (16, 19)** cm, bind off all sts.

2) Cut yarn; switch to larger needles and Partner 6, and then continue in garter stitch.

1) With smaller needles and Phil Douce, cast on **35 (37, 39)** sts. Work 4 rows of garter stitch (= 2 "ridges").

Assembly and finishing

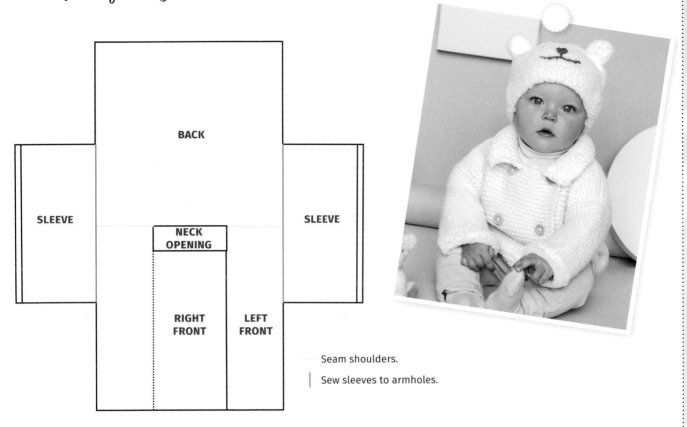

Seam shoulders.

Sew sleeves to armholes.

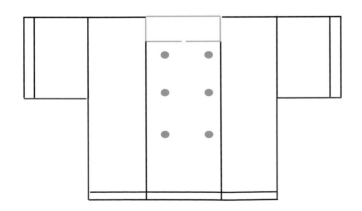

Seam sides of jacket and undersides of sleeves.

Sew collar around edge of neck opening, placing ends of collar about 2 in / 5 cm from edges (when jacket is buttoned, the ends of the collar will be next to each other).

Make 2 lines of 3 buttonholes each (the knitting should be elastic enough for you to push a pencil or knitting needle between a couple stitches and gently widen a hole). The first line should start about ⅜ in / 1 cm below front neck, with 1 group of buttonholes 4 sts away from edge and the second group 10 sts further over.

Space buttonholes evenly, as shown. Sew buttons in position, opposite the buttonholes.

Weave in ends neatly on wrong side.

24. Cardigan

Worked in garter stitch, using Tendresse and U.S. size 7 / 4.5 mm needles.

23. Shirt

Worked in stockinette and garter stitch, using Partner 3,5 and U.S. size 4 / 3.5 mm needles (or using Tendresse and U.S. size 8 / 5 mm needles).

23. Shirt

Sizes

3 months (6 months, 12 months)

The instructions include all 3 sizes; the order above corresponds to the order in which instructions will be given for each size throughout. For example: for the 6-month size, always look for the first of two numbers in parentheses—in the materials list, the written instructions, and all the diagram labels showing size or length measurements.

Materials

◊ CYCA #2 (sport/baby) Phildar Partner 3,5 (50% polyamide, 25% combed wool, and 25% acrylic; 137 yd / 125 m / 50 g): 2 (3, 3) skeins of Blanc or CYCA #4 (worsted/afghan/aran) Phildar Tendresse (75% viscose, 25% polyamide; 107 yd / 98 m / 50 g): 3 (4, 4) skeins of Blanc
◊ U.S. size 4 / 3.5 mm needles, if using Partner 3,5
◊ U.S. size 8 / 5 mm needles, if using Tendresse
◊ 1 button

Stitches used

◊ **Garter stitch**
  Row 1 (right side of work): Knit.
  Row 2: Knit.
  Repeat Rows 1 and 2.
◊ **Stockinette**
  Row 1 (right side of work): Knit.
  Row 2: Purl.
  Repeat Rows 1 and 2.

Gauges

• 23 sts and 30 rows in stockinette using U.S. size 4 / 3.5 mm needles and Partner 3,5 = 4 x 4 in / 10 x 10 cm.
• 23 sts and 45 rows in garter stitch using smaller needles and Partner 3,5 = 4 x 4 in / 10 x 10 cm.
OR
• 21 sts and 30 rows in stockinette using needles and Tendresse = 4 x 4 in / 10 x 10 cm.
• 21 sts and 44 rows in garter stitch using U.S. size 8 / 5 mm needles and Tendresse = 4 x 4 in / 10 x 10 cm.
Adjust needle sizes to obtain correct gauge if necessary.

Patterns

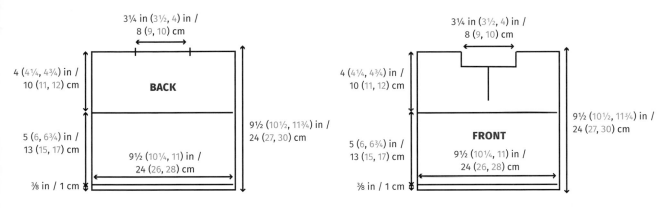

BACK

3¼ in (3½, 4) in / 8 (9, 10) cm

4 (4¼, 4¾) in / 10 (11, 12) cm

5 (6, 6¾) in / 13 (15, 17) cm

9½ (10¼, 11) in / 24 (26, 28) cm

9½ (10½, 11¾) in / 24 (27, 30) cm

⅜ in / 1 cm

FRONT

3¼ in (3½, 4) in / 8 (9, 10) cm

4 (4¼, 4¾) in / 10 (11, 12) cm

5 (6, 6¾) in / 13 (15, 17) cm

9½ (10¼, 11) in / 24 (26, 28) cm

9½ (10½, 11¾) in / 24 (27, 30) cm

⅜ in / 1 cm

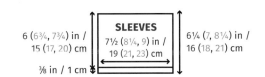

SLEEVES

6 (6¾, 7¾) in / 15 (17, 20) cm

7½ (8¼, 9) in / 19 (21, 23) cm

6¼ (7, 8¼) in / 16 (18, 21) cm

⅜ in / 1 cm

Instructions (using Partner 3,5)

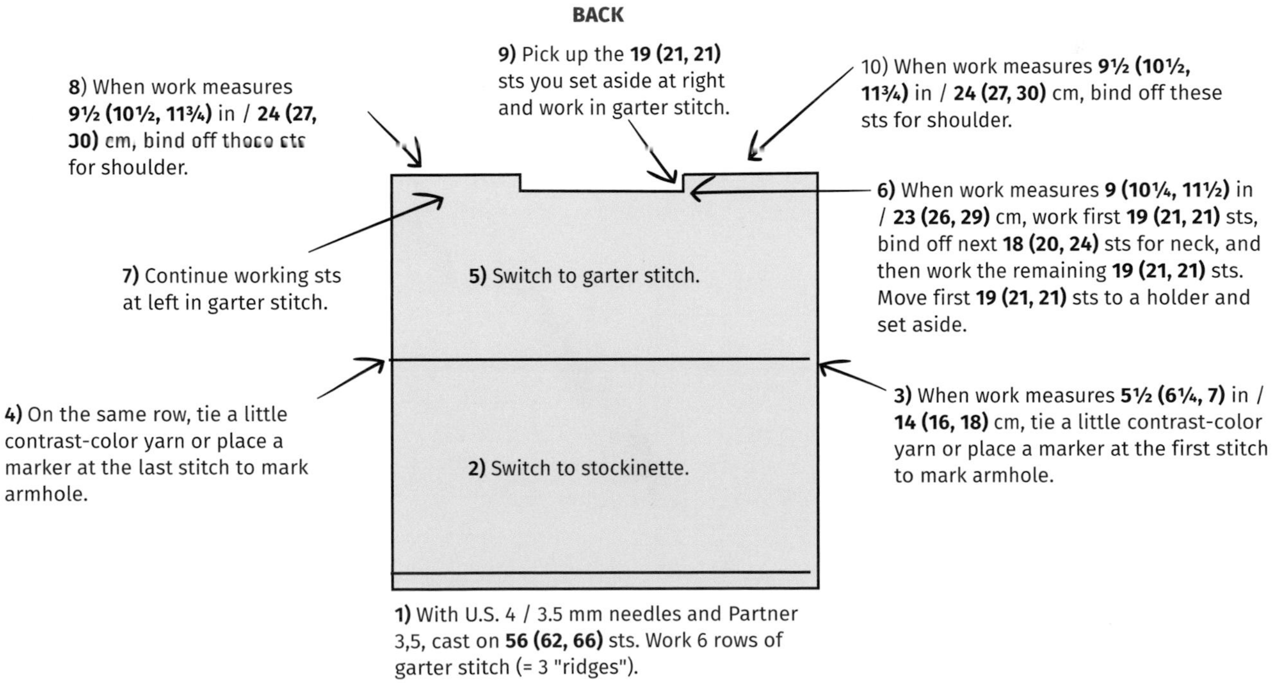

BACK

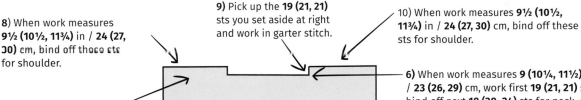

8) When work measures **9½ (10½, 11¾)** in / **24 (27, 30)** cm, bind off these sts for shoulder.

9) Pick up the **19 (21, 21)** sts you set aside at right and work in garter stitch.

10) When work measures **9½ (10½, 11¾)** in / **24 (27, 30)** cm, bind off these sts for shoulder.

7) Continue working sts at left in garter stitch.

5) Switch to garter stitch.

6) When work measures **9 (10¼, 11½)** in / **23 (26, 29)** cm, work first **19 (21, 21)** sts, bind off next **18 (20, 24)** sts for neck, and then work the remaining **19 (21, 21)** sts. Move first **19 (21, 21)** sts to a holder and set aside.

4) On the same row, tie a little contrast-color yarn or place a marker at the last stitch to mark armhole.

2) Switch to stockinette.

3) When work measures 5½ (6¼, 7) in / 14 (16, 18) cm, tie a little contrast-color yarn or place a marker at the first stitch to mark armhole.

1) With U.S. 4 / 3.5 mm needles and Partner 3,5, cast on **56 (62, 66)** sts. Work 6 rows of garter stitch (= 3 "ridges").

Instructions (using Partner 3,5)

FRONT

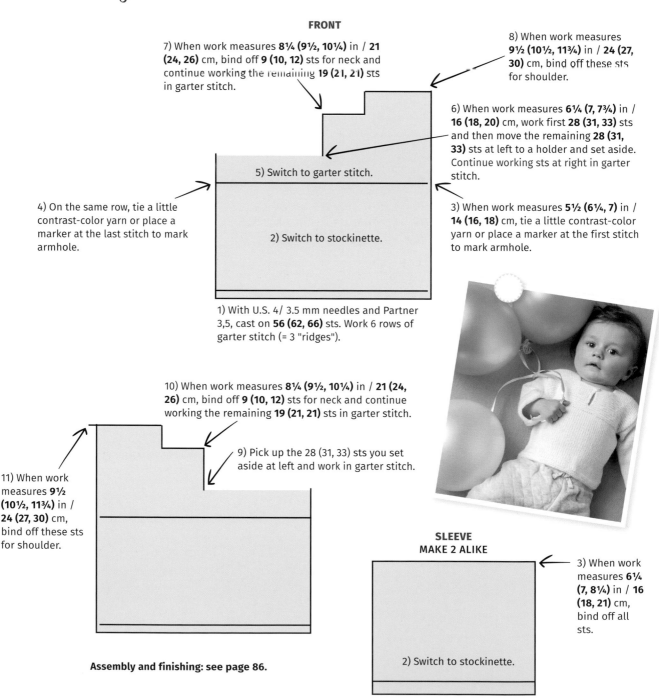

7) When work measures **8¼ (9½, 10¼)** in / **21 (24, 26)** cm, bind off **9 (10, 12)** sts for neck and continue working the remaining **19 (21, 21)** sts in garter stitch.

8) When work measures **9½ (10½, 11¾)** in / **24 (27, 30)** cm, bind off these sts for shoulder.

6) When work measures **6¼ (7, 7¾)** in / **16 (18, 20)** cm, work first **28 (31, 33)** sts and then move the remaining **28 (31, 33)** sts at left to a holder and set aside. Continue working sts at right in garter stitch.

5) Switch to garter stitch.

4) On the same row, tie a little contrast-color yarn or place a marker at the last stitch to mark armhole.

3) When work measures **5½ (6¼, 7)** in / **14 (16, 18)** cm, tie a little contrast-color yarn or place a marker at the first stitch to mark armhole.

2) Switch to stockinette.

1) With U.S. 4/ 3.5 mm needles and Partner 3,5, cast on **56 (62, 66)** sts. Work 6 rows of garter stitch (= 3 "ridges").

10) When work measures **8¼ (9½, 10¼)** in / **21 (24, 26)** cm, bind off **9 (10, 12)** sts for neck and continue working the remaining **19 (21, 21)** sts in garter stitch.

9) Pick up the 28 (31, 33) sts you set aside at left and work in garter stitch.

11) When work measures **9½ (10½, 11¾)** in / **24 (27, 30)** cm, bind off these sts for shoulder.

Assembly and finishing: see page 86.

SLEEVE
MAKE 2 ALIKE

3) When work measures **6¼ (7, 8¼)** in / **16 (18, 21)** cm, bind off all sts.

2) Switch to stockinette.

1) With U.S. 4 / 3.5 mm needles and Partner 3,5, cast on **46 (50, 54)** sts. Work 6 rows of garter stitch (= 3 "ridges").

Instructions (using Tendresse)

BACK

9) Pick up the **18 (19, 20)** sts you set aside at right and work in garter stitch.

10) When work measures **9½ (10½, 11¾)** in / **24 (27, 30)** cm, bind off these sts for shoulder.

8) When work measures **9½ (10½, 11¾)** in / **24 (27, 30)** cm, bind off these sts for shoulder.

6) When work measures **9 (10¼, 11½)** in / **23 (26, 29)** cm, work first **18 (19, 20)** sts, bind off next **16 (18, 20)** sts for neck and then work the remaining **18 (19, 20)** sts. Move the first **18 (19, 20)** sts to a holder and set aside.

7) Continue working sts at left in garter stitch.

5) Switch to garter stitch.

4) On the same row, tie a little contrast-color yarn or place a marker at the last stitch to mark armhole.

3) When work measures **5½ (6¼, 7)** in / **14 (16, 18)** cm, tie a little contrast-color yarn or place a marker at the first stitch to mark armhole.

2) Switch to stockinette.

1) With U.S. 8 / 5 mm needles and Tendresse, cast on **52 (56, 60)** sts. Work 4 rows of garter stitch (= 2 "ridges").

FRONT

7) When work measures **8¼ (9½, 10¼)** in / **21 (24, 26)** cm, bind off **8 (9, 10)** sts for neck and continue working the remaining **18 (19, 20)** sts in garter stitch.

8) When work measures **9½ (10½, 11¾)** in / **24 (27, 30)** cm, bind off these sts for shoulder.

6) When work measures **6¼ (7, 7¾)** in / **16 (18, 20)** cm, work the first **26 (28, 30)** sts and then move the remaining 26 (28, 30) sts at left to a holder and set aside. Continue working sts at right in garter stitch.

5) Switch to garter stitch.

4) On the same row, tie a little contrast-color yarn or place a marker at the last stitch to mark armhole.

3) When work measures **5½ (6¼, 7)** in / **14 (16, 18)** cm, tie a little contrast-color yarn or place a marker at the first stitch to mark armhole.

2) Switch to stockinette.

1) With U.S. 8 / 5 mm needles and Tendresse, cast on **52 (56, 60)** sts. Work 4 rows of garter stitch (= 2 "ridges").

10) When work measures **8¼ (9½, 10¼)** in / **21 (24, 26)** cm, bind off 8 (9, 10) sts for neck and continue working the remaining **19 (21, 21)** sts in garter stitch.

11) When work measures **9½ (10½, 11¾)** in / **24 (27, 30)** cm, bind off these sts for shoulder.

9) Pick up the **26 (28, 30)** sts you set aside at left and work in garter stitch.

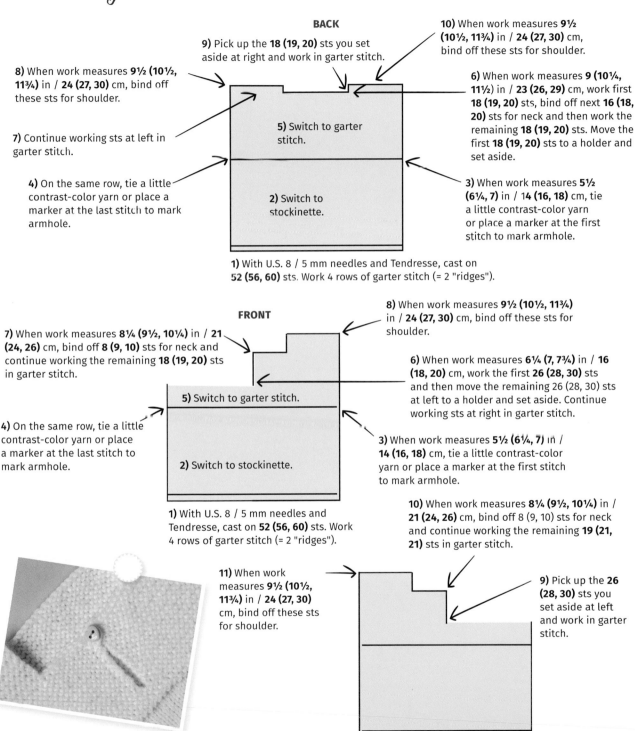

Instructions (using Tendresse)

**SLEEVE
MAKE 2 ALIKE**

2) Switch to stockinette.

3) When work measures **6¼ (7, 8¼)** in / **16 (18, 21)** cm, bind off all sts.

1) With U.S. 8 / 5 mm needles and Tendresse, cast on **42 (46, 50)** sts. Work 4 rows of garter stitch (= 2 "ridges").

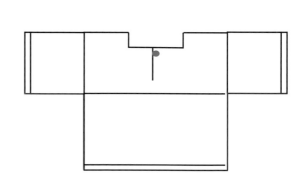

Assembly and finishing

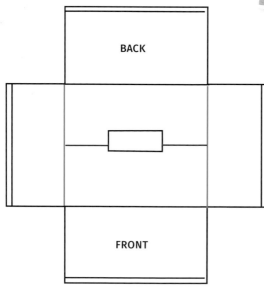

BACK

FRONT

— Seam shoulders.

— Sew sleeves to armholes.

— Seam sides of shirt and undersides of sleeves.

● Make 1 buttonhole at front neck (the knitting should be elastic enough for you to push a pencil or knitting needle between a couple stitches and gently widen a hole) and sew the button in position opposite.

Weave in ends neatly on wrong side.

24. Cardigan

Sizes

3 months (6 months, 12 months)

The instructions include all 3 sizes; the order above corresponds to the order in which instructions will be given for each size throughout. For example: for the 6-month size, always look for the first of two numbers in parentheses—in the materials list, the written instructions, and all the diagram labels showing size or length measurements.

Materials

◊ CYCA #4 (worsted/afghan/aran) Phildar Tendresse (75% viscose, 25% polyamide; 107 yd / 98 m / 50 g): 4 (5, 5) skeins of Faïence or CYCA #2 (sport/baby) Phildar Partner 3,5 (50% polyamide, 25% combed wool, 25% acrylic; 137 yd / 125 m / 50 g): 3 (4, 4) skeins of Ciel
◊ U.S. size 7 / 4.5 mm needles, if using Tendresse
◊ U.S. size 4 / 3.5 mm needles, if using Partner 3,5
◊ 5 buttons

Stitches used

◊ **Garter stitch**
Row 1 (right side of work): Knit.
Row 2: Knit.
Repeat Rows 1 and 2.

Gauges

22 sts and 44 rows in garter stitch using U.S. 7 / 4.5 mm needles and Tendresse = 4 x 4 in / 10 x 10 cm.
23 sts and 45 rows in garter stitch using U.S. 4 / 3.5 mm needles and Partner 3,5 = 4 x 4 in / 10 x 10 cm.
Adjust needle sizes to obtain correct gauge if necessary.

Patterns

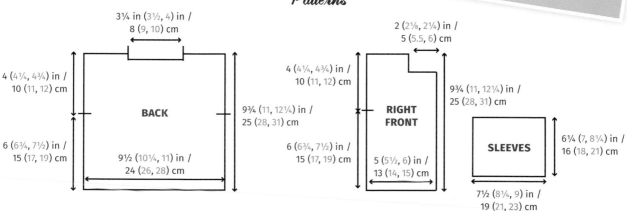

BACK
3¼ in (3½, 4) in / 8 (9, 10) cm
4 (4¼, 4¾) in / 10 (11, 12) cm
9¾ (11, 12¼) in / 25 (28, 31) cm
6 (6¾, 7½) in / 15 (17, 19) cm
9½ (10¼, 11) in / 24 (26, 28) cm

RIGHT FRONT
2 (2⅛, 2¼) in / 5 (5.5, 6) cm
4 (4¼, 4¾) in / 10 (11, 12) cm
6 (6¾, 7½) in / 15 (17, 19) cm
5 (5½, 6) in / 13 (14, 15) cm

SLEEVES
9¾ (11, 12¼) in / 25 (28, 31) cm
6¼ (7, 8¼) in / 16 (18, 21) cm
7½ (8¼, 9) in / 19 (21, 23) cm

Instructions

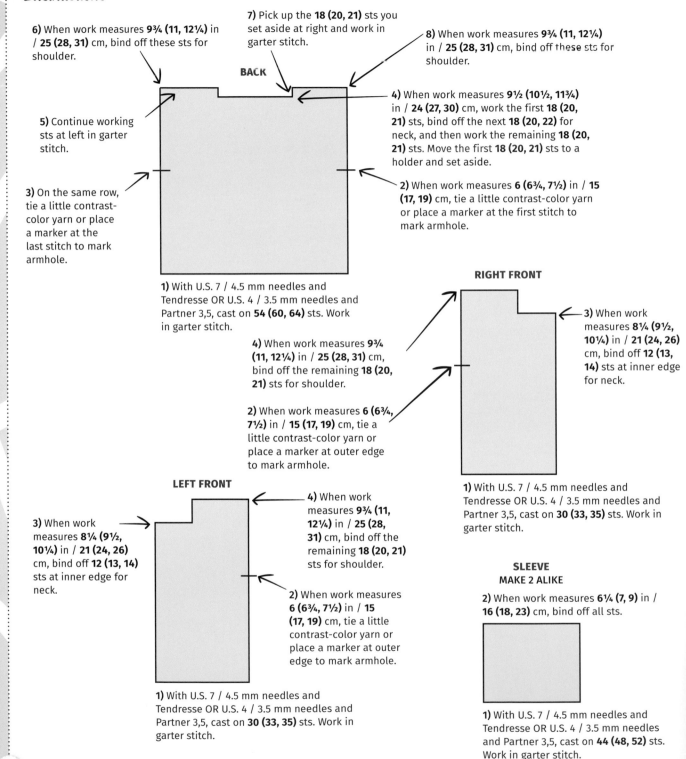

6) When work measures **9¾ (11, 12¼)** in / **25 (28, 31)** cm, bind off these sts for shoulder.

7) Pick up the **18 (20, 21)** sts you set aside at right and work in garter stitch.

8) When work measures **9¾ (11, 12¼)** in / **25 (28, 31)** cm, bind off these sts for shoulder.

BACK

5) Continue working sts at left in garter stitch.

4) When work measures **9½ (10½, 11¾)** in / **24 (27, 30)** cm, work the first **18 (20, 21)** sts, bind off the next **18 (20, 22)** for neck, and then work the remaining **18 (20, 21)** sts. Move the first **18 (20, 21)** sts to a holder and set aside.

3) On the same row, tie a little contrast-color yarn or place a marker at the last stitch to mark armhole.

2) When work measures **6 (6¾, 7½)** in / **15 (17, 19)** cm, tie a little contrast-color yarn or place a marker at the first stitch to mark armhole.

1) With U.S. 7 / 4.5 mm needles and Tendresse OR U.S. 4 / 3.5 mm needles and Partner 3,5, cast on **54 (60, 64)** sts. Work in garter stitch.

RIGHT FRONT

4) When work measures **9¾ (11, 12¼)** in / **25 (28, 31)** cm, bind off the remaining **18 (20, 21)** sts for shoulder.

3) When work measures **8¼ (9½, 10¼)** in / **21 (24, 26)** cm, bind off **12 (13, 14)** sts at inner edge for neck.

2) When work measures **6 (6¾, 7½)** in / **15 (17, 19)** cm, tie a little contrast-color yarn or place a marker at outer edge to mark armhole.

1) With U.S. 7 / 4.5 mm needles and Tendresse OR U.S. 4 / 3.5 mm needles and Partner 3,5, cast on **30 (33, 35)** sts. Work in garter stitch.

LEFT FRONT

4) When work measures **9¾ (11, 12¼)** in / **25 (28, 31)** cm, bind off the remaining **18 (20, 21)** sts for shoulder.

3) When work measures **8¼ (9½, 10¼)** in / **21 (24, 26)** cm, bind off **12 (13, 14)** sts at inner edge for neck.

2) When work measures **6 (6¾, 7½)** in / **15 (17, 19)** cm, tie a little contrast-color yarn or place a marker at outer edge to mark armhole.

1) With U.S. 7 / 4.5 mm needles and Tendresse OR U.S. 4 / 3.5 mm needles and Partner 3,5, cast on **30 (33, 35)** sts. Work in garter stitch.

SLEEVE
MAKE 2 ALIKE

2) When work measures **6¼ (7, 9)** in / **16 (18, 23)** cm, bind off all sts.

1) With U.S. 7 / 4.5 mm needles and Tendresse OR U.S. 4 / 3.5 mm needles and Partner 3,5, cast on **44 (48, 52)** sts. Work in garter stitch.

Assembly and finishing

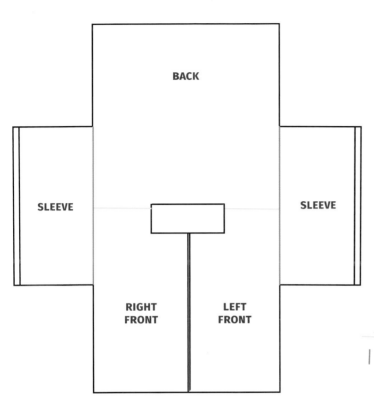

— Seam shoulders.

| Sew sleeves to armholes.

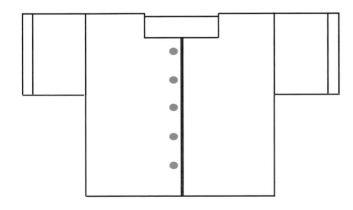

— Seam sides of cardigan and undersides of sleeves.

● Make 5 buttonholes on right front (the knitting should be elastic enough for you to push a pencil or knitting needle between a couple stitches and gently widen a hole), 3 sts in from side edge, with the lowest at 1¼ (1¼, 1¼) in / **3 (3, 3)** cm from bottom edge and the others 1½ (2, 2⅛) in / **4 (5, 5.5)** cm apart.

Sew buttons in position, opposite buttonholes.

Weave in ends neatly on wrong side.

25. Short-sleeved shirt

Worked in stockinette stripes with finishing in garter stitch, using Phil Coton 4 and U.S. size 6 / 4 mm needles.

26. Shorts

Worked in stockinette with finishing in garter stitch, using Phil Coton 4 and U.S. size 6 / 4 mm needles.

25. Short-sleeved shirt

Sizes

3 months (6 months, 12 months)

The instructions include all 3 sizes; the order above corresponds to the order in which instructions will be given for each size throughout. For example: for the 6-month size, always look for the first of two numbers in parentheses—in the materials list, the written instructions, and all the diagram labels showing size or length measurements.

Materials

◊ CYCA #3 (DK/light worsted) Phildar Phil Coton 4 (100% cotton; 93 yd / 85 m / 50 g): 2 (2, 3) skeins of Faïence; 1 (1, 1) skein of Blanc
◊ U.S. size 6 / 4 mm needles
◊ 3 buttons
◊ 2 snaps

Stitches used

◊ **Garter stitch**
  Row 1 (right side of work): Knit.
  Row 2: Knit.
  Repeat Rows 1 and 2.
◊ **Stockinette**
  Row 1 (right side of work): Knit.
  Row 2: Purl.
  Repeat Rows 1 and 2.
◊ **Stockinette stripes**
  Row 1 (right side of work): With Blanc, knit.
  Row 2: With Blanc, purl.
  Row 3, Row 5: With Faïence, knit.
  Row 4, Row 6: With Faïence, purl.
  Repeat Rows 1-6.

Gauge

22 sts and 28 rows in stockinette stripes = 4 x 4 in / 10 x 10 cm.
Adjust needle sizes to obtain correct gauge if necessary.

Patterns

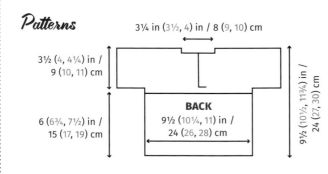

3¼ in (3½, 4) in / 8 (9, 10) cm

3½ (4, 4¼) in / 9 (10, 11) cm

6 (6¾, 7½) in / 15 (17, 19) cm

BACK
9½ (10¼, 11) in / 24 (26, 28) cm

9½ (10½, 11¾) in / 24 (27, 30) cm

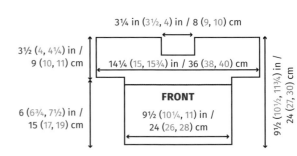

3¼ in (3½, 4) in / 8 (9, 10) cm

3½ (4, 4¼) in / 9 (10, 11) cm

14¼ (15, 15¾) in / 36 (38, 40) cm

6 (6¾, 7½) in / 15 (17, 19) cm

FRONT
9½ (10¼, 11) in / 24 (26, 28) cm

9½ (10½, 11¾) in / 24 (27, 30) cm

Instructions

6) When work measures **6¼ (7½, 8¾)** in / **16 (19, 22)** cm, work 3 sts garter stitch, **38 (40, 42)** sts stockinette, and 3 sts garter stitch across right half of row. Move remaining stitches at left to a holder and set aside.

9) When work measures **9½ (10½, 11¾)** in / **24 (27, 30)** cm, bind off these **32 (33, 34)** sts for shoulder.

8) When work measures **9 (10¼, 11½)** in / **23 (26, 29)** cm, bind off **12 (13, 14)** sts for neck at inner edge and then work 3 sts garter stitch, **26 (27, 28)** sts stockinette, and 3 sts garter stitch across remaining stitches.

BACK

7) When work measures **8¾ (9¾, 11)** in / **22 (25, 28)** cm, begin working 3 sts garter stitch at outer edge, **26 (27, 28)** sts stockinette, and **15 (16, 17)** sts garter stitch at inner edge.

5) Switch from stockinette only to working 3 sts garter stitch, **76 (80, 84)** sts stockinette, and 3 sts garter stitch across.

3) When work measures **6 (6¾, 7½)** in / **15 (17, 19)** cm, work across row and then cast on **14 (13, 13)** additional sts to form a sleeve = **68 (73, 77)** sts.

4) On next row, work across and then cast on **14 (13, 13)** additional sts on other edge to form a second sleeve = **82 (86, 90)** sts.

2) Switch to stockinette stripes: *2 rows Blanc, 4 rows Faïence*; repeat from * to * 5 (6, 7) more times and then end with 2 rows Blanc. Cut yarn and switch to Faïence, and continue in stockinette.

1) With Faïence, cast on **54 (60, 64)** sts. Work 4 rows of garter stitch.

13) When work measures **9½ (10½, 11¾)** in / **24 (27, 30)** cm, bind off these **32 (33, 34)** sts for shoulder.

12) When work measures **9 (10¼, 11½)** in / **23 (26, 29)** cm, bind off **12 (13, 14)** sts for neck at inner edge and then work 3 sts garter stitch, **26 (27, 28)** sts stockinette, and 3 sts garter stitch across the remaining stitches.

BACK

11) When work measures **8¾ (9¾, 11)** in / **22 (25, 28)** cm, begin working **15 (16, 17)** sts garter stitch at inner edge, **26 (27, 28)** sts stockinette, and 3 sts garter stitch at outer edge.

10) With Faïence, cast on 6 sts and then pick up the **38 (40, 42)** sts you set aside at left and work across: 3 sts garter stitch, **38 (40, 42)** sts stockinette, and 3 sts garter stitch.

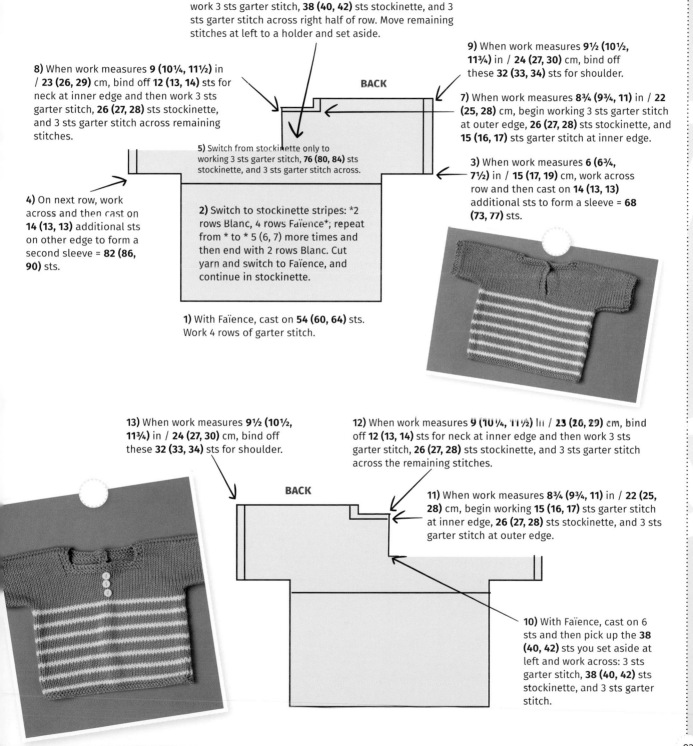

Instructions

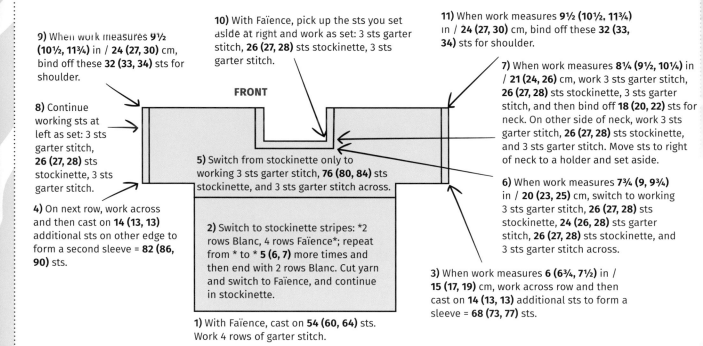

9) When work measures **9½ (10½, 11¾)** in / **24 (27, 30)** cm, bind off these **32 (33, 34)** sts for shoulder.

8) Continue working sts at left as set: 3 sts garter stitch, **26 (27, 28)** sts stockinette, 3 sts garter stitch.

4) On next row, work across and then cast on **14 (13, 13)** additional sts on other edge to form a second sleeve = **82 (86, 90)** sts.

10) With Faïence, pick up the sts you set aside at right and work as set: 3 sts garter stitch, **26 (27, 28)** sts stockinette, 3 sts garter stitch.

FRONT

5) Switch from stockinette only to working 3 sts garter stitch, **76 (80, 84)** sts stockinette, and 3 sts garter stitch across.

2) Switch to stockinette stripes: *2 rows Blanc, 4 rows Faïence*; repeat from * to * **5 (6, 7)** more times and then end with 2 rows Blanc. Cut yarn and switch to Faïence, and continue in stockinette.

1) With Faïence, cast on **54 (60, 64)** sts. Work 4 rows of garter stitch.

11) When work measures 9½ (10½, 11¾) in / **24 (27, 30)** cm, bind off these **32 (33, 34)** sts for shoulder.

7) When work measures **8¼ (9½, 10¼)** in / **21 (24, 26)** cm, work 3 sts garter stitch, **26 (27, 28)** sts stockinette, 3 sts garter stitch, and then bind off **18 (20, 22)** sts for neck. On other side of neck, work 3 sts garter stitch, **26 (27, 28)** sts stockinette, and 3 sts garter stitch. Move sts to right of neck to a holder and set aside.

6) When work measures **7¾ (9, 9¾)** in / **20 (23, 25)** cm, switch to working 3 sts garter stitch, **26 (27, 28)** sts stockinette, **24 (26, 28)** sts garter stitch, **26 (27, 28)** sts stockinette, and 3 sts garter stitch across.

3) When work measures **6 (6¾, 7½)** in / **15 (17, 19)** cm, work across row and then cast on **14 (13, 13)** additional sts to form a sleeve = **68 (73, 77)** sts.

Assembly and finishing

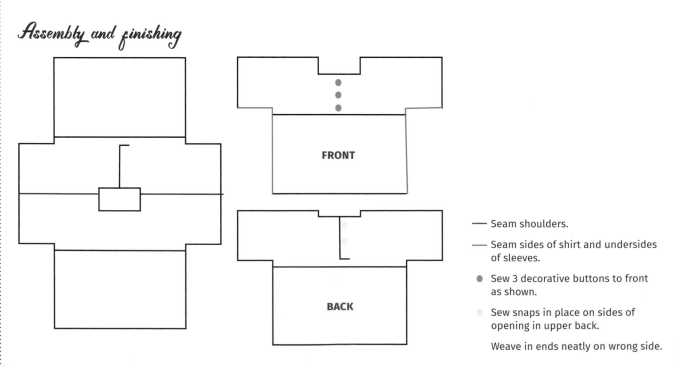

FRONT

BACK

— Seam shoulders.

— Seam sides of shirt and undersides of sleeves.

● Sew 3 decorative buttons to front as shown.

○ Sew snaps in place on sides of opening in upper back.

Weave in ends neatly on wrong side.

26. Shorts

Sizes

3 months (6 months, 12 months)

The instructions include all 3 sizes; the order above corresponds to the order in which instructions will be given for each size throughout. For example: for the 6-month size, always look for the first of two numbers in parentheses—in the materials list, the written instructions, and all the diagram labels showing size or length measurements.

Materials

◊ CYCA #3 (DK/light worsted) Phildar Phil Coton 4 (100% cotton; 93 yd / 85 m / 50 g): 2 (2, 3) skeins of Faïence
◊ U.S. size 6 / 4 mm needles
◊ 4 buttons
◊ 13¾ (15¾, 17¾) in / 35 (40, 45) cm of elastic, 1 in / 2.5 cm wide, for waistband

Stitches used

◊ **Garter stitch**
Row 1 (right side of work): Knit.
Row 2: Knit.
Repeat Rows 1 and 2.
◊ **Stockinette**
Row 1 (right side of work): Knit.
Row 2: Purl.
Repeat Rows 1 and 2.

Gauge

22 sts and 28 rows in stockinette = 4 x 4 in / 10 x 10 cm. Adjust needle sizes to obtain correct gauge if necessary.

Patterns

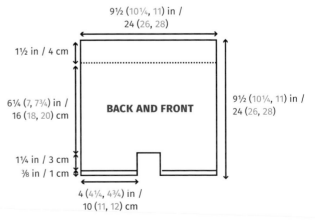

9½ (10¼, 11) in / 24 (26, 28)

1½ in / 4 cm

6¼ (7, 7¾) in / 16 (18, 20) cm

BACK AND FRONT

9½ (10¼, 11) in / 24 (26, 28)

1¼ in / 3 cm
⅜ in / 1 cm

4 (4¼, 4¾) in / 10 (11, 12) cm

Instructions

**BACK/FRONT
MAKE 2 ALIKE**

9) When piece measures **9½ (10¼, 11)** in / **24 (26, 28)** cm, bind off all sts.

8) When piece measures **8 (8¾, 9½)** in / **20 (22, 24)** cm, tie a little contrast-color yarn or place a marker in first and last sts to mark start of waistband.

7) Work across the resulting **54 (60, 64)** sts in stockinette.

6) When work measures **1½ in / 4 cm**, work **22 (25, 27)** sts, cast on 10 additional sts, and then pick up the **22 (25, 27)** sts you set aside for first leg.

Begin with first leg.

3) When work measures **1½ in / 4 cm**, move sts to a holder and set aside.

2) Switch to stockinette.

5) Switch to stockinette.

1) Cast on **22 (25, 27)** sts. Work 4 rows of garter stitch.

4) Cast on **22 (25, 27)** sts. Work 4 rows of garter stitch.

Begin with second leg.

Assembly and finishing

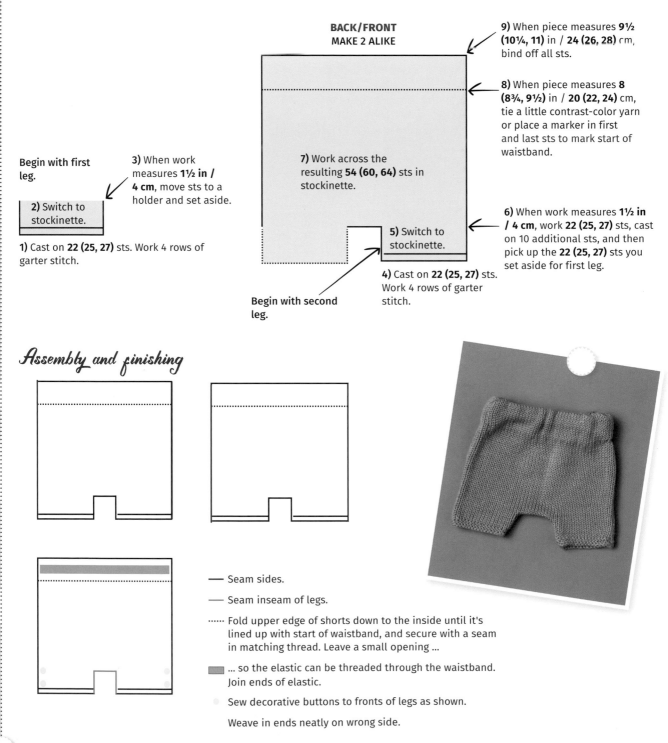

—— Seam sides.

—— Seam inseam of legs.

······ Fold upper edge of shorts down to the inside until it's lined up with start of waistband, and secure with a seam in matching thread. Leave a small opening …

▬ … so the elastic can be threaded through the waistband. Join ends of elastic.

○ Sew decorative buttons to fronts of legs as shown.

Weave in ends neatly on wrong side.

27. Hoodie

Worked in stockinette stripes
and stockinette, using Aviso
and U.S. size 7 / 4.5 mm and
U.S. size 8 / 5 mm needles.

27. Hoodie

Sizes

3 months (6 months, 12 months)

The instructions include all 3 sizes; the order above corresponds to the order in which instructions will be given for each size throughout. For example: for the 6-month size, always look for the first of two numbers in parentheses—in the materials list, the written instructions, and all the diagram labels showing size or length measurements.

Materials

◊ CYCA #4 (worsted/afghan/aran) Phildar Aviso (60% cotton, 40% acrylic; 74 yd / 68 m / 50 g): 3 (4, 4) skeins of Horizon; 2 (2, 3) skeins of Anthracite
◊ U.S. size 7 / 4.5 mm and U.S. size 8 / 5 mm needles
◊ 6 buttons

Stitches used

◊ **Garter stitch**
   Row 1 (right side of work): Knit.
   Row 2: Knit.
   Repeat Rows 1 and 2.
◊ **Stockinette**
   Row 1 (right side of work): Knit.
   Row 2: Purl.
   Repeat Rows 1 and 2.
◊ **Stockinette stripes, back and left front**
   Rows 1, 3, 5, 7, 9 (right side of work): With Horizon, knit.

Rows 2, 4, 6, 8, 10: With Horizon, purl.
Rows 11, 13, 15, 17, 19 (right side of work): With Anthracite, knit.
Rows 12, 14, 16, 18, 20: With Anthracite, purl.
Repeat Rows 1-20.
◊ **Stockinette stripes, right front**
   Rows 1, 3, 5, 7, 9 (right side of work): With Anthracite, knit.
   Rows 2, 4, 6, 8, 10: With Anthracite, purl.
   Rows 11, 13, 15, 17, 19 (right side of work): With Horizon, knit.
   Rows 12, 14, 16, 18, 20: With Horizon, purl.
   Repeat Rows 1-20.
◊ **Stockinette stripes, sleeves**
   Rows 1 and 3: With Anthracite, knit.
   Rows 2 and 4: With Anthracite, purl.
   Rows 5 and 7: With Horizon, knit.
   Rows 6 and 8: With Horizon, purl.
   Repeat Rows 1-8.

Gauge

16 sts and 23 rows in stockinette or stockinette stripes using larger needles = 4 x 4 in / 10 x 10 cm.
Adjust needle sizes to obtain correct gauge if necessary.

Patterns

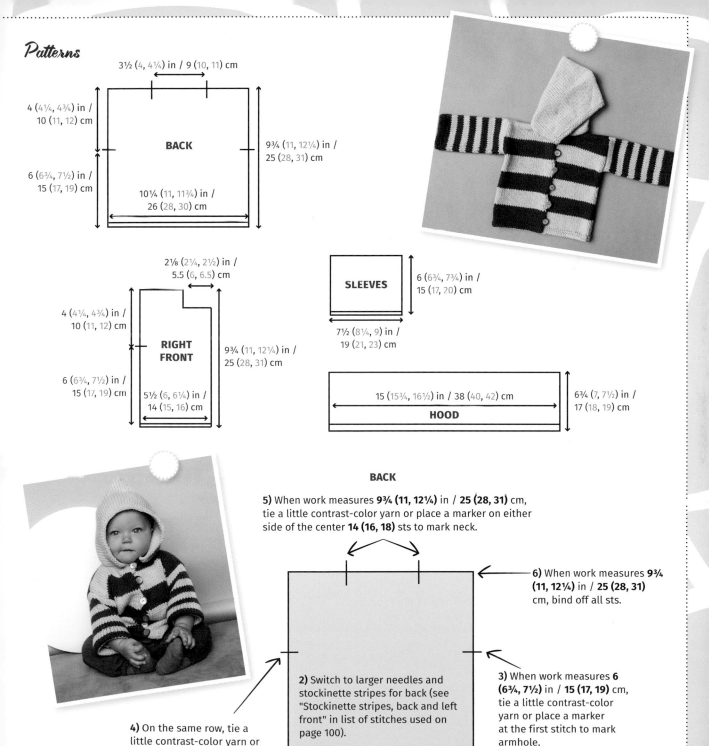

BACK

3½ (4, 4¼) in / 9 (10, 11) cm

4 (4¼, 4¾) in / 10 (11, 12) cm

9¾ (11, 12¼) in / 25 (28, 31) cm

6 (6¾, 7½) in / 15 (17, 19) cm

10¼ (11, 11¾) in / 26 (28, 30) cm

RIGHT FRONT

2⅛ (2¼, 2½) in / 5.5 (6, 6.5) cm

4 (4¼, 4¾) in / 10 (11, 12) cm

9¾ (11, 12¼) in / 25 (28, 31) cm

6 (6¾, 7½) in / 15 (17, 19) cm

5½ (6, 6¼) in / 14 (15, 16) cm

SLEEVES

6 (6¾, 7¾) in / 15 (17, 20) cm

7½ (8¼, 9) in / 19 (21, 23) cm

HOOD

15 (15¾, 16½) in / 38 (40, 42) cm

6¾ (7, 7½) in / 17 (18, 19) cm

BACK

5) When work measures **9¾ (11, 12¼)** in / **25 (28, 31)** cm, tie a little contrast-color yarn or place a marker on either side of the center **14 (16, 18)** sts to mark neck.

6) When work measures **9¾ (11, 12¼)** in / **25 (28, 31)** cm, bind off all sts.

3) When work measures **6 (6¾, 7½)** in / **15 (17, 19)** cm, tie a little contrast-color yarn or place a marker at the first stitch to mark armhole.

4) On the same row, tie a little contrast-color yarn or place a marker at the last stitch to mark armhole.

2) Switch to larger needles and stockinette stripes for back (see "Stockinette stripes, back and left front" in list of stitches used on page 100).

1) With smaller needles and Horizon, cast on **44 (46, 50)** sts. Work 4 rows of garter stitch.

Instructions

RIGHT FRONT

5) When work measures **9¾ (11, 12¼)** in / **25 (28, 31)** cm, bind off all **15 (15, 16)** sts for shoulder.

4) When work measures **8¾ (9¾, 10½)** in / **22 (25, 27)** cm, bind off **9 (11, 12)** sts at inner edge for neck.

2) Switch to larger needles and stockinette stripes for right front (see "Stockinette stripes, right front" in list of stitches used on page 100).

3) When work measures **6 (6¾, 7½)** in / **15 (17, 19)** cm, tie a little contrast-color yarn or place a marker at outer edge to mark armhole.

1) With smaller needles and Anthracite, cast on **24 (26, 28)** sts. Work 4 rows of garter stitch.

SLEEVE
MAKE 2 ALIKE

3) When work measures **6 (6¾, 7¾)** in / **15 (17, 20)** cm, bind off all sts.

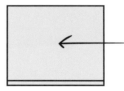

2) Switch to larger needles and stockinette stripes for sleeves (see "Stockinette stripes, sleeves" in list of stitches used on page 100).

1) With smaller needles and Anthracite, cast on **32 (36, 38)** sts. Work 4 rows of garter stitch.

HOOD

3) When work measures **6¾ (7, 7½)** in / **17 (18, 19)** cm, bind off all sts.

2) Switch to larger needles and stockinette.

1) With smaller needles and Horizon, cast on **62 (66, 70)** sts. Work 4 rows of garter stitch.

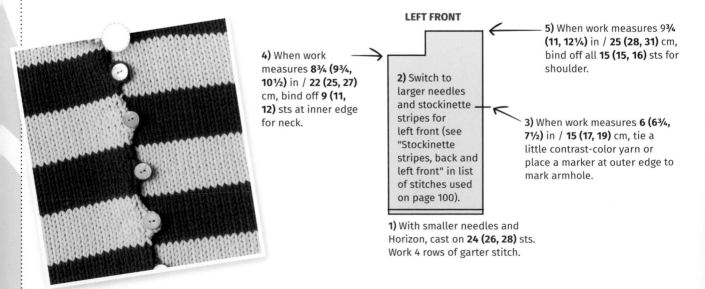

LEFT FRONT

5) When work measures **9¾ (11, 12¼)** in / **25 (28, 31)** cm, bind off all **15 (15, 16)** sts for shoulder.

4) When work measures **8¾ (9¾, 10½)** in / **22 (25, 27)** cm, bind off **9 (11, 12)** sts at inner edge for neck.

2) Switch to larger needles and stockinette stripes for left front (see "Stockinette stripes, back and left front" in list of stitches used on page 100).

3) When work measures **6 (6¾, 7½)** in / **15 (17, 19)** cm, tie a little contrast-color yarn or place a marker at outer edge to mark armhole.

1) With smaller needles and Horizon, cast on **24 (26, 28)** sts. Work 4 rows of garter stitch.

Assembly and finishing

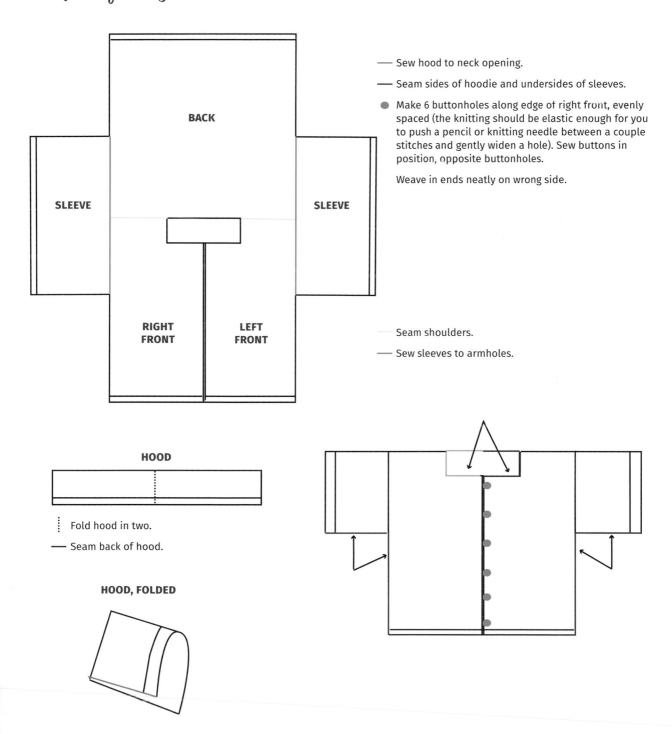

— Sew hood to neck opening.

— Seam sides of hoodie and undersides of sleeves.

● Make 6 buttonholes along edge of right front, evenly spaced (the knitting should be elastic enough for you to push a pencil or knitting needle between a couple stitches and gently widen a hole). Sew buttons in position, opposite buttonholes.

Weave in ends neatly on wrong side.

BACK

SLEEVE

SLEEVE

RIGHT FRONT

LEFT FRONT

— Seam shoulders.

— Sew sleeves to armholes.

HOOD

⋮ Fold hood in two.

— Seam back of hood.

HOOD, FOLDED

28. Short-sleeved jacket

Worked in garter stitch, using Phil Thalassa and U.S. size 2.5 / 3 mm needles.

29. Short-sleeved jacket

Worked in garter stitch, using Partner 3,5 and U.S. size 2.5 / 3 mm needles.

30. Booties

Worked in garter stitch, using Partner 3,5 and U.S. size 2.5 / 3 mm needles.

28. Short-sleeved jacket

Sizes

3 months (6 months, 12 months)

The instructions include all 3 sizes; the order above corresponds to the order in which instructions will be given for each size throughout. For example: for the 6-month size, always look for the first of two numbers in parentheses—in the materials list, the written instructions, and all the diagram labels showing size or length measurements.

Materials

◊ CYCA #4 (worsted/afghan/aran) Phildar Phil Thalassa (75% cotton, 25% tencel; 89 yd / 81 m / 50 g): 3 (3, 4) skeins of Corail
◊ U.S. size 2.5 / 3 mm needles
◊ 1 button

Stitches used

◊ **Garter stitch**
Row 1 (right side of work): Knit.
Row 2: Knit.
Repeat Rows 1 and 2.

Gauge

21 sts and 47 rows in garter stitch = 4 x 4 in / 10 x 10 cm.
Adjust needle sizes to obtain correct gauge if necessary.

Patterns

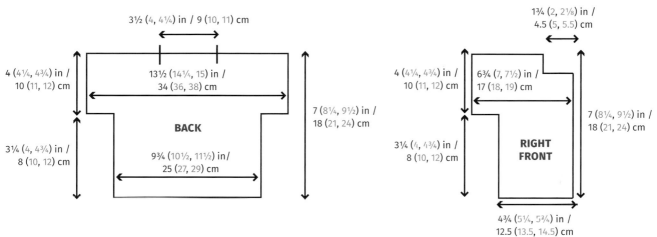

BACK

3½ (4, 4¼) in / 9 (10, 11) cm

13½ (14¼, 15) in / 34 (36, 38) cm

4 (4¼, 4¾) in / 10 (11, 12) cm

7 (8¼, 9½) in / 18 (21, 24) cm

3¼ (4, 4¾) in / 8 (10, 12) cm

9¾ (10½, 11½) in / 25 (27, 29) cm

RIGHT FRONT

1¾ (2, 2⅛) in / 4.5 (5, 5.5) cm

6¾ (7, 7½) in / 17 (18, 19) cm

4 (4¼, 4¾) in / 10 (11, 12) cm

7 (8¼, 9½) in / 18 (21, 24) cm

3¼ (4, 4¾) in / 8 (10, 12) cm

4¾ (5¼, 5¾) in / 12.5 (13.5, 14.5) cm

Instructions

BACK

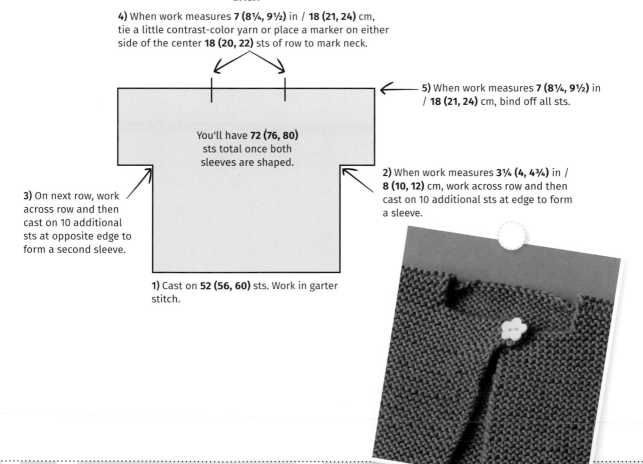

4) When work measures **7 (8¼, 9½)** in / **18 (21, 24)** cm, tie a little contrast-color yarn or place a marker on either side of the center **18 (20, 22)** sts of row to mark neck.

5) When work measures **7 (8¼, 9½)** in / **18 (21, 24)** cm, bind off all sts.

You'll have **72 (76, 80)** sts total once both sleeves are shaped.

2) When work measures **3¼ (4, 4¾)** in / **8 (10, 12)** cm, work across row and then cast on 10 additional sts at edge to form a sleeve.

3) On next row, work across row and then cast on 10 additional sts at opposite edge to form a second sleeve.

1) Cast on **52 (56, 60)** sts. Work in garter stitch.

Instructions

RIGHT FRONT

4) When work measures **7 (8¼, 9½)** in / **18 (21, 24)** cm, bind off all **27 (28, 29)** sts remaining for shoulder.

You'll have **36 (38, 40)** sts total after forming sleeve.

3) When work measures **6 (7, 7¾)** in / **15 (18, 20)** cm, bind off **9 (10, 11)** sts at inner edge for neck.

2) When work measures **3¼ (4, 4¾)** in / **8 (10, 12)** cm, cast on 10 additional sts at outer edge to form a sleeve.

1) Cast on **26 (28, 30)** sts. Work in garter stitch.

LEFT FRONT

4) When work measures **7 (8¼, 9½)** in / **18 (21, 24)** cm, bind off all **27 (28, 29)** sts remaining for shoulder.

3) When work measures **6 (7, 7¾)** in / **15 (18, 20)** cm, bind off **9 (10, 11)** sts at inner edge for neck.

You'll have **36 (38, 40)** sts total after forming sleeve.

2) When work measures **3¼ (4, 4¾)** in / **8 (10, 12)** cm, cast on 10 additional sts at outer edge to form a sleeve.

1) Cast on **26 (28, 30)** sts. Work in garter stitch.

Assembly and finishing

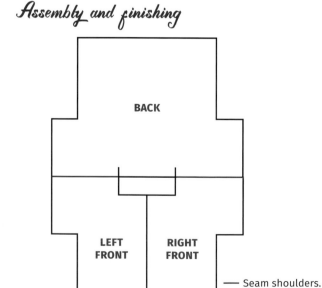

BACK

LEFT FRONT

RIGHT FRONT

Seam shoulders.

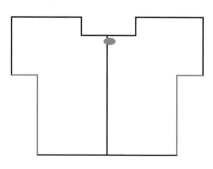

— Seam sides of jacket and undersides of sleeves.

● Make a buttonhole high on right front (the knitting should be elastic enough for you to push a pencil or knitting needle between a couple stitches and gently widen a hole) and sew a button in position opposite.

Weave in ends neatly on wrong side.

29. Short-sleeved jacket

Sizes

3 months (6 months, 12 months)

Materials

◊ CYCA #2 (sport/baby) Phildar Partner 3,5 (50% polyamide, 25% combed wool, 25% acrylic; 137 yd / 125 m / 50 g): 2 (3, 3) skeins of Jade
◊ U.S. size 2.5 / 3 mm needles
◊ 5¾ in / 40 cm of ribbon, ⅜ in / 1 cm wide

Patterns

Stitches used

◊ **Garter stitch**
  Row 1 (right side of work): Knit.
  Row 2: Knit.
  Repeat Rows 1 and 2.

Gauge

23 sts and 46 rows in garter stitch = 4 x 4 in / 10 x 10 cm.
Adjust needle sizes to obtain correct gauge if necessary.

Instructions

BACK

5) As you are binding off (or after bind-off is complete), tie a little contrast-color yarn or place a marker on either side of the middle **21 (23, 25)** sts of row to mark neck.

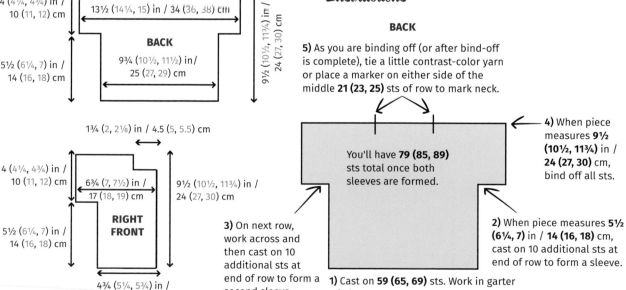

BACK

3½ (4, 4¼) in / 9 (10, 11) cm

4 (4¼, 4¾) in / 10 (11, 12) cm

13½ (14¼, 15) in / 34 (36, 38) cm

9¾ (10½, 11½) in / 25 (27, 29) cm

9½ (10½, 11¾) in / 24 (27, 30) cm

5½ (6¼, 7) in / 14 (16, 18) cm

1¾ (2, 2⅛) in / 4.5 (5, 5.5) cm

RIGHT FRONT

4 (4¼, 4¾) in / 10 (11, 12) cm

6¾ (7, 7½) in / 17 (18, 19) cm

9½ (10½, 11¾) in / 24 (27, 30) cm

5½ (6¼, 7) in / 14 (16, 18) cm

4¾ (5¼, 5¾) in / 12.5 (13.5, 14.5) cm

You'll have **79 (85, 89)** sts total once both sleeves are formed.

4) When piece measures 9½ **(10½, 11¾)** in / **24 (27, 30)** cm, bind off all sts.

3) On next row, work across and then cast on 10 additional sts at end of row to form a second sleeve.

2) When piece measures 5½ **(6¼, 7)** in / **14 (16, 18)** cm, cast on 10 additional sts at end of row to form a sleeve.

1) Cast on 59 (65, 69) sts. Work in garter stitch.

For an explanation of reading sizes, **see** page 106.

Instructions

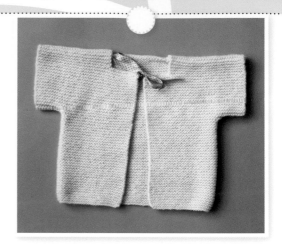

RIGHT FRONT

4) When piece measures **9½ (10½, 11¾)** in / **24 (27, 30)** cm, bind off all **31 (32, 33)** sts remaining for shoulder.

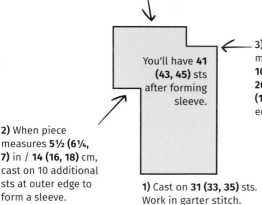

You'll have **41 (43, 45)** sts after forming sleeve.

3) When piece measures **8¼ (9½, 10¼)** in / **21 (24, 26)** cm, bind off **10 (11, 12)** sts at inner edge for neck.

2) When piece measures **5½ (6¼, 7)** in / **14 (16, 18)** cm, cast on 10 additional sts at outer edge to form a sleeve.

1) Cast on **31 (33, 35)** sts. Work in garter stitch.

LEFT FRONT

4) When piece measures **9½ (10½, 11¾)** in / **24 (27, 30)** cm, bind off all **31 (32, 33)** sts remaining for shoulder.

You'll have **41 (43, 45)** sts after forming sleeve.

3) When piece measures **8¼ (9½, 10¼)** in / **21 (24, 26)** cm, bind off **10 (11, 12)** sts at inner edge for neck.

2) When piece measures **5½ (6¼, 7)** in / **14 (16, 18)** cm, cast on 10 additional sts at outer edge to form a sleeve.

1) Cast on **31 (33, 35)** sts. Worked in garter stitch.

Assembly and finishing

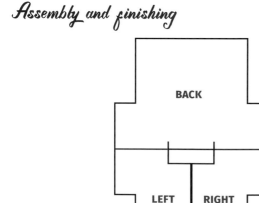

BACK

LEFT FRONT

RIGHT FRONT

— Seam shoulders.

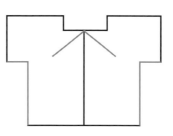

— Seam sides of jacket and undersides of sleeves.

\ Cut the ribbon in two and sew a piece to either side of front neck.

Weave in ends neatly on wrong side.

30. Booties

One size

Suitable for 3 months

Materials

◊ CYCA #2 (sport/baby) Phildar Partner 3,5 (50% polyamide, 25% combed wool, 25% acrylic; 13/ yd / 125 m / 50 g): 1 skein of Jade
◊ U.S. size 2.5 / 3 mm needles
◊ 70 cm of ribbon, ⅛ in / 1 cm wide

Stitches used

◊ **Garter stitch**
  Row 1 (right side of work): Knit.
  Row 2: Knit.
  Repeat Rows 1 and 2.

4¾ in / 12 cm

1½ in / 4 cm

1½ in / 4 cm

2¾ in / 7 cm

6 in / 15 cm

6¾ in / 17 cm

Instructions

BOOTIE
MAKE 2 ALIKE

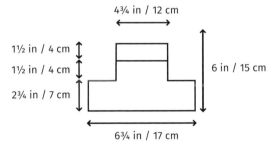

5) When work measures **6 in / 15 cm**, bind off all sts.

4) When work measures **3¼ in / 8 cm**, work a row of eyelets (knit 3 sts, *1 yarnover, knit 2 together, knit 1 st*; repeat from * to * across this row and then knit last 2 stitches).

3) When work measures **2¾ in / 7 cm**, bind off 7 more sts at other edge = 29 sts remaining.

1) Cast on 43 sts. Work in garter stitch.

2) When work measures **2¾ in / 7 cm**, bind off 7 sts at one edge = 36 sts remaining.

Assembly and finishing

⋮ Fold each bootie in two.

— Seam sole, instep, and ankle of bootie.

— Fold top of ankle down about 1½ in / 4 cm.

⋮ Weave a strand of Jade through the stitches at the toe opening, and then pull tight to draw the toe closed. Poke ends through to inside of bootie.

- - - Cut ribbon in two.

— Weave ribbon through row of eyelets and then tie in a bow at front.

31. Poncho

Worked in stockinette and garter stitch with finishing embroidery, using Rapido and Partner 6, and U.S. size 10½-11 / 7 mm needles.

32. Hat

Worked in garter stitch and stockinette with finishing embroidery, using Partner 6 and U.S. size 9 / 5.5 mm needles.

31. Poncho

Sizes

3-6 months (12 months)

The instructions include both sizes; the order above corresponds to the order in which instructions will be given for each size throughout. If you want to make the 3-6-month size, always look for the first number, outside the parentheses—in the materials list, the written instructions, and all the diagram labels showing size or length measurements. If you want to make the 12-month size, look inside the parentheses instead.

Materials

◊ CYCA #6 (super bulky, roving) Phildar Rapido (50% polyamide, 25% combed wool, 25% acrylic; 45 yd / 41 m / 50 g): 4 (4) skeins of Œillet
◊ CYCA #5 (chunky, craft, rug) Phildar Partner 6 (50% polyamide, 25% combed wool, 25% acrylic; 71 yd / 65 m / 50 g): 1 (1) skein of Écru
◊ U.S. size 10½-11 / 7 mm needles

Stitches used

◊ **Garter stitch**
  Row 1 (right side of work): Knit.
  Row 2: Knit.
  Repeat Rows 1 and 2.
◊ **Stockinette**
  Row 1 (right side of work): Knit.
  Row 2: Purl.
  Repeat Rows 1 and 2.
◊ **Embroidery, backstitch and cross stitch**

Gauge

11 sts and 16 rows in stockinette = 4 x 4 in / 10 x 10 cm. Adjust needle sizes to obtain correct gauge if necessary.

Pattern

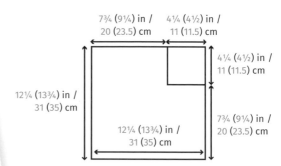

7¾ (9¼) in / 20 (23.5) cm

4¼ (4½) in / 11 (11.5) cm

4¼ (4½) in / 11 (11.5) cm

12¼ (13¾) in / 31 (35) cm

7¾ (9¼) in / 20 (23.5) cm

12¼ (13¾) in / 31 (35) cm

Instructions

SIDE 1

4) When work measures **12¼ (13¾)** in / **31 (35)** cm, bind off all sts.

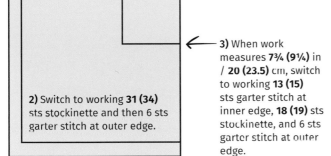

2) Switch to working **31 (34)** sts stockinette and then 6 sts garter stitch at outer edge.

3) When work measures **7¾ (9¼)** in / **20 (23.5)** cm, switch to working **13 (15)** sts garter stitch at inner edge, **18 (19)** sts stockinette, and 6 sts garter stitch at outer edge.

1) With Œillet, cast on **37 (40)** sts. Work 10 rows of garter stitch (= 5 "ridges").

SIDE 2

4) When work measures **12¼ (13¾)** in / **31 (35)** cm, bind off all sts.

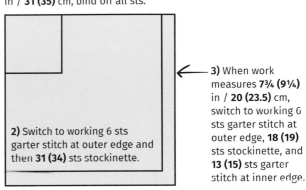

2) Switch to working 6 sts garter stitch at outer edge and then **31 (34)** sts stockinette.

3) When work measures **7¾ (9¼)** in / **20 (23.5)** cm, switch to working 6 sts garter stitch at outer edge, **18 (19)** sts stockinette, and **13 (15)** sts garter stitch at inner edge.

1) With Œillet, cast on **37 (40)** sts. Work 10 rows of garter stitch (= 5 "ridges").

Assembly and finishing

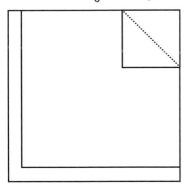

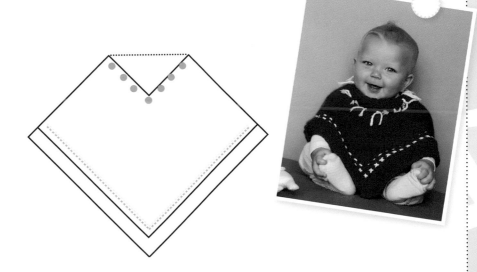

— Lay sides against each other, right sides facing, and seam edges up to the change to garter stitch for collar.

⋱ Fold corners of collar outward.

⋯ With Écru, embroider a line of cross stitch along the 2nd row of stockinette, following shape of corner as shown (each cross stitch should cover 1 st in 1 row). One row above and one st inward from cross stitch, embroider a line of backstitch (each backstitch should cover 1 st, with 1 st between stitches, when embroidering along the length of a row; or should cover 2 rows, with 1 row between stitches, when embroidering across rows).

● Make a bunch of small tassels out of a few strands of Écru and attach them to outer edge of collar.

Weave in ends neatly on wrong side.

32. Hat

Sizes

3-6 months (12 months)

The instructions include both sizes; the order above corresponds to the order in which instructions will be given for each size throughout. If you want to make the 3-6-month size, always look for the first number, outside the parentheses—in the materials list, the written instructions, and all the diagram labels showing size or length measurements. If you want to make the 12-month size, look inside the parentheses instead.

Materials

◊ CYCA #5 (chunky, craft, rug) Phildar Partner 6 (50% polyamide, 25% combed wool, 25% acrylic; 71 yd / 65 m / 50 g): 2 (2) skeins of Grenadine; 1 skein of Écru
◊ U.S. size 9 / 5.5 mm needles

Stitches used

◊ **Garter stitch**
  Row 1 (right side of work): Knit.
  Row 2: Knit.
  Repeat Rows 1 and 2.
◊ **Stockinette**
  Row 1 (right side of work): Knit.
  Row 2: Purl.
  Repeat Rows 1 and 2.
◊ **Embroidery, backstitch and cross stitch**

Gauge

15 sts and 21 rows in stockinette = 4 x 4 in / 10 x 10 cm. Adjust needle sizes to obtain correct gauge if necessary.

Pattern

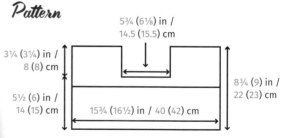

5¾ (6⅛) in / 14.5 (15.5) cm

3¼ (3¼) in / 8 (8) cm

5½ (6) in / 14 (15) cm

15¾ (16½) in / 40 (42) cm

8¾ (9) in / 22 (23) cm

Instructions

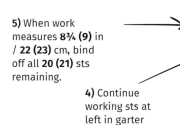

6) Pick up the **20 (21)** sts you set aside at right and work in garter stitch.

7) When work measures **8¾ (9)** in / **22 (23)** cm, bind off all **20 (21)** sts remaining.

5) When work measures **8¾ (9)** in / **22 (23)** cm, bind off all **20 (21)** sts remaining.

4) Continue working sts at left in garter stitch.

2) When work measures **5½ (6)** in / **14 (15)** cm, switch to garter stitch.

1) With Grenadine, cast on **62 (66)** sts. Work in stockinette.

3) When work measures **7 (7½)** in / **18 (19)** cm, work the first **20 (21)** sts, bind off next **22 (24)** sts, and move remaining sts at right to a holder and set aside.

Assembly and finishing

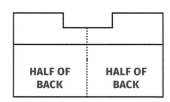

| HALF OF BACK | HALF OF BACK |

····· Fold hat in two.

— Seam hat with matching thread.

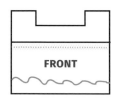

FRONT

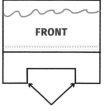

FRONT

··· With Écru, embroider a line of backstitch below the change to garter stitch (each backstitch should cover 1 st, with 1 st between stitches). A row above the backstitch, embroider a line of cross stitch as shown (each cross stitch should cover 1 st in 1 row). A row above the cross stitch, embroider a second line of backstitch (each backstitch should cover 1 st, with 1 st between stitches).

〜 Weave a strand of Grenadine through the sts at 1¾ in / 4.5 cm from cast-on row and then pull tight to gather top of hat. Poke ends through to inside of hat.

With 12 strands of Grenadine per braid, make 2 braids about 5½ in / 14 cm long and attach to the corners over the ears.

33. Blanket

Worked in garter stitch and welt stitch, using Rapido and U.S. size 11 / 8 mm needles

34. Cuddly friend

Worked in stockinette, using Partner 6 and U.S. size 9 / 5.5 mm needles; finishing with milled I-cord and embroidery, using Partner 3,5.

33. Blanket

Dimensions

19¾ x 27½ in / 50 x 70 cm

Materials

◊ CYCA #6 (super bulky, roving) Phildar Rapido (50% polyamide, 25% combed wool, 25% acrylic; 45 yd / 41 m / 50 g): 8 skeins of Danube
◊ U.S. size 11 / 8 mm needles

Stitches used

◊ **Garter stitch**
  Row 1 (right side of work): Knit.
  Row 2: Knit.
  Repeat Rows 1 and 2.

◊ **Stockinette**
  Row 1 (right side of work): Knit.
  Row 2: Purl.
  Repeat Rows 1 and 2.
◊ **Welt stitch (1x3)**
  Row 1: Knit.
  Row 2: Purl.
  Row 3: Knit.
  Row 4: Knit.
  Repeat Rows 1-4.

Gauge

25 sts and 27 rows in 1x3 welt stitch = 8 x 4 in / 20 x 10 cm.
Adjust needle sizes to obtain correct gauge if necessary.

Pattern

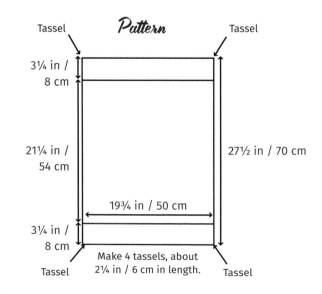

Tassel   Tassel

3¼ in / 8 cm

21¼ in / 54 cm

27½ in / 70 cm

19¾ in / 50 cm

3¼ in / 8 cm

Make 4 tassels, about 2¼ in / 6 cm in length.

Tassel   Tassel

Instructions

4) When work measures **27½ in / 70 cm**, bind off all sts.

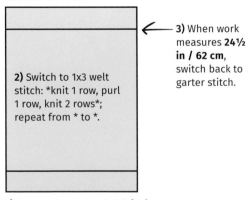

3) When work measures **24½ in / 62 cm**, switch back to garter stitch.

2) Switch to 1x3 welt stitch: *knit 1 row, purl 1 row, knit 2 rows*; repeat from * to *.

1) Cast on 64 sts. Work **3¼ in / 8 cm** of garter stitch.

34. Cuddly friend

Materials

◊ CYCA #5 (chunky, craft, rug) Phildar Partner 6 (50% polyamide, 25% combed wool, 25% acrylic; 71 yd / 65 m / 50 g): 1 skein of Piscine
◊ CYCA #2 (sport/baby) Phildar Partner 3,5 (50% polyamide, 25% combed wool, 25% acrylic; 137 / 125 m / 50 g): 1 skein of Soufre; 1 skein of Rose; 1 skein of Jade; 1 skein of Grenadine
◊ U.S. size 9 / 5.5 mm needles
◊ Spool knitter or knitting mill for small tubes
◊ Fiberfill

Stitches used

◊ **Stockinette**
   Row 1 (right side of work): Knit.
   Row 2: Purl.
   Repeat Rows 1 and 2.
◊ **Reverse stockinette**
   Row 1 (right side of work): Purl.
   Row 2: Knit.
   Repeat Rows 1 and 2.
◊ **Embroidery, straight stitch and stem stitch**

Gauge

15 sts and 21 rows in stockinette = 4 x 4 in / 10 x 10 cm. Adjust needle sizes to obtain correct gauge if necessary.

Pattern

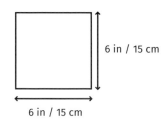

6 in / 15 cm

6 in / 15 cm

Instructions

2) When piece measures **6 in / 15 cm**, bind off all sts.

SIDE 1

1) With Piscine, cast on 24 sts. Work in stockinette.

2) When piece measures **6 in / 15 cm**, bind off all sts.

SIDE 2

1) With Piscine, cast on 24 sts. Work in reverse stockinette.

Assembly and finishing

Stockinette

Reverse stockinette

— Place stockinette face against reverse stockinette face.

— Seam sides, leaving a small opening for stuffing, and then turn right side out.

Make 3 spool-knit cords with Jade, about **5¼ in / 13 cm** long, and 1 cord **10¼ in / 26 cm** long.

Make 3 spool-knit cords with Rose, about **5¼ in / 13 cm** long.

Make 3 spool-knit cords with Grenadine, about **5¼ in / 13 cm** long.

Make 3 spool-knit cords with Soufre, about **5¼ in / 13 cm** long.

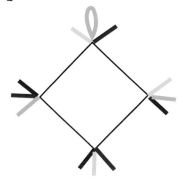

Fold the Jade cord measuring **10¼ in / 26 cm** so that it forms a loop, and attach to one corner.

Attach remaining cords to other corners as shown. Lightly stuff interior and then seam the small opening.

With Jade, embroider eyes with straight stitch.

With Grenadine, embroider nose with straight stitch.

With Rose, embroider mouth with stem stitch.

Poke any ends through to inside.

Acknowledgments

A big thank you to Mya, Eloise, Anatole and Yann, our little models, and to their agency, Cute.

Anatole

Eloïse

Yann

Mya

Suppliers

LoveKnitting.com
www.loveknitting.com/us

If you are unable to obtain any of the yarn used in this book, it can be replaced with a yarn of a similar weight and composition. Please note, however, the finished projects may vary slightly from those shown, depending on the yarn used. Try www.yarnsub.com for suggestions.

For more information on selecting or substituting yarn, contact your local yarn shop or an online store; they are familiar with all types of yarns and would be happy to help you. Additionally, the online knitting community at Ravelry.com has forums where you can post questions about specific yarns. Yarns come and go so quickly these days and there are so many beautiful yarns available.

Background canvases, ROUGIER & PLÉ. (painted by Marie Claire Déco). www.rougier-ple.fr

Rack, pants, and chair, VERTBAUDET. www.vertbaudet.fr

Balloons and little bear, CHOCOLAT
SHOW. www.chocolatshow.fr

Cushions and pillows, MAISON DE VACANCES.
www.maisondevacances.com

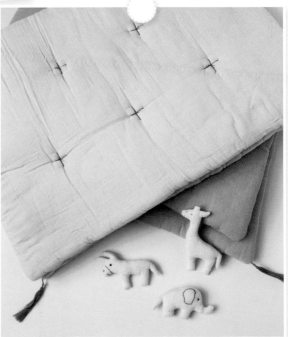

Blankets and stuffed animals,
NUMÉRO 74. numero74.com